ELLI

LIVIA E. BITTON JACKSON

Times
BOOKS

ELLI

*Coming
of
Age
in the
Holocaust*

Published by TIMES BOOKS, a division
of Quadrangle/The New York Times Book Co., Inc.
Three Park Avenue, New York, N.Y. 10016

Published simultaneously in Canada by
Fitzhenry & Whiteside, Ltd., Toronto

Library of Congress Cataloging in Publication Data

Jackson, Livia E. Bitton.
  Elli: coming of age in the holocaust.
  1. Holocaust, Jewish (1939–1945)—Personal
narratives. 2. Jackson, Livia E. Bitton. I. Title.
D810.J4J125 1980   940.53'1503'924   [B]   79–66863
ISBN 0–8129–0882–1

Manufactured in the United States of America

To my children
for whom I was spared,
and who share my pain
over the million
Jewish children who were not.

MY HUSBAND's gentle prodding kept igniting the spark of inspiration needed for the agonizing task of remembering. My mother's brilliant memory revived forgotten details. My friend Avner Beringause helped discipline my thoughts into readable sentences, dispel self-doubt. My family bore with me with varying degrees of patience. They all share my gratitude.

ELLI

SOMORJA IS a small, sunny town at the foot of the Carpathian mountains. The familiar hills loom in a blue haze toward the west. To the south a forest rises, near and immediate, an inviting green oasis stretching to the bank of the Danube a kilometer away. And the Danube, this cool, rapid river, is the heart of our town. It pulsates with the promise of life, of perpetual motion. I love this clear, blue, surging river. I love to swim in its rippling waters and lie in the shade of the bushes hugging its edge.

Swarms of children splash all summer in the Danube. Families picnic on the grass, the soccer team has its practice ground nearby, and the swimming team trains for its annual meet. Even the army camp empties once a day its sweaty contents of hundreds of recruits into the cleansing waters of the river.

Toward the evening, as the sun moves beyond the hills, herds of sheep and cattle arrive at the Danube. The shepherds drive the sheep first and then the horses and cows into the water, cursing louder and louder, and drive us children out. The mosquitoes arrive, too, with the dusk, and then it is time to go home.

The walk through the open pasture is pleasant and cool, but the town is hot and dusty when we get home. The sheep arrive before us, and it is they who churn up the dust. But soon the dust settles, and so does the night. A dark velvety blanket of silence wraps the town snugly against the intrusion of the outside world. The stars one by one light up the dirt roads and the single paved street of the town. By nine o'clock all is quiet. Only a restless dog barks here and there. Soon the dogs, too, go to sleep.

Lying in my bed, I can hear when the orchestra of insects begins its song, the harmony interrupted by the croaking of a single frog. There is a small swamp beyond the last houses of our street surrounded by tall grass. In the tall grass mystery lurks, deep dark secrets of a hidden world.

With eyes closed I lie for hours and daydream. Life is a mystery to me. A beautiful, secret mystery. In my dreams I am a great poet. Beautiful, talented, and very famous. My poems open the secret heart of the world and its embrace carries me far away.

Secretly, every evening I am studying Latin. I hope to pass entrance examinations to the gymnasium and thus persuade Daddy to let me enroll. The gymnasium is in Budapest, the capital.

It is a big and beautiful city with wide streets and very tall buildings and yellow streetcars whizzing around corners. All the streets are paved. In our town we have only one paved street, the main street. And of course it is not so wide as the streets of Budapest. And we have no tall buildings. The tallest building is the city hall, two stories high. There are no streetcars in our town. Only horse-drawn wagons and only two automobiles. One of them belongs to my friend's father.

The thousand-wing-insect orchestra lulls me to sleep. At five in the morning I am awakened by the tooting of the shepherd's horn. The cows moo a response, and the horses neigh restlessly. The gates open, one by one, and the beasts march dutifully down the street. The shepherd cracks his whip and the stench of manure fills the morning air.

When the cows and horses turn the bend in the road, and the shepherd's horn and curses become a distant sound, the second shepherd's horn penetrates the air. A deeper sound. Again the gates open. Goats and sheep pour into the street. A somewhat less noisy, less dusty, less smelly procession.

Then come the pigs. A stampeding herd of swine is the noisiest, the messiest thing in the world. Oh, I do hate the pigs!

When the pigs, too, pass around the corner, the gates open for the fourth time. In every door a housewife appears with a long wicker-broom. Good morning! Good morning! And within minutes the streets are swept clean of the round flat markings of the cows, the yellow corn muffins of the horses, and the small black pebbles of the goats. Good morning! Good morning!

As the last gate closes shut, I go back to sleep. To dream. Our little town is made for dreaming.

TWO

THE SUMMER passed and my brother, Bubi, left for Budapest. He is a student at the Jewish Teachers' Seminary. Next year I will join him!

He did not have to fight for Daddy's permission. He is a boy and he is older, I am told. Besides, he has natural ability, and I have only ambition. You see, I get good grades because I like to study, but my brother gets good grades without ever opening a book. Mommy is very proud of him. Daddy praises me for my ambition. He says ambition is sometimes more important than ability. People often accomplish more with ambition than with ability. I wonder: Does having ambition mean that I have no natural ability? Or talent? How will I ever become a famous poet if I have no talent? With ambition alone?

Dark, rainy days of autumn froze into glistening white stiffness of winter. The gloom of the Hungarian occupation, the slow drag of the war, increasing food shortages and lack of news of our soldiers on the fronts thickened the chill winter fog. Hitler's speeches were broadcast daily and his shrill shrieks struck panic in my heart. One of his broadcasts became a catch phrase with the Hungarian Nazis: "We will play football with the heads of Jews."

When Daddy saw I became frightened at hearing this, he reassured me: "Don't worry, little Elli. It is only a manner of speaking. Don't take it literally, God forbid. They say these things to reduce the Jews to an oppressed, intimidated group. All they want is to frighten and humiliate us." Sharp lines of pain etched his square, handsome face. His deep, brown eyes were sad and a wan smile accompanied the touch of his hand on my shoulder: "Don't even think about these things, Ellike. Just forget you ever heard them."

But I could not put the vision out of my mind. Bloody heads rolling on the dusty football field of Somorja became a recurring nightmare.

The proud, erect figure of my father seemed to grow somewhat slack as the winter wore on. His silences became longer, the shadows under his cheekbones, deeper. Ever since the Hungarian occupation three years ago when our business was confiscated, Daddy was becoming more and more distant. His famous wit became more caustic, his laughter, a rare treat. He seemed to derive pleasure only from study, and the endless winter evenings found him poring over huge folios of the Talmud or leather-bound volumes of Biblical commentaries.

Now the winter is over, and I am glad. It was long and unusually cold. On my birthday, February 28, the snow started to melt and spring was in the air. Even Daddy cheered up a little, and it made my heart sing with delight. It promises to be a wonderful spring. Soft, mellow, full of sunshine. A light, chirpy spring. I am thirteen.

Yesterday Jancsi Novack said hello. I was wearing my new navy-blue coat with the shoulder pads. I look at least fifteen in that coat. The shoulder pads make me look less thin and more mature. As I was passing Banga's General Store, Jancsi Novack came out and noticed me. He smiled and said: "Oh, hello."

Novack is a senior, and the dream of every girl in the class. He used to walk with the prettiest girls. He never ever even noticed me before. Now he singled me out with a smile and a big hello. What a wonderful, wonderful spring!

Many other wonderful things are happening. I passed the examinations with high marks and Daddy agreed. I have written for application forms to the Jewish Gymnasium in Budapest, and Mommy wrote to her cousin who lives near the school, asking if I can live with them. My dreams are coming into sharper focus with every passing day.

I am writing a long letter to Bubi tonight. It will be simply marvelous to live in Budapest and meet him after school, go places with him. He is handsome and tall and knows everything about Budapest. Tonight my daydreams are not laced with painful longing. They are anticipatory, real. I fall asleep in a glow of excitement.

There is a sharp knock on the window near my bed. In the next room my parents are stirring. They speak in hushed tones.

"They are here again," my father whispers. "I wonder what do they want this time?"

"Please, be polite to them," says Mommy. "It is always better to be courteous even if they are rude. Please. We must avoid trouble."

"I will open the storefront. I prefer it that way. Let them enter through the store."

Daddy in his dressing gown tiptoes through my room leaving the door to the store ajar. I can hear him unbolt the storefront. Nothing happens. There is no one there. Now there is pounding at the rear entrance of the house.

"They are at the rear. Hurry. They will break down the door if we don't open immediately. Hurry, please." He quickly rebolts the storefront and hurries to the back of the house. Mother follows him. She closes my bedroom door carefully behind her. The illuminated clock says 2:30 A.M.

They always come unexpectedly in the middle of the night.

The Hungarian military police, with their tall cock-feathers tucked in black helmets. They always come pounding on windows or doors, four or five of them. High-heeled boots, guns perched on their shoulders. They are the dread of the Jews in the occupied territories. They stage raids, *razzias*, in the middle of the night, looking for concealed weapons, they say. They raid our houses turning everything upside down, rudely poking furniture with bayonets, ordering my father around as if he were a criminal.

"You Jews are harboring enemy aliens! You are collaborating with the enemy. You want the Czechs back, we know. You want to sell out Hungary to the enemy."

And with that they enter the store and take whatever they like, packets of coffee, tea, chocolate. They put things in their satchels and move through the house once again.

They open closets and drawers, spill the contents on the floor. Our most precious belongings. They are looking for spies, they say. They poke at the furniture with their bayonets, and stand in their muddy boots on our best upholstered chairs, on the petit-point dining room chairs. They are looking for hidden radio equipment, they say. The Jews are in contact with the enemy, feeding information through secret equipment. We know, they say to my father, and one day we will find out. And they slip a watch, a bracelet, a fountain pen, a silk scarf, or an embroidered kerchief into their cases.

I see all this from under my covers. I am not allowed to get out of bed. Mommy orders me covered up. She tells me not to move. I pretend to sleep. But I see their faces menacing my father, I hear them speaking to him in loud, rude tones, and I see my father biting his lips. My father is a very tall man, but they are much taller in their cock-feathers. He is thin and they are sturdy.

They usually find some violation. Once they officially "expropriated" my mother's heavy winter coat. It was English wool, they said, enemy fabric. Another time they took a box of tea, claiming it was Russian tea—imported from the enemy. Once they carted away cartons of soap, another time, cases of cotton thread. It was American cotton, French soap. Consorting with the enemy in secret. It was merchandise, Hungarian manufactured, labeled, merchandise left over from the store. It is four years now since our store has been closed. By order of the Hungarian Royal Republic. You are lying, they say to my father. Jews always lie. An official summons for the violations is left on the dining room table.

The next morning my father has to appear at the police station with the summons. He politely answers an endless row of questions and then signs a "confession" to the crimes he committed. Concealing English wool, Russian tea, French soap, and American cotton under Hungarian labels. The fine is always steep. He has to pay promptly. Sometimes my mother would be arraigned, too. Once the charge was that we failed to follow air-raid regulations carefully and a beam of light escaped from our kitchen window "to warn enemy planes." They held both of them all day. Another time they claimed we bought white flour on the black market. A neighbor denounced us, they said. The neighbor saw my mother bake *halot* for Shabbat. Sometimes they detained my father for days. We lived in agony during those days. Are they torturing him? Will they release him alive?

There are voices in the kitchen. The lights are on, and I can hear voices in the kitchen. When will they come to the rooms? Why are they staying in the kitchen for so long? I begin to tremble. Against my mother's orders I tiptoe to the kitchen door and peer through the sheer curtain. There, right in the middle of the kitchen, stands my brother in his overcoat, his face flushed, talking excitedly. My father and mother flank him on both sides. No one else is in the kitchen. Where are the police?

"Bubi!" My surprise and joy knows no bounds. I rush into the kitchen, barefoot, hugging him. "Bubi!"

"Shh. Let's keep still." My father is pale.

"Let's all sit down. Now, Bubi, tell us slowly, quietly, what happened."

THREE

THE GERMANS invaded Budapest! Bubi saw German tanks roll down Andrassy Ut this morning. He saw the flag with the swastika on the building of the Parliament. He saw German flags elsewhere. And a long column of tanks and armored vehicles.

He was on his way to school. He immediately decided to come home, took the next streetcar to the railway station, bought a ticket, and got on the next train. He has been traveling since morning.

My father shakes his head. Gently he puts his hand on my brother's shoulder. "It is impossible. It is simply impossible. How could the Germans have invaded Budapest and we know nothing about it? Nothing. Nothing in the newspapers. On the radio. Not a word. How can it be?"

"Let's go to sleep. We will see in the morning. The morning papers will headline it. Then we will know. Let's go to bed quietly." Mommy's voice is tense.

In the morning nothing happens. No mention of a German invasion anywhere. My father comes home from the synagogue with the reassuring news. Not a sign of invasion. He is worried about my brother.

"Bubi, I did not tell anyone you came home. By now I am sure it was a false alarm. I am absolutely sure. Something, or someone, frightened you, son. I don't blame you for coming home. These are frightening times."

Bubi's eyes catch a strange flame. But he says nothing.

"I don't blame you for coming home when you thought there was trouble. But there is no reason for you to stay home and miss your classes. I think it best if you go right back. To school. There is an express for Budapest at one P.M."

"But, Dad, I saw them. I saw them with my own eyes. The tanks on Andrassy Ut. And the flags. Flags with swastikas, everywhere, everywhere. The crowds at first were silent, but then began shouting: '*Heil* Hitler!' As I ran to the streetcar I kept hearing the shouts, people everywhere repeating it: '*Heil* Hitler!' "

"It must have been a demonstration of some kind. Some kind of Nazi rally. Bubi, there is no point in your staying home. If you leave with the one P.M. train, you can be in school on time tomorrow morning. You shall have missed only one day of classes."

Bubi averts his eyes. Father is to be obeyed. Mother concurs as well. No point in remaining here. Father is always careful in his judgment. He is never rash, never jumps to unreasonable conclusions.

Mommy packs a food parcel for my brother. But before he leaves for the train, Dad goes to see Mr. Kardos, the lawyer down the block whose son was also studying in Budapest. But Mr. Kardos has no news from his son. Bubi is embarrassed. He was the only one to run home.

When I kiss my brother good-bye, I feel a wild pain.

We do not walk him to the station so as not to arouse suspicion. People will ask questions. We have no answers.

He leaves for Budapest with the one P.M. train. At 1:20 Mr. Kardos comes running to our house. He has received a telegram from his son: The Germans invaded Budapest! He wants to know whether we have heard anything from my brother.

Father turns pale.

"At this moment my son is on his way back to Budapest."

"What! He was here? And he knew? You knew? You knew and did not say anything?"

"Yes. Bubi came home last night and told us he saw the Germans marching into Budapest. Came home immediately. But . . . I did not believe him. No one had heard anything. There was nothing in the papers. On the radio. What shall we do now?"

"I am going to Budapest at once. To bring home my son."

This is the first time in my life that I see my mother cry. She is a strong woman, always cheerful and full of hope. But today she walks about with lips set tight, eyes brimming and red. She is busy with her housework and does not speak. My father smokes incessantly. His face is ashen and his hands tremble each time he lights a cigarette. He paces the kitchen floor. I want to scream.

The next morning the news pours in. The headlines roar: WE ARE LIBERATED! THE GLORIOUS ARMY OF HITLER IN BUDAPEST! ORDER RESTORED! The radio blares "Deutschland über Alles," all day long. The country is agog with the news. Two days late.

Other news reaches us. Jews are being arrested on sight. On the streets, on streetcars, at their places of work, at railroad stations. They are herded into freight trains. The trains are locked, some chained shut. They are taken away. Where? No one knows.

Father stops pacing the floor: "I cannot stand it any longer. I am going to Budapest after him. There is a train at eight P.M. I am going."

"You can't. It is too late. They will arrest you, too. You won't be of any help to him that way. Stay here with us. God will help us. God will be with us and save him."

Mother's voice trembles. I hug her and she begins to cry openly. Father's tall, erect frame seems almost fragile. I feel pain choke my throat. God, if only Bubi were here!

During the night Bubi arrives from Budapest.

Mr. Kardos has not returned. Neither has his son, Gyuri. Nothing was ever heard of them again.

FOUR

BUBI SUCCEEDED in getting to Budapest undetected, thanks to his blond hair, blue eyes, Aryan looks. He managed to evade the black-booted SS patrolling the streets until he reached his apartment. His landlady was shocked to see him. What insanity to return to Budapest! Pack and go home immediately!

Instead, Bubi listened to Father, took his briefcase and went off to school.

As he approached the school building he saw students carrying school furniture—benches, desks, chairs—and piling them on the sidewalk. Like robots, they moved with a deliberate, unanimated speed. Bubi understood. The work was supervised by SS guards stationed at the entrance and scattered on the sidewalk. His classmates at the Jewish Teachers' Institute were under arrest! They were doomed, within a few feet of him!

With this realization, Bubi felt his feet rooted into the ground. He could not move. Transfixed, he stood there staring at the scene. A truck came. From its hulk, men, women, and children poured onto the street accompanied by SS men, gesticulating, shouting, herding them into the building. Bubi's school was being converted into a concentration camp. Only three days after the occupation. The Germans had wasted no time.

Suddenly, Bubi saw Sanyi carrying a chair. Cousin Sanyi was a senior at the Institute. He noticed Bubi and motioned to him to run. As the SS guard was about to turn around, Bubi ducked into a doorway. Quickly, he removed his navy blue school cap with the gold emblem of the Institute and stuffed it into his pocket. Unnoticed, he slipped out of the doorway and headed for the nearest trolley. Back to the railway station for home.

The railroad station was packed with long rows of freight cars, army trucks, and SS men rushing about. Huge yellow stars were crudely painted on the wagons which held men, women and children. Others were being dragged off the trucks and loaded onto the train shrieking, crying and pleading. Some were screaming messages from narrow windows, from slits in the doors; they were screaming names, names of children, husbands, sisters.

As if in a dream, Bubi bought a ticket and boarded a passenger train. On the platform Hungarian police demanded identification of everyone in sight. My brother, the tall, thin, unobtrusive, blond teen-ager, slipped by.

The train stood still for over an hour. A group of Hungarian military police combed through the compartments, checking identity papers. Jews were automatically placed under arrest, pulled off the train, and handed over to the SS. From his corner seat Bubi saw them shoved into the wagons. Once again the police passed him by.

During the five-hour ride home the Hungarian police entered the cars at every station and dragged off passengers whose identity papers revealed they were Jews. Shocked and uncomprehending, men and women were thrown onto waiting trucks and driven off. Bubi huddled in his corner, paralyzed with fear. Finally at 2 A.M. he arrived home. Shaken and pale and tired, but safe.

Or so we felt for the moment.

FIVE

NOTHING HAPPENED during that week in town.

The small Jewish community waited in silence. No one knew what was happening elsewhere. There was no news of other Jews in other towns. No news at all. No Jew from another town came to our place, and no Jew left the town. Our Gentile neighbors confirmed Bubi's report that on trains and buses Jews were arrested on sight and put into cattle cars. The cattle cars were locked and driven off.

Fear sealed every Jew into his home. Mommy's words of comfort did little to ease the tension in our house. Bubi kept up his schoolwork with difficulty despite Mommy's encouragement and exhortations to carry on, all this would pass soon, and he would pick up in school where he left off. It was the twelth hour of the war, she said. Daddy paced the floor of our spacious kitchen like a caged lion. What was to be done?

I alone continued my routine. School was as usual, nothing has changed there. There was no sign of the German occupation either on the street or in the classrooms. It was an escape into normalcy. It was a relief to leave my house every morning and enter the familiar world of unaltered schedules of classes and recesses, carefree camaraderie with fellow students and absorption in lectures unrelated to the world threatening to engulf the Jew.

Then, suddenly, on Saturday morning all schools were ordered closed.

It was March 25, 1944—three months before graduation. Our homeroom teacher made the announcement in terse, staccato sentences: "Class, the Royal Hungarian Ministry of Education has terminated instruction in all schools of the country —to safeguard our interest."

Her voice broke. Tears welled in her eyes. Almost inaudibly she said: "Good-bye, class . . . children. You can all go home now."

That is all? Not a word of explanation? What are we to do now? Will we graduate? Will we get our report cards? Mrs. Kertész left the classroom without giving us a chance to ask questions. No mention of the German occupation. No indication of what was to happen next. Of what awaited us.

We looked at each other, shocked. Confused. Then, one by

one, my classmates stood up and began filing out of the room.

I got up, too, and looked around. The dark, oil-stained floor. The worn wooden benches. The white-washed walls with their threadbare maps and faded pictures. It was all so, familiar, so reassuring. Even the dark-green crucifix above the door. For almost four years I had struggled, sweated, and, sometimes triumphed among these walls, in front of this blackboard. The stale smell of the oiled floor mingled with rising chalk dust, with fear, with jealousy, or joy.

Will I ever sit behind my narrow desk in the last row? Will I ever see my classmates? Will I ever sense the substance of childhood filtered through the ambience of this room again?

Perhaps soon the schools will reopen. Perhaps soon the country will settle down under German occupation and everything will be just as before. Classes will resume and our group will graduate as planned. I was certain of that. I was quite certain.

I decided to leave by the main entrance. The boys' classes use the main entrance. Maybe Jancsi Novack will be leaving just now, too. I wanted to see him for the last time.

As I turned into the hallway leading to the main staircase, an arm reached out and blocked my way. I looked up, astonished. It was not Novack. A stocky, pimply-faced boy with dark hair slicked back stood in my way, grinning. He raised his right arm in the Nazi salute and said: "*Heil*, Hitler!" A group of fifteen boys lined both sides of the stairs. And they echoed: "*Heil* Hitler!" Grinning.

As I passed them, they began to chant: "*Heil*, Hitler! *Sieg heil! Sieg heil! Sieg heil!*" I ran down the stairs. The stocky boy shouted: "Down with the Jews! Down with the Jews!"

I flew down the stairs and out to the street. I ran and ran. Far down the block I heard them sing the popular ditty, the vulgar army marching song: "*Hej, zsidó lány, zsidó lány . . .*" Hey, Jew girl, Jew girl . . .

The sounds followed me home. Mocking, taunting, devastating. Sounds that can penetrate and bruise and pierce.

Sounds that can kill. As I ran, one of my braids got undone. Tears choked my throat. I reached my house as my temples throbbed and sweat ran down my back.

No one was home. My parents were still at the synagogue—it was Sabbath morning. I fished the key from under the mat and slammed the great oak door behind me. As I buried my face in my pillow I cried for my world which had just collapsed. This was the beginning of the end.

SIX

THE END came rapidly. The dizzying pace of our "liquidation" and the methodical rhythm of the well-oiled machinery of the system divested us of initiative of any kind. It was easiest to be swept along by the swift current of events. Like lifeless matter we were carried along on a powerful conveyor belt toward an unknown fate. The professional efficiency of the process, the smooth operation, was vaguely reassuring. It was easiest to give up. The dreaded moment had come; what we had feared had come to pass. We are in the hands of the SS: There is no escape. The struggle is over. Perhaps. No, not perhaps. Surely it is God's will.

On Monday morning all Jews were ordered to appear at the town hall. We had to deliver all jewelry, radios, and vehicles. We had to line up, and we were counted, registered, and supplied with tags. Like children before leaving for summer camp. Or pets after leaving the pet shop.

I had to part with my new Schwinn bicycle. It was a present from my parents on my last birthday. My only real possession. The realization of years of yearning, daydreaming. At first I thought I would not be able to give it to them. It is intimately mine. How can they just tell me to take it to the town hall and just leave it there in a pile? How can they just tell you one day that the next morning you give up your most precious possession. Without a sound of protest. Without even demanding explanation. At first I thought I could not do it. I thought such things were impossible.

It was a bright-yellow girls' bike with bright red-and-yellow webbing on the back wheel. It had a dark-yellow leather seat and the shiny chrome handlebars were tucked into handles matching the seat. It was beautiful.

On Sunday afternoon when with a face frozen into a mask of defiance my father brought the news, I began to scream. I was not going to do it! Let them kill me, I was not going to let them take my new bike I had not even ridden yet. I had been waiting for spring to try it out. Spring was just beginning. The snow had just begun to melt, and I was going to take my new, shiny Schwinn on the street as soon as the mud cleared. I cannot part from it now! In my panic and rage I felt helpless, exposed. Violated.

"As soon as this is over, all this madness, I will buy you another Schwinn. Never mind this one, Elli. Never mind. You will have the most beautiful bike money can buy. A full-size girls' bike. Bigger than this one and even more beautiful." Father's voice was choked with anger and pain. He spoke very low, almost in a whisper.

"I don't want another bike. I have not even tried this one out. What right do they have to take it? I have just received it from you; you gave it to me as my birthday present. It is mine. How can they just *take* it?"

Daddy's soft hands on my cheeks soothed my sobbing. Over and over, he repeated: "Never mind, Ellike. Never mind."

On Monday morning, as I walked next to my father leading his bicycle and my brother leading his own Schwinn, I felt no more rage or panic or loss. Only humiliation. And when I saw my bright, shiny bike lined up against the wall among the many battered, lackluster old bicycles, I felt the ground slip under me. The long tables in the courtyard of the city hall were piled high with jewelry, silverware, radios, and cameras. I saw our antique candlesticks in the pile and some of Mommy's best silver. My bracelets and earrings were somewhere in the heap. I saw the faces as they turned from the table. Humiliation and shame flickered in every eye. Degradation.

That night Father took me down into the cellar. In the far corner of the dank dark underground room the flashlight revealed a rough spot on the earthen floor.

"Look, Elli. Here on this spot I buried our most precious pieces of jewelry, about twenty-five centimeters deep. Mommy and Bubi also know the spot. Each one of us should know where the jewels are buried. We don't know which of us will return. Will you remember?"

I refused to look: "I don't want to know! I don't want to remember!"

He put his arm about my shoulders: "Elli . . . Ellike . . ." he repeated softly. Then slowly, with heavy steps he led me up the stairs.

In the kitchen Mommy turned from the stove and asked Daddy in a matter-of-fact tone: "Have you showed her?"

With a nod of his head Daddy was about to forestall anymore discussion of the subject, when I burst out crying: "Why should Daddy show me the spot? Why? Why do I have to know about the jewels? Why? Tell me, why? Tell me! I don't want to know! I don't want to be the one to survive! I don't want to survive alone! Alone, I don't want to live! Oh, God, I don't want to live if you don't! I don't want to know about anything!"

My sobs were the only sounds in the kitchen. Dead silence followed my outburst. In utter misery I went to bed. Pulling the blanket over my head, I continued sobbing for a long time.

The next morning, the sounds of the town crier woke me. I did not run to the square as I used to every time the intriguing drumbeat sounded and the high-pitched, singsong proclamation began. I opened my window and through the fluttering muslin curtains the words reached me: "Hear ye! Hear ye! As of eight A.M. this Tuesday morning, the twenty-eighth day of the month of March, in the nineteen hundred and forty-fourth year of our Lord Jesus Christ, all Jews must wear a yellow star on the left side of the chest. The star must be of canary-yellow fabric, of six equal points, eight centimeters in diameter. Any Jew seen on the street without the star will be arrested. Likewise, a canary-yellow six-pointed star of one meter in diameter shall be painted on the exterior wall of every Jewish home to the left of the main entrance of the house. Tomorrow morning at eight o'clock the residents of any Jewish house not marked by the star shall be arrested. This proclamation be duly . . ."

I shut the window. My God, what next? A yellow star? The Middle Ages, evil tales of long ago. I used to hate Jewish history in the after-school Hebrew class. I hated the misery, the suffering, the badge. The Jew badge.

I refused to leave the house. I am not going to wear the yellow star! I am not going to appear in public with the Jew badge. I can't be seen wearing that horrible, horrible thing. I will die if any of my schoolmates see me. My brother made a brave joke of the whole thing. He made believe he had been awarded a medal: On a cardboard star he fastened glistening bright yellow silk. It really looked like a gold military medal. This he pinned on his chest and marched about the streets with a smile of triumph. His "medal" became the envy of his friends; they began to imitate him. Soon other young boys were wearing decorative yellow stars, feigning distinction, denying the badge was meant to humiliate them. I could not understand them. All I felt was bitter resentment. Deep hurt and anger.

My brother's attitude made me sad. When I saw him, the tall, handsome seventeen year old wearing his "medal" with mock pride, his brave attempt to turn humiliation into triumph made me want to cry. It was a bitter joke. My anger turned to raw pain.

I sat indoors for over a week. Mother pleaded, her voice gentle and sad: "Elli, let us thank God for being alive. Let us thank God for being together, in our own house. What is a yellow star on a jacket? It does not kill or condemn. It does not harm. It only means you are a Jew. That is nothing to be ashamed of. We are not marked for being criminals. Only for being Jews. Aren't you proud of being a Jew?"

I did not know if I was proud to be a Jew. I had never thought about it. But I knew I did not want to be marked as a Jew or as anything else. I knew I was hurt and outraged at being made to wear a glaring mark, a thing intended to set me apart and humiliate me. Jew, or criminal, what is the difference in their intent? What is the difference in my shame of helplessness? I was no longer a human being, I was singled out at will, an object.

Daddy seemed oblivious to the star. Each time he left the house Mommy had to remind him to wear his jacket with the star on it. One could not simply pin a star on whatever one was wearing: A star had to be sewn onto every garment with small stitches. Mommy solved this problem by stitching stars to several outer garments and we wore those each time we went outdoors.

The canary-yellow star did not detract from Daddy's elegant appearance. Always impeccably dressed and with a proud bearing, he continued to exude an air of quiet dignity. His seeming lack of awareness of this humiliating mark puzzled me. How can he ignore it so completely?

The nasal, grating tones of the town crier carried a new message which broke my resolution of never being seen with the yellow star. Report cards were being distributed at all schools. Schools will not reopen. All school children must appear in person to pick up report cards, diplomas, certificates. I have to appear in person at ten o'clock. Our diplomas are to be handed out in our homeroom. The entire class will be there! Like a reunion for the last time.

I was thrilled. Then I remembered the star. My heart sank. I went to my closet, and there on my spring jacket was the horrible thing, left of the zipper. On me it looked even larger, more glaring. What if I met the *heil*-Hitler gang? Was I actually afraid of them? Even worse, Jancsi Novack. What would he say?

I hung the jacket back into my closet.

"Coward." It was my brother.

"I am not. I am not a coward."

"Then what are you? Why haven't you left the house for over a week? And now your report card, even your diploma. I know what they mean to you. But you are afraid to wear the star. Isn't that cowardice?"

No one will call me a coward. I snatched the jacket and not turning to say good-bye to my brother, left the house. On the street, brilliant sunshine splashed into my face. The acacia tree in front of our house was the brightest green I have ever seen. The huge yellow star on the front wall was shockingly brilliant. I had not seen it until now.

I walked fast. When I got to the school, I quickly removed my jacket and carried it folded inside out, hiding the star. The corridors were empty. The distribution of report cards was under way in every classroom.

When I entered my classroom, Mrs. Kertész was speaking to the class. She was saying farewell to us. With tears in her eyes, she wished us all success and told us of her plans to return to her native town in Upper Slovakia in early retirement. We all drank in her words with the thirst of those who know that this is their last few moments of water supply. Something final was happening in our lives. Early in our lives we were arriving at a terminal. It was frightening.

Then Mrs. Kertész started distributing the report cards together with the diplomas—alphabetically. When I stepped to her desk, Mrs. Kertész paused. "Class," she said, "Livia Elvira Friedmann received . . ." My heart began beating rapidly and my temples throbbed. I did not hear her words. But I knew. For in the next few moments I was clutching the coveted honor scroll. It had been a dream, unattainable. "Congratulations. I am happy for you, Livia Elvira," she said with warmth.

In a state of delirium I walked to my seat, squeezing hands stretched out in the aisle. A heady feeling of joy. Warm glances of shared happiness. The warm glow of bliss. Is it really happening?

When it was all over, diplomas handed out and final embraces made, I headed for home, still in a glow of unreality. A cold breeze greeted me at the exit of the school. As I absently put on my jacket, my glance fell on the yellow star. Almost simultaneously I heard someone from behind me call, "Congratulations. You got the class honor scroll. Congratulations."

I turned. It was Jancsi Novack. For a moment I forgot about the star.

"Thank you. How did you know? The scroll, I mean. I mean, that I got the honor scroll."

This is the first time Jancsi Novack spoke to me. Suddenly, I remembered the star. I blushed. It was too late. He must have seen it already. As he spoke there was no hint that he noticed it. Not a flicker of embarrassment. "I saw the list. Your name was posted on the honor roll," he said.

"Posted? Where?"

"In the main corridor, on the wall. Next to the picture of Miklos Horthy and the flag. I saw your name on the column for girls—Livia E. Friedmann. A nice name."

I blushed again. "I did not know it was posted. They had never posted the names before."

"This year it's different. This year there won't be any yearbook. Posting takes the place of the yearbook. This year everything is different. No yearbook. No graduation. We were looking forward to it. And now, nothing. Well, not quite nothing. We received the honor scroll, didn't we? At least that much."

"You, too? Congratulations!"

He was pleased with my enthusiasm. We reached the front entrance of my house, and I was relieved. We had not met anyone. Jancsi stretched out his hand: "Good luck. Perhaps I

will see you again? Every Thursday I will be coming to
Somorja, and then I will be going to the library. Perhaps I can
see you there. In the afternoon?"

As he shook my hand, his eyes held an unfathomable sad-
ness. It astounded me. Then he averted his gaze from the star.
I promised to meet him at the library. But the glow was gone.
Suddenly I felt unbearably bruised.

His sadness was too much to bear.

SEVEN

I NEVER saw Jancsi Novack again. On Wednesday morning the
town crier announced that "Jews are forbidden under penalty
of immediate arrest to have intercourse of any kind with Gentiles. They are forbidden to speak, greet, acknowledge greeting,
correspond, deliver to or receive objects from Gentiles. Gentiles are enjoined to observe the same. Jews are further forbidden under penalty of immediate arrest to enter public
places—theaters, cinemas, restaurants, cafes, schools, parks,
post office, city hall, or library. Gentiles are enjoined to in-
form on any Jew seen entering the aforementioned places."

We are virtually under house arrest. Even getting staples
from the grocery store is becoming painful. I dread meeting
our neighbors on the street; entering the store without greeting
is sheer agony. I walk stiffly, averting my gaze from every face
in constant fear of disobeying the order. What if I forget and
say hello? Or respond to a greeting? Or what if, in meeting a
friend, we remember to observe the order, and pass each other
like strangers? Is that possible?

It was possible. It happened. Meeting neighbors was unavoidable. As nonexistent shadows we moved on the streets

unrecognized, unacknowledged, unseen. The awkwardness I feared never materialized. Our Gentile friends and neighbors observed the restrictions without apparent conflict. A sense of isolation pervaded our every waking moment. Alienation was becoming more tangible with every passing day.

A week passed. Another announcement from the drumbeat of the town crier. The worst. The one we dread most and had believed would not come. All Jews of Somorja are to be concentrated in a ghetto in another town—Nagymagyar, fourteen kilometers away. In five days every Jewish family must stand ready for deportation to the ghetto. One room of furniture and personal possessions may be packed, everything else to be left behind; keys delivered to police headquarters.

Five more days. The weather has turned from early spring to early summer and the fragrance of violets fills the air. Five-day feverish packing culminates in the arrival of the cock-feathered military police. Under their supervision our belongings are laden on peasant carts. Food stuffs, pieces of furniture, clothing. Even firewood. Mother is in charge. She organizes the packing operation, dispatches carts that are filled, talks to the police, calms my father. He is tense. My brother is efficient. He helps my mother the most. I am having an excruciating stomachache. We have to hurry. By 1 P.M. Somorja must be *Judenrein*.

It is eleven o'clock. All the carts are laden. My father is sitting on the furniture cart, Mommy's sister, Aunt Szerén, who lives at the end of town, on the cart with the clothing and food. Mommy tells my brother to join my aunt on the cart. As he jumps up in the back, we wave good-bye to them and to my father on the first cart. The coachmen snap their whips and the carts are off to an early start. Mommy and I will follow them on the cart with the firewood. But first she wants to go to the cemetery. Her parents are buried in the old Jewish cemetery, near the next village, a forty-minute walk. My grandfather, the revered scholar and *tzaddik*, and my grandmother, the cheerful, kind lady—I had not known them. Both died before my birth.

But I know the graves. I used to accompany Mommy to the cemetery. And now, perhaps for the last time, I am to accompany her again. The cart stands before the house, waiting, while Mommy and I are going to the cemetery: "Your keys. Hand over the keys, missus." The cock-feathered Hungarian was grim.

"Ah, yes. The keys. You want them now? Can you wait until we get back from the cemetery? We won't be long. We will be back before the deadline. Before one o'clock." Her voice pleaded.

"Now," said the policeman.

She hands him the keys. And in her eyes a veiled look of terror.

In our hurry to the cemetery we walk along the length of our town past half-laden carts, past wide-open gates through which men and women busily carry belongings in a sense of haste and load them onto the wagons. They do not even glance at us. A burden of fear drives them on.

We hurry. More carts, more people scurrying in and out of gates, loading bundles onto carts. Some friends notice us briefly and wave silently, then move on. We pass the synagogue at the end of town. Mr. Stern, the old *shohet*, stands facing the western wall of the synagogue, praying. Mommy motions to me to stop. We wait for him to finish his prayer. Slowly, he closes the prayerbook and kisses the wall. He just stands there, his eyes closed, his face touching the wall. We approach him silently. He is motionless. Tears are trickling down his thin white beard. Mommy touches him lightly on the shoulder:

"Mr. Stern. Good-bye. God be with you."

He turns around. As if lost, he looks at my mother. The synagogue yard is deserted. All the families are gone. He is left, alone. An old man, a thin, stooped and fragile figure, against a backdrop of desolation. He does not answer.

"Mr. Stern, what did you pray for just now? We are on our way to the cemetery, tell me what should we pray?"

His voice is barely audible: "I said the Prayer of the Road. We are going on a long road. A very long road. The road may never end. We may not live to see the end of the road. . . . Perhaps we will never come back."

He begins to cry loudly. Mother takes his arm and leads him into his house behind the synagogue.

On the open road my stomachache lessens a little. The sun shines brightly and the graves glisten white. While Mommy prays I lie down in the grass, pressing my aching belly against the moist ground. It is 12:30 P.M. We have to hurry back.

On the main street all carts are gone. The gates of the Jewish houses are wide open. I can see scattered furniture, pots, and pans, lying about in the yards, doorways, and even on the sidewalk. But no living soul. Where are the Gentile neighbors? Their doors and windows are shut, shades drawn on every window. There is only one solitary sign of life in the town. The lonely cart with its horse impatiently slapping its tail in front of our house, the driver like a stone statue in the seat and cock-feathered police pacing the sidewalk. It is five minutes to one. Two Jewish women are still on the loose polluting the pure Aryan air of Somorja.

Without a word mother gets on the cart next to the driver. I follow her climbing onto the small seat facing the pile of wood. The peasant cracks his whip, *"Gyutteee!"* and the cart rolls out onto the open road. A sharp stab of pain in my stomach. From the bend in the road I can see the receding outline of our house. The yellow star glistens brightly.

From my seat I cannot see the road ahead. I am facing the road we are leaving behind. I am facing the past receding rapidly. The steel-spiked wooden wheels of the cart churn up tiny pebbles and a cloud of dust. I am leaving my birthplace behind. Perhaps forever. The parting is etched in my memory through a haze of dust and stomachache.

EIGHT

I HAD had a dream several weeks earlier. My father and I, the two of us, stood in the middle of our storage room called *kamra*. In this room we kept sacks of flour, animal feed, chopped-up wood, and other odds and ends. I hated the *kamra*. It was a dark, bleak place. When mother sent me there for flour or wood, I hurried out as soon as I could. When I was little I used to believe there were evil spirits in the dark corners of the *kamra* and was terrified to enter it.

But in my dream I was standing in the middle of the *kamra* with my father, without an apparent purpose. We just stood there, silently, our backs to the entrance whence a dim light was filtering into an otherwise dark place. The flour sacks stood menacing against the wall and the pile of wood was harboring a strange brooding stillness. Suddenly, a bird flew into the *kamra*. An unusual bird with an egg-shaped body covered with golden feathers, and large, greenish-yellow wings. As it flew into the *kamra*, a bright light streamed in with it, following it as it fluttered about. It hovered above my father's head, the light growing ever brighter until bathing the bird in a glittering flood of blinding sparkle. But the room remained cloaked in dark. And we, too—my father and I—remained wrapped in the shadows.

"Look at that bird!" said my father, pale with shock. He was deeply moved. Not frightened, but strangely moved by the awesome sight.

I glanced at the bird and then averted my eyes. I dared not look at it. It was too awful, too frightening. I began to tremble. My father gripped my arm and said again: "Look at that bird!" He stood transfixed, not moving his gaze from the horrible beauty of the bird. His grip tightened on my arm. When I looked at him he was no longer a living figure but a gray statue with eyes lifted to the heights. But his lips, motionless, kept whispering: "Look at that bird. . . ."

When I awoke I had a clear, dreadful knowledge that I would lose my father soon. And it was then that a slow pain had crept into my stomach and stayed there. But I did not tell anyone of my dream.

Sitting on the cart facing the dusty past, the hours grind away on the bumpy road. I remember the dream. Oh, God, help us all.

NINE

THE CART pulls into a narrow dirt road which widens into the main street of Nagymagyar. At the far end of the long, winding street is the synagogue, a simple white structure surrounded by small houses and a tall, wire fence. This is the ghetto.

Our cart comes to a halt in the synagogue yard before one of the small houses, the house of the ritual slaughterer. Our family has been assigned to share their apartment. An elderly couple with two tiny rooms and a tiny kitchen. We are to move in there. Father, Aunt Szerén, and Bubi, who arrived before us, are standing about helplessly in the yard with heaps of furniture, bundles of clothes, pots and pans, mattresses, baby carriages, sacks of flour, and metal stoves. There is no room in any of the houses for our things. The finest pieces of furniture from our house are now in the midst of a mountain of objects piled in the yard.

Over five hundred families are crowded into this enclave for twenty. How are we to manage? Each family brought the allocated amount of furniture and clothing, foodstuffs, and per-

sonal effects—but no room for any of it here. No room for the
people who are herded into this small area from fifteen com-
munities of the region. People are milling about, mothers and
infants, elderly men and women, small children.

"That's the sofa from our living room!" A girl about my age
is pointing to a deep scarlet satin corner protruding from the
heap. I am thinking of our dining room chairs with the
Gobelin seats. They are my favorite. Where are they? I cannot
see them anywhere. The pile of precious possessions is too
high and deep.

By the evening the yard is cleared of people. The hustle and
bustle subside. Every available space is utilized. People move
into storage rooms, tool sheds, attics, basements, stairwells,
and into the synagogue itself. But the mountain of belongings
remains in the yard. In the little apartment of Mr. and Mrs.
Blumenfeld a bed is put into the kitchen for my brother. Father, Mother, Aunt Szerén, and I sleep in one room, the
Blumenfelds in the other. I share a bed with Mommy; Daddy
sleeps on the cot, and Aunt Szerén on the sofa.

We are lucky. Six, seven, or eight families are crowded into
other houses. People put bathtubs, stoves, and washstands into
the yard; kitchens and bathrooms serve as living quarters.
Beds and cots are everywhere. Simply everywhere. It is hilari-
ous.

There are cots even in the entrance hall to the synagogue.
Those who sleep in the synagogue have to get up before the
morning prayers and wait until after the evening prayers to go
to sleep. I think it is rather convenient. You simply have to
poke your nose from under your covers, and you are in the
synagogue for morning prayers!

"You should live in the shul," I say to my brother. "Your
problems would be solved."

He has trouble getting up for early morning prayers.
Mommy used to jerk his covers off; nothing else worked in
waking him. Then it is a long sleepy drag until he makes it to
the synagogue, usually late. Now he could have a built-in ar-

rangement. With one foot off the bed he could join the prayers on time.

The women cook in the yard: All the stoves are there. It is a pleasant, warm, sunny May, and most of life's activities take place in the yard. In one corner several women are cooking at one stove. A few yards away, a mother is bathing three children in a tub. A long line forms before the public toilet, another one before the public bath. And, alongside the tall wire fence, a row of Hungarian soldiers, looking at the spectacle. They are our guards, in addition to the military police.

We are aware of their presence. I feel quite self-conscious of their looks. But perhaps less so today than I did in the beginning. Gradually they are becoming part of the present scene.

Our life is taking a bearable course. The early confusion changes into a deliberate hustle and bustle, a harmonious coexistence. Together we prepare meals or eat at long tables in the yard, retire for the night or rise for prayers. Debates and discussions are the order of the day. The mood is becoming more positive and optimistic every day, even confident. There is a hopeful tone to the rhythm of life here. The worst is over. We have been uprooted from our homes and our property has been confiscated. We have been humiliated, crowded like cattle, and reduced to living behind a fenced-in enclosure like animals in a zoo. Yet, God in his mercy made it all manageable. And bearable. We are not cattle or captured beasts in a zoo. We have succeeded in carving out a dignified life style even within these confines. We are going to make it. We are making it.

I like the ghetto. The first day of our arrival here I meet more interesting, congenial, pleasant people than ever before. There are more people in this world I can identify with than I had realized. Girls my age, good-looking boys just a little older, well-dressed ladies, impressive men, and lovely little children. And they are all so exposed to you—in the yard. Their intimate habits, their privacy, open to your observation.

Families at their dinner table, washing up for the night, play-ing with their children, suckling their infants, studying with their adolescents, embraces and scoldings, tears and laughter, cries of pain and joy, lines for the toilet—all in the yard.

I like it all. I am part of every life. And every life is partly mine. I cease to be an individual. I am a limb of a larger body. In this I find solace.

I like the toilet line the best. It is long and moves slowly. You have time to meet and talk. There is so much to listen to and learn. So many people with so much to tell. I drink it all in with a thirst I had not been aware of. This is a shared fate and the communication is light, free-flowing, other-embracing. The toilet line is my love feast: I revel in it.

For the first time in my life I am happy to be a Jew. I am happy to share this peculiar condition. This condition of Jew-ishness, of distinction and chosenness even if for humiliation and suffering but selectively, carefully designated—all in one. All the select, designated, carefully despised and persecuted people together. Their handsome, teen-age boys, pretty ladies, beautiful babies, gray-bearded old men—all under one roof, in one backyard of oppression, together. I like being a Jew. I meet Jews closely, very closely, for the first time, and I like them. The soldiers are beyond the fence, and the cock-feath-ered policemen who had trampled on our sofas and our self-respect. The Gentile neighbors who were afraid to wave good-bye as we left, the Jancsi Novacks, the kind, gentle friends who nevertheless have not attempted to send a note of sympathy or farewell, the peasant drivers of the laden carts who dutifully accepted wages from us for delivering us to the enemy, the villagers who lined the roads as our cart passed and kept their silence. . . . They are on the other side of the fence. A world separates us because they do not understand. But we all within the fence, we understand. We put up sheets around bathtubs in the yard to take a bath, and we cook on open stoves, stand on long lines for the toilet . . . and understand. No compassion, friendship, or love binds as this deep, spontaneous, easy, mutuality. . . . It makes the Jewish condition comprehensible.

Naturally, I fall in love again in the ghetto. He is Pinhas, a tall, thin, pale boy, with dark earlocks, and large dark eyes. I noticed one day that he was watching me as I sat on a pile of firewood and wrote. I was copying my poems into a notebook I had brought from home.

I have over a hundred poems. When I was eight years old, my first poem attracted the attention of my teacher who deemed it acceptable for the program at the annual Mother's Day celebration. I recited the poem about a ship being tossed by angry waves on a stormy sea to an appreciative audience, and became an instant celebrity of sorts. The epithet "poet" entitled me to a flow of invitations to recite my poetry at the town's charitable functions and sometimes to the frequent derision of my peers. "Poet" is a strange creature, she is "different" at best. Being different reduced my popularity and created a wall of isolation. Yet, writing became central to my self-image, my aspirations, and dreams. I wrote lyric lines about the seasons and nature, epic poems about historical figures, elegies about my moods. I wrote almost constantly, often feverishly, inspired by a landscape, a kitten, rain, or the slaughter of a chicken. And, as my poems grew in popularity among the grown-ups, I dropped in popularity among the children.

They are all sad, my poems. Pain is the common denominator to each.

"Why? Why all this weltschmerz? Why don't you write cheerful little verses about trees, birds, animals? Why the lurking tragedy behind every blade of grass?" Mommy would inquire in puzzled annoyance.

"Because she is truly a poet. A poet knows," Father would reply. "The true poet knows life is laced with pain. Human life is fashioned for tragedy."

Most of my poems are scribbled on scraps of paper, and

now I am copying them into one book. Daily, I work hours at it when not helping mother with the cooking, playing with the children, or standing on lines.

At first I thought he was watching me out of curiosity. But then I caught him watching me from behind the door of the synagogue when he was supposed to be inside praying. And I was not writing. I was just sitting on a pail peeling potatoes.

Next time I saw him I smiled at him, and he smiled back. I was in love. And when Bobbi, my best friend, said he was handsome, in fact looked interesting, I could barely contain my happiness. "Interesting" was top evaluation.

Pinhas became central to my life in the ghetto. I anticipated meeting him on lines, watching for him as he went to shul, looked for him in any part of the yard. Everything else is somewhat receded in the background. A glimpse of Pinhas seems to pale everything else. Bobbi is right. He is handsome. And very interesting.

I took to endless brushing of my hair, experimenting with new styles. It is my only strong point.

"Just let it hang down, it is most striking that way. Just let it hang in two braids, it is best. Nobody has hair as long as yours, or as rich in texture. Or as brilliantly blonde. Just let it simply hang in braids."

Mother admires my hair. Its color, its shine, its thickness. She likes nothing else about me. But my hair makes up for it, I think. Even though she says she was disappointed when I turned out blonde. She had hoped for dark-haired, dark-eyed children, and both my brother and I are blond with blue-green eyes. But at least my brother has curly hair which Mommy has always wanted. My hair is as straight as freshly combed linen. "And as the rays of sun," my Aunt Cili used to say. But that is Aunt Cili. Mother had been disappointed with my hair. It is only recently that she has started to approve of it, even admire it. Thank God for my hair.

I try to pin my braids rolled around my head. It makes me look older. But it is not becoming. Finally, I hit on a style. I am crisscrossing the braids in the back, tying each end to the other side at the neck, each with a ribbon. It is quite elegant. Noticeable. I wonder if Pinhas will notice the difference.

He saw me a little later, on my way to the well to bring a pail of water for cooking. He stopped, looked at me in surprise, and smiled. He just stood there watching me while I stood on line for water. His eyes followed me back to our stove. He did not move. I almost dropped the pail from excitement. When he began walking away, he kept turning around. He was not smiling anymore. Just looking back, again and again.

My day is made. I help around the house cheerfully, not objecting even to kneading the dough. The trough is set up in the yard near our kitchen and I can watch people from afar.

"And people can watch and see that my little sister is working hard. Isn't that the idea?"

I ignore my brother's remark. I am anxious to catch another glimpse of Pinhas. My world is filled with newfound hope. Perhaps next time he will speak to me. We will become friends. It is all very, very exciting.

News, rumors reach the ghetto. Impending "liquidation." Rumors about internment camps. Labor camps. Concentration camps. Rumors, recurrent rumors, about camps where Jews are relocated from ghettos in Hungary. They are somewhere in Austria. Many Hungarian Jews have already been deported there. Many ghettos have been liquidated according to rumor and their inhabitants taken away by trains.

One day Father came back from the synagogue with the news that our ghetto was the only ghetto in the entire region. The others have all been liquidated. When? Where to? No one knows.

Other rumors. Younger men, from eighteen to forty-five, are rounded up and sent to the Russian front. To dig ditches for the Nazis. Older men, women, and children are put in labor camps. Where? In Hungary. Or maybe in Austria.

Mother began to worry about food. Our supply is running

low. Especially flour. Our flour sack is nearly empty. And we are cut off from the outside. We are forbidden to leave the ghetto and people on the outside are forbidden to enter. Even to approach the fence. We cannot buy food. We can't hold out indefinitely. What will happen when we run out of food?

Suddenly I remember a verse from the Bible. It was read in the synagogue three weeks ago. "If you shall refuse to heed my commandments . . . ten women shall bake in one oven . . . women shall devour their children." I shudder. The sudden moment of dread passes quickly, however. The verse, the dire warning of long ago, does not refer to us. It can't. Somehow we will get food when the time comes. As for now, there is still food left.

Aunt Szerén has been transformed since the move to the ghetto. Her good-natured humor is all gone. Her calm, patient smile is gone. And she has stopped singing. I used to love to listen to her voice—a soft, melodious, warm voice. My father used to tease her that she sang every song as if it were a lullaby.

Now she is silent. Not once has she sung in the ghetto. She is silent and sad, as if a sudden veil of gloom settled over her every aspect. She barely talks, and then only in soft whispers. On Friday nights she does not seem to hear even the kiddush but stares silently into the candlelight. As if she left her soul in her small, simple home on the outskirts of our little town.

"Wherever they take us, it will be better than to starve to death here. Our food is almost gone. I am glad they are taking us to labor camps. At least we can work for our food. Here they don't let us get even a loaf of bread!"

Mother has always been practical and optimistic. Suddenly she makes us all feel better about the deportations. But when will they begin? Days pass and we use up the last scrapings of food. The flour sack is now empty. This morning I kneaded bread from the last batch of flour.

There is a commotion at the gate. I join some people who are running to see what's going on. There's always something

going on. Yesterday a baby was born. The day before someone got a letter from the Budapest ghetto.

A rosy-cheeked, buxom peasant woman is arguing with the
young soldier on guard. It seems that she wishes to enter the
ghetto, and the soldier refuses to allow her to come near the
gate. She is making a lot of fuss, loudly scolding the young
soldier. I know that soldier. The other day, when I approached
the fence, he called out to me and asked my name. I told him,
even though I knew I was not supposed to talk to the soldiers.
But he looked kind. And very young. Brown eyes and a blond
fuzz for a mustache. He told me he was from beyond the
Danube. And I told him I was from Somorja.

Suddenly I catch sight of a girl partially covered by the
ample body of the peasant woman still in noisy shouting
match with the young soldier. She is Márta Kálmán, my
schoolmate from Somorja.

"Márta!"

She turns and sees me. In a flash she is at the fence. "Elli!
Oh, Ellike!" Her cheeks flush with excitement. "Ellike! We
found you!"

She runs to her mother and tugs at her sleeve. "Mother!
Mother! Quick. Come here. It's Ellike. She is here. Come." She
is dragging the excited woman away from the soldier to where
I stand at the fence.

Now I recognize Mrs. Kálmán. I had seen her once when
she drove her daughter from Gutor to our house. I was helping Márta with math and German.

Mrs. Kálmán is about to extend her hand through the bars
of the fence to shake mine. The young soldier catches up with
her.

"You can't do that. It's against the rules." Then he saw
me.

"Good morning."

"Good morning. These are my friends. May I talk to them
for a few minutes?"

"O.K. But be careful. Just a few minutes."

"Oh, Ellike! I am so happy to see you. We thought they killed you, all of you. And here you are. My God!"

"Hush," the mother interrupts. "We brought you some things. Flour, eggs, a goose. We owe you so much. You know, Márta passed her math, and in German she got a high mark. . . . I would have brought these things earlier, but we did not know where to find you. They wouldn't tell us anything."

The soldier returns. He is worried. The other soldiers, stationed further alongside the fence, are beginning to take notice of the commotion. A huge crowd gathers inside the fence.

"Please, they must leave now."

"Listen, officer. I brought some things to this young lady. She is my daughter's best friend. Can I give them to her?"

He looks at me. My eyes are pleading. "Do it fast. Let no one see."

Mrs. Kálmán and Márta hurry to the cart and bring to the gate the sack of flour, a white bundle containing at least twenty eggs, and the live goose. I quickly take the goose and the eggs. The sack of flour lands on a boy's shoulder who hurriedly carries it toward our room. Mrs. Kálmán holds me in her embrace.

"God be with you, Miss Friedmann."

Márta has tears in her eyes as she waves good-bye.

The goose in my arms feels warm. It brings back a rush of memories. Of geese in our backyard, of white fluffy geese I loved and held in my lap, and of geese I carried to the ritual slaughterer as if I myself were walking to the guillotine. Memories of recent past. Of another era.

Choked with embarrassment, I manage to whisper thanks to the young soldier and carry my precious cargo to our lodgings at the head of a deputation of men, women and children joined in the celebration of this miracle.

Thank you, God, for your providence.

TEN

WE ARE not to use any of the foodstuffs the Kálmáns brought. The end begins sooner than expected, and differently.

On Sunday, shortly after midnight, my father was ordered to the gate, and a telegram was handed to him. He is summoned to the Komarom labor camp immediately. At 5 A.M. he is to report to the gate.

Every man between the ages of eighteen and forty-five received a similar summons during the night. Rumors are turning into reality.

The arrival of the summonses is a shock wave throughout the ghetto. It was preceded by the arrival of a fresh truckload of military police who quickly surrounded the ghetto with guns drawn ready for action. What action? What is going to happen next? So this is how "liquidation" begins.

Grim, tight-lipped, and pale, Mother is packing Father's knapsack. Mommy, who only recently was looking forward to labor camp, is now paralyzed into panic. She had not expected this. She had not expected Daddy to be taken separately from us. And the suddenness. The military police. It does not bode well. I hear Mommy moving about in the darkened room, packing noiselessly. Daddy is in the kitchen talking to my brother in a low murmur. As I huddle in bed, my entire body is twisted in stomachache like a rubber hose.

"If I fall asleep, Mommy, will you promise to wake me at four-thirty?"

"Okay, I'll wake you. Just go to sleep."

My head, the only part of me free of stomachache, is whizzing with a million thoughts. Daddy had called me to the

kitchen and told me to take care of Mommy. "You are strong,
Elli. Don't be frightened, the Almighty is going to be with you.
He will take care of you. He will take care of my family.
Remember to help Mommy in every way." He took my face in
his two soft yet firm, muscular hands and slowly drew it to his
own. Time stood still, and I thought that my heart would
break. I wanted to speak but words drowned somewhere in the
morass of pain and helplessness. I wanted to tell him I loved
him. And that I knew he loved me. I wanted to tell him I knew
he thought I had nice legs and it made me happy and proud.
And that our long walks, our long, silent walks together were
the happiest times of my life. And our swimming together in
the Danube on hot, summer afternoons were the happiest afternoons of my life. I wanted to tell him how I loved him for his
fast walk and fast swimming, for his silences, and for his
youthful, athletic figure, for his youthful, quick movements. I
loved him with a yearning born of the distance between us, of
the enigmatic nature of his fatherhood. And I wanted to tell it
to him. But I could not bridge that distance now with words. I
held him, my arms gripping his slim back, my face buried in
his neck. I did not cry. I was numb and stupid with a horrible
foreknowledge of finality.

Gently he loosened my grip. "Go to sleep now, Ellike. It is
very late."

"Daddy, I want to speak to you in the morning. I want to
tell you something."

"Okay. In the morning." Quietly he walked me to the bedroom door. And then he sat down at the table in the kitchen
with a huge folio of the Talmud. Mommy beckoned to Bubi
and the two of them began to study the Talmud in hushed
tones. "This is how I wish to part from you," he said to my
brother, "learning a passage of the Talmud. Remember this
passage when you remember me."

I hear the murmur in the kitchen, Aunt Szerén restlessly
tossing about on the sofa and Mommy undressing quietly.

Outside my window the ghetto has settled down. It must be about 2 A.M.

The sound of clattering carriage wheels wakes me. The room is dark and empty. All the beds and sofa are empty. Everyone is gone.

I run out of the house in my nightgown, barefoot. In the early dawn I can see the silhouette of a small crowd at the gate. I reach the gate, the crowd, out of breath. Mother, Aunt Szerén, and Bubi are there among a handful of men and women. But Daddy is not. Daddy! I push my way to the open gate flanked by armed military police. Daddy! The last carriage is only dimly visible now, but I can see Daddy's erect figure sitting among several men. His back is turned, the outline of his shoulders and neck is etched with a sharp stomachache in my mental vision. And then, rapidly, a rising dust cloud swallows everything.

A sudden, violent shiver shakes my body. It is a chilly dawn rapidly brightening into a clear morning. Mother becomes aware of my presence.

"Elli! You are in your nightgown! And barefoot!"

"How could you do it? You promised to wake me! How could you do this to me? I did not even say good-bye to Daddy. I could not even kiss him good-bye. How could you do this?"

My hysterical sobs surprise everyone. I am aware of the astonishment my violent display causes. I am conscious of the unwritten taboo. But I am powerless against my wild grief. I am totally powerless in the face of the sense of doom that now grips me. The sense of unbearable loss. I know what I wanted to tell my father in the moments of parting, and those moments are no more. I was robbed of those moments. The knowledge that I will never see him again is now a certainty. The knowledge that I have been harboring ever since my dream of the golden bird in the *kamra*, the terror that has clawed at my intestines with brutal intensity ever since, now exploded. All the self-delusions of the ghetto suddenly melted away. The delusions which had lulled me into a false sense of security and had made the gnawing subside were suddenly part of the cloud of dust which swallowed the last sights of my father. Oh, Daddy! You are gone. How could you leave without my good-bye? How could you leave me?

It is weeks later, in another time and space dimension, when I am able to speak of this again and ask Mother if Father had said anything about me before he left. "Yes," Mommy says, "he said to tell you to remember what you had talked about that night. He kissed you in your sleep. He was very tense and barely spoke to any of us," recalls Mommy. Then she adds: "You know him. He hates sentimentality."

The departure of the men plunges the ghetto into gloom. Movement slows down, sounds are muffled, crowds are smaller and scatter quickly. Fear stalks my favorite hangouts.

Only the crying of the children is louder and more frequent. That is almost the only and prevailing sound. Why do the children cry?

Another sound is added. The sound of chanting the Psalms. The older men left behind in the ghetto now sit on the ground in the synagogue and chant the Psalms. Aloud. All day long. All night long. The chanting and the children crying. A slow rhythmic stupor lulls me to sleep. The sounds reverberate in my aching belly.

The chanting continues for six more days and nights until it becomes a dull refrain in my soul. Until the time came for our deportation.

ELEVEN

A HUNGARIAN police officer reads the order. On Sunday morning, at 5 A.M., the ghetto at Nagymagyar will be liquidated. Every person is permitted to take along of his possessions as much as he or she can carry, but not exceeding 50 kilograms in weight. Belongings must be carried in sacks on the back, no suitcases allowed. Be prepared to carry your sack for long distances.

Sunday! That is less than three days. Backpacks must be sewn, preparations made. What to cram into a sack small enough to be carried for long distances? Food? Clothing? Valuables? Where are they taking us? A cold climate? Then warm clothes are most important. Will they feed us on the journey? If not, food is the most important. How about gold or silver, or even china? Converted into cash, these may prove the most important. Who knows? I wish Daddy were here.

The chanting of the Psalms is more insistent. Only three more days.

Mother tears up sheets and makes knapsacks for each of us. Bubi insists on having the largest. He wants to carry the family burden. Instead of Father. He makes Mommy pack all the heavy things in his sack.

"You cannot carry all that. It is more than 50 kilos. It will break your back."

But he coaxes Mother into helping him swing the sack onto his back. It is a staggering load. But my prematurely tall, thin seventeen-year-old brother walks with feigned ease under its weight. "You see. It's nothing."

Then he helps me put my sack on. I tumble under the sudden weight. I cannot regain my balance. "I can't carry all this. I can't even stand up. How could I ever walk with this?"

"Don't be a sissy. Try."

Mother is worried. "No. She can't manage such a load. We will take a few things out of the sack."

I am embarrassed and hurt. I so wish to carry as much as my brother. Every article of clothing, every piece of food may be essential. Perhaps, precisely the thing we remove from my load would be the thing we will need. Why don't I have the courage to face carrying a heavy load? I hate my weakness.

Aunt Szerén volunteers. "Why don't you add those things to my sack? My pack is too light anyway. You know I can carry much more."

But we all know she cannot. She is a frail, gentle widow in her late fifties. She has been in poor health most of her life. As children we learned to avoid rough games and loud noises in her proximity. My kindly, soft-spoken, delicate aunt has always been my special relative. Ever since I was born she has pampered me with a thousand little attentions, a thousand little ways of showing love. She would share every favorite dish, every special delicacy with me even if it took hours before I showed up at her house for my daily visit. I remember her dish of roast pigeon, her cocoa-roll, her candied orange peels. Oranges themselves used to be rarities in our country. One could buy oranges only in the spring, and then the price was high. Szerén *néni* would buy an orange and wait for my visit. We would sit on the veranda, and she would peel the orange slowly, carefully separating the slices. She would hand me a slice, taking for herself every second. Each slice of orange would be a tender offering of love. Each slice of orange would link us closer.

"Forget it. We don't need these anyway. Forget it."

Mommy quickly puts the things back into the closet. Now my pack is bearable. It still feels like a drag on my shoulders, but I manage to walk upright with it. Mother's knapsack is as large and as heavy as that of my brother. After she finishes packing, she starts helping Mr. and Mrs. Blumenfeld with their packing. They are totally helpless since their son, Chaim, was sent to a labor battalion on the Russian front. Their dependence on her grows with his absence. Mother has sewn knapsacks for them and now advises them what and how to pack.

The news of liquidation struck the ghetto like a thunderbolt. A heavy silence descended on the yard. In silence people move about the task of preparation. With averted gaze people pass each other, muffling even the sound of footsteps.

Is this the pall of defeat?

The chanting is getting louder. The young boys have joined the chanters as well. Bubi is also sitting among them on the ground of the synagogue. The drawn-out sound of wailing has an eerie quality in the dead silence of the ghetto. Centuries-old Jewish wailing. Jews wailing again and again. Forever. For three more days.

The Hungarian police officer is back with another announcement. It is an order read in somewhat harsher tones than the first. All documents, books, papers of every kind have to be surrendered immediately. Valuables still in the possession of every Jew—gold, silver, gems—have to be surrendered immediately. Money above fifty pengö per person has to be surrendered, immediately.

Tables are set up in the middle of the yard next to which a row of Hungarian military policemen are stationed. Lines of ghetto inhabitants queue up, delivering piles of books of every size and color: prayerbooks and Bibles, notebooks and picture albums, identity papers and passports, huge folios of the Talmud and the Torah scrolls from the synagogue. A mountain of paper. Human lives, loves, identities piled high in obscene casualness in the middle of the yard.

"This, too?" A young woman clutches a pile of family photos.

"Everything." The mustachioed Hungarian is firm.

"Can I keep this one, perhaps? Just one?" A picture of a baby is in a trembling hand.

"Everything."

The glossy snapshot flutters on top of the pile.

"Will we get these back? When we come back, I mean."

"Oh, of course. You'll get them all back."

With hesitant footsteps she moves on. My brother is next in line. He dumps our books and quickly steps aside. I bring the documents, my parents' marriage certificate, our birth certificates and report cards, paper clippings, my father's business books, and all my best notebooks saved throughout the years. Except one. The notebook into which I had carefully copied all my poems—one hundred and five in all. This I quickly hide inside my blouse when I see the total disarray in which the paper articles are dumped on the ground. How will all this be sorted out? I am not going to chance losing my precious possession. With my right elbow supporting the notebook under my blouse, I hand the papers to the officer and hurry on. I do not want to tarry. I have no jewelry to deliver. Those not buried in the cellar we had submitted to the authorities in Somorja.

Piles of valuables lie on the tables alongside mounds of money. Jeweled watches, sapphire earrings, diamond rings, gold necklaces and bracelets glitter in vulgar abandon next to the incongruous pile of green paper weighed down by a heaving sea of silver coins.

Perhaps someday we will dig up the jewelry from the belly of our cellar floor. Or will it be someone else?

My hurried footsteps carry me to our crowded little room in the back of the synagogue yard. I must hide the notebook with my poems before anyone sees it. Even Mommy must not know. She would worry over the grave infraction. Quickly I tuck the notebook deep into my knapsack all packed for departure. With suppressed excitement I run back to the yard.

I stop, paralyzed. Oh, my God! Wild flames are dancing about the pile of books. A column of dark smoke is rising from the middle of the heap. They are burning our books! I walk as if in a dream. Ash particles are flying in the hot breeze and the pungent smell of smoke fills the air. Men, women and children crowd about the conflagration, which leaps higher and higher churning up blinding clouds of smoke.

The Torah scrolls! The fire is dancing a bizarre dance of death with one large scroll in the middle, clutching and twisting and twisting in an embrace of cruel passion. Aged folios of Jewish wisdom and faith tumble and explode into fiery particles, spluttering pellets of ash. Volumes of the Bible, leather-bound Pslams, phylacteries turn and twist and burst into myriad fragments of agony. Pictures and documents flutter as weightless speckles of ash at the perimeter of the savage torch. Our identity. Our soul. Weightless speckles of ash rising, fleeing the flames into nothingness.

"Almighty God, forgive us our sins! Woe to the generation which witnesses its Torah burned to ashes! Woe to the generation which witnesses its sacred trust trampled to the ground!"

The rabbi's voice. He stands with flaming eyes, tears rolling down his long, brown beard. "Woe to us, my friends, we witnessed the burning of the Torah! Woe to us and our children. God forgive us our sins!"

He slowly grips his overcoat and rends a tear in it. The sound of the ripping cloth jars my insides. All the men who stand near follow his example. They rend their clothes one by one, and begin the chant *El mole rahamin* . . . The chant for the dead.

Below my feet the flames are dancing no more. A huge, flat heap of gray ashes, a fluttery flat heap framed by a wide edge of scorched earth. The accumulation of hundreds of lives. Mementoes of the past and affirmations of the future. My brother's *teffilin* and my diploma. My grandparents' picture that hung above my bed, and the novel I had been writing. My father's letters and all his Talmud. All transformed into this light, fluttery, gray mass. How many times can one witness the end?

I have seen the Torah scroll twist and turn in the flames before I have ever had the chance of touching it. How does the Torah feel to the touch? Will I ever know?

My poems are safe. What does it matter now?

The pain in my stomach is now laced with a surge of nausea. I get to the public latrine in time. In the deep ditch, layers of bank notes cover the human waste. Thousands of pengos with the proud uniformed figure of Miklos Horthy on a white horse soaked in excrement, large notes of one thousand, five hundred, and one hundred denominations. I have never seen so much money. I was not the only one to sabotage the order.

I vomit again and again. But the taste of ashes is not extricated from my insides. Neither is the pain from my stomach.

The night is hot. Stifling air mingles with the smell of soot and the incessant chant from the synagogue. God, will they ever stop?

One more day.

TWELVE

EARLY MORNING. The police officer is back with a new order. All beards and earlocks have to be shorn off immediately.

What! Even the rabbi? Tomorrow is Shabbat. Can we leave the beards on for Shabbat? Just one more day. At dawn on Sunday all men will be clean-shaven for deportation. Please.

"No. Immediately."

Without his beard the rabbi of Nagymagyar looks like a young Gentile. He is quite handsome. Approachable. Pinhas looks strange without his earlocks. Paler. Sadder. Frightened.

Like shadows we pass each other, not seeing. The dread knowledge of the last few days hangs like a heavy veil. I look after him and wonder: Will I ever see him again?

The Shabbat approaches like a frightened stranger. Old Mr. Blumenfeld makes kiddush in Daddy's absence. His voice is barely above a whisper. We sip his homemade raisin wine and eat in silence. Mr. Blumenfeld begins to sing. "This day is honored, honored above others . . . this day above others . . . the sacred day of Shabbat." We all join in slowly, one by one. To coax the Shabbat. Tentative, tearful voices. But the Shabbat would not spread her wings. She crouches thinly, miserably in a corner while we move about, eat and pray, fearful to realize our inability to make the Shabbat welcome. And thus the day drags on, its holy splendor beyond our grasp.

The loss of Shabbat is one more painful blow.

In the evening we test our backpacks. Wear them for some minutes around the room. Will we be able to carry them for long distances?

Suddenly, Aunt Szerén begins to scream: "I am not going anywhere! I am not leaving here! I am not going anywhere! And I will not let them have anything else! Nothing! Nothing!"

She runs to the closet. She holds a cup of her fine china. It flies and crashes against the wall. One by one she smashes the entire set.

"They will not have this! And this!" Now she is holding a magnificent Dresden coffeepot. Stunned, we watch her smash it with astonishing force against the wall. A crystal vase is now in her hand.

Mother runs to her. She clutches her older sister in her arms: "Please, stop. Please, Szerénke, stop this. Please, calm down. My darling, do not do such terrible things. Oh, no, don't, I beg you. Everything will be all right. You will see."

I am hugging her frantically and begin to sob.

"Aunt Szerén, please. Please, sit down with me on the sofa."

But she sees only Mother. Fiercely, she turns on her: "Why do you say everything is all right? Don't you see? They will kill us all. Everyone of us. Don't you see? First they take everything from us. Then they take us far away from home. To murder us. I am not going! Let them kill me here. And they will take nothing from me. No more!"

She grabs her pillow and in an instant tears it open. Feathers fill the room, fluttering like wild snowflakes above the debris of broken china and glass.

Bubi rushes out of the room. Mother and I soothe Aunt Szerén. Finally she sits down on the bed and begins to cry softly. Mommy is crying, too. And I sob, my head buried in my pillow.

Then slowly Mommy stands up and begins to clean up the feathers and broken china. Bubi returns, and we all work with heavy limbs. Now, to sleep. At dawn we are to leave the ghetto.

THIRTEEN

IT IS dark when Mommy wakes me. She tells me to pray *shaharit*, the morning prayer and the prayer for journey. I gulp a glass of milk but the slice of brown bread I am unable to swallow.

It is chilly outside even in my overcoat with the large pack on my back. At the gate there is a large crowd, and outside the fence a long row of people with sacks on their backs. An endless row. Like so many "wandering Jews." I recognize the sight. It was a sketch of a medieval ghetto: bearded Jews with bundles on their backs, weeping women and ragged children. I am part of the picture now, one of the figures in the stilted scene. Mommy in her blue raincoat, a brilliant background for her yellow star, with an outsized sack on her back, my brother wearing Daddy's overcoat and hat, bent under the weight of his bundle, and Aunt Szerén, silent and withdrawn, are all parts of the long-forgotten sketch.

It is dawn. The lines start to move. With a strange momentum the rows of men, women and children are set into motion that sweeps the motley crowd along the main dirt road out of the village. On and on we march, silently wearing our burdens, clinging to each other for support.

Gates open. Faces appear. Silent, furtive faces. I do not know these faces. This is a strange village. I do not know if they are curious faces or sad. Dogs bark as we pass. Some children run into the street. I am not turning my head to look at any of them. Embarrassment is controlling my every motion. My every thought.

The daylight grows brighter. The road does not seem to end.

At the edge of the village stand horse-drawn wagons of every kind. Waiting for us. The Hungarian military police is busy ordering us about. There is an army unit here, too, directing the heavy traffic of horses, coachmen, and Jews. We get on the wagons in groups of six, seven, or even ten. Mother, Aunt Szerén and I get on a large, drab peasant coach together with the old couple Blumenfeld and others, but Bubi gets on a bright-yellow buggie. He waves to us with a triumphant smile and the prancing horse draws into the line of carriages and carts already in motion toward the open road. Dust, noise and confusion accompany the caravan of about a hundred clattering vehicles. Each vehicle is guarded by two military personnel.

As we are boarding, the young soldier from the ghetto notices me. He hurries to the wagon. "I will be on your cart, Ella."

"My name is Elli."

"Oh, yes. Elli. Now I remember."

He motions to another soldier and the two of them get on the cart. The other one sits next to the coachman up front, but he sits next to me on the narrow seat in the back. I am embarrassed. I shoot a sideways glance at Mommy. How does she like it? I, sitting next to a soldier? Is she wondering, how does he know my name? But Mommy is preoccupied with Aunt Szerén who, now shrunk and pale, huddles soundlessly next to her on the seat. My darling aunt, pale and shrunk. Defeated. Betrayed into submission.

The young soldier wants to know my age and how I feel about this all.

"Are you afraid?" he asks.

"Yes. I am afraid. Very afraid. So afraid that I stopped thinking."

"Do you know where they are taking you?"

"I? We? We do not know anything. How can we know? Do *you* know where they are taking us?"

No, he does not. His orders are to accompany us to Dunaszerdahely and stay there until further orders. I confide in him and tell him of my secret hope. I have not told it to anyone. It is my secret hope that a miracle will occur before we will board the trains at Dunaszerdahely. The news of a change of plans or an end to the war or something. I feel something will happen to save us. I can think of nothing else since last night. Since Aunt Szerén's outburst. My hope is becoming, strangely, a kind of certainty. He looks at me and does not answer.

"Do you know," he says after a while, "that you look very much like my sister. She, too, has freckles and a small nose. But your eyes are different. She has brown eyes. Yours are blue."

I do not correct him. The Hungarian csárdás, "blue eyes, blue eyes, beautiful is the one with blue eyes," made blue eyes the standard of beauty. I am glad he does not notice my eyes are blue-green.

The journey lasts over two hours. The soldier, Pista, talks about his life, his hopes, his family. He, too, hopes to get a higher education. And live in Budapest. Before we reach Dunaszerdahely I decide to confide in him. My heart beats with fear and excitement as I tell him of the notebook with my poems and ask him if he would keep it for me until the end of the war. If I return, I will look for him in his village beyond the Danube. If not, he can keep it.

"You will come back, Elli. I know you will. And I will be waiting. I will take good care of your poems, and you will get them back safe and sound."

I hope Mommy will not notice me rummaging in my knapsack and ask questions. She is sitting now grimly gazing ahead. I find the notebook on the bottom of the sack and hand it to him shielded by the bulk of the sack in order to avoid the notice of the others on the cart. Pista is unaware of my fear. He opens it with eager interest. "May I?" he asks.

"Oh, no! Please, don't! Someone might see it."

He forgot the order. The burning of all papers and books. Uncomprehending, he looks at me. "Why not? What's wrong?"

"The books. All books had to be burned. I saved this from the flames. It's against the order. Didn't you know?"

He knew, but had forgotten. Quickly, he closes the notebook and puts it in his green canvas satchel. "Don't worry, Elli Friedmann, I'll take care of it. No one will find out."

I thank him and my voice trembles.

He tells me his last name is Szivós and promises to visit me in the Dunaszerdahely ghetto.

The cart is now rolling on the cobblestoned streets of Dunaszerdahely. It is almost noon. The streets are crowded with gawking people. The young soldier grows silent, and I become aware of a renewed churning in my stomach.

The cart caravan rattles through the winding streets of the small town and comes to a halt before the synagogue. I know this town and this synagogue. It holds happy memories. I used to come to Dunaszerdahely to visit my brother on Purim. My brother studied here in the Yeshiva and on Purim I was always invited to the family he boarded with to spend the holiday. Dunaszerdahely has a large Jewish community and Purim was much more of an event here than in Somorja. Children wore costumes and masks on the street on Purim, and grown men were dancing in the synagogue yard. There was a merry celebration in the Yeshiva, and Purim plays were performed in different places. To me Dunaszerdahely meant

Purim . . . songs, music, dancing, an endless variety of sweets.
I wonder if I will be able to go to visit the Grünwalds now that
we are in Dunaszerdahely. The wagons do not pass the street
they live on, but the synagogue is not far from there. Perhaps
tomorrow I can find out whether I would be allowed to go and
see them. The thought makes me happy for a moment. I would
see Chavi again. And Rochel. And the rest of the children. I
have not seen them since last Purim.

The synagogue yard is surrounded by a heavy cordon of
sinister-looking soldiers in a strange dark-gray uniform, black
arm bands.

"The SS!" Bubi exclaims with horror. "We are being handed
over to the Germans."

"We are in God's hands. Hungarians, Germans—what's the
difference? God is with us. God is with Daddy, wherever he is.
He protects him, and He will protect us wherever we are.
Remember, wherever we put down our knapsack, there is our
home. And God is right above us. He is with us everywhere."

I do so wish I felt like Mommy. For, right now, the SS look
to me very stark and stern, very frightening. And there are so
many of them! They are much more frightening than the
Hungarians with their green uniforms and expressive faces.
The SS do not look human, and their faces do not look like
faces at all. They are grim masks. And their voices sound like
angry barks.

As we get off the carts, the SS shout orders herding us into
the synagogue yard crowded with people—men, women, children, and invalids of all kind, camping on the ground leaving
barely enough room to pick our way past carefully so as not to
step on a foot or head sprawling on a knapsack. I turn to see
what happened to the cart. The two Hungarian soldiers are
now sitting next to the coachman up front. The coachman is
spurring the horses on, and the cart moves in line with the
others. When he sees me looking at him, Pista Szivós shrugs
his shoulders—a gesture of resignation. He is not to be stationed in Dunaszerdahely after all. Here the Jews are guarded

solely by Germans. The Hungarians are returning with the horse-drawn wagons to Nagymagyar. As the cart pulls away, Szivós waves good-bye and points to his breast pocket: My poems are safe. Thank you, Pista. But I am afraid to wave good-bye.

There are no Hungarian soldiers or police to be seen. As Mother leds the way toward the synagogue building, we pass a wall of SS men urging us in choppy German tones to move faster. We, too, are eager to move out of this crowded yard into the building. Here one cannot even stop or rest one's knapsack. There is simply no room.

The synagogue presents a staggering spectacle. The large interior of the men's section is crowded to the brim with a tumultuous mass—people, baggage, and baby carriages packed densely on top of each other. Some stand, others crouch on the ground, many sit on their knapsacks. The noise rises to an unbearable pitch. Children crying, men arguing, and women comforting. And an endless stream of newcomers surging in. Where to?

"There is no room here. Not even standing room." One of our neighbors from Nagymagyar blocks our advance with his knapsack in one hand and infant daughter in the other. His wife and the two bigger children huddle helplessly next to him.

"Where are all the others?"

"The others are still coming in. We were among the first to get off the wagons."

"Where will they all go? We have no place either."

I wait for my mother to come up with an idea. She always does. "Let's go upstairs to the ladies' section. Perhaps there is room there."

We turn to the crowded hall and climb the stairs. The ladies' section presents an identical sight. The crowding is humanly inconceivable. There are families camping even on the stairwell. But here it is less noisy. One can at least size up the situation. The huge area downstairs crammed with utter bedlam made thinking impossible. Now I manage to collect my thoughts.

"Who are all these people?" I ask the woman crouching in the corner at the entrance, with her infant in her lap and three other children sleeping on a blanket spread on top of two knapsacks.

"The Jews of the whole county were brought in here. We are here since yesterday."

"Where are you from?"

"We are from Dunaszerdahely."

"Dunaszerdahely? The Jews of Dunaszerdahely are here, too? All the Jews? That's impossible! There are at least three thousand Jews in Dunaszerdahely."

"They are all here. And the Jews of Nagymagyar, Nagymegyer, Patony, Somorja . . ."

"We are from Somorja."

"So you see. The whole county is here."

"That must be more than six thousand Jews. How can everyone be put in one synagogue?"

"You saw how. There are people everywhere. Some are sleeping in the sheds and storage shacks behind the synagogue. And more are coming all the time."

"Stop talking and let's find a corner for ourselves." Mother is in charge, once again.

There is no such corner. But we find a stairwell and climb up to the attic. A comparative paradise. The place is dusty and dark. People are lying on blankets spread on the ground. Instead of the unbearable din of the lower floors, here a pall of gloom dominates. Silently, they lie on their backs staring at the ceiling. No children. Men and women, some elderly, seem to evaporate into the dusk of the attic's gloom. Fear and apprehension take on a taste. Tragedy is tangible up here in the attic of the Dunaszerdahely synagogue.

We open our knapsacks and spread out a blanket. Bubi has another blanket in his knapsack and he spreads that, too, next to the first. There is enough room for both. We eat our sand-

wiches, and I go downstairs to see if I can see the Grünwalds
or anyone else I know. I have one special person secretly in
mind. He is Ali, the tall boy who used to come to our house
once a year for a few days. He came to Somorja to take the
exams at the secondary school. His parents knew my parents,
and so it was arranged that he stay with us during the exams.
He is dark, handsome, artistic, and intelligent. We used to have
long talks. When I showed him my poems, he was visibly im-
pressed. He seemed to consider me his equal, even though he
is four years older. He is seventeen now. Each year when he
came to us, he brought me a small present. It would always be
something he made himself. A drawing, a pin made of pearls,
or a small mosaic box. Everything he made was done with
sensitivity and taste. Ali is my most exciting adventure. Even
though he never indicated anything but friendliness in his
manner, I have worshipped him, hoping for the day when he
too will be consumed by similar passion. Of course, I knew at
thirteen one is not taken seriously yet, but I was willing to wait
for the day when he will notice me as a woman.

My latest conquests gave me a new self-confidence. My
friendship with the soldier, the obvious ogling of Pinhas, and
even the short-lived affair with Jancsi Novack in Somorja
were indications that I am not a child anymore. If others noticed it, perhaps Ali will, too.

In the yard and the synagogue the crowding is even greater
now than before. But there is less noise and confusion. The
new arrivals settled down in several ingeniously devised ways.
Blankets are hung, hammock-fashion, between columns, ac-
commodating little children. Some are sleeping in washbowls
on top of the arch and the pews, allowing more room for
grown-ups. Baggage is arranged to serve as resting place. With
familiarity, fear subsides and so does the shouting and wailing.
It is easier to move around. I pass through the hallways, the
backyard and the main hall, hoping to meet Ali or one of the
Grünwald children. My stomachache has disappeared. I even
feel elated at the prospect of meeting friends unexpectedly.

After two hours of hopeless search I give up. I am dizzy and tired from looking into a sea of faces, stepping over sleeping bodies, apologizing incessantly for a thousand infractions of etiquette by shoving and elbowing my way in a forest of human flesh. Inadvertently, I cause countless cups of coffee to spill and cigarette ashes to sprinkle as I make my circuitous way through densely packed hallways and stairways and basements, as I climb to lofts in the storage rooms and circle the synagogue building amid sprawling humanity in the yard. I upset bowls of soup and cereal placed in precarious positions, perched on knees and banisters; I disturb snoozing old men and little children, rub against injured limbs, and cause discomfort to many who have to draw up tired legs to let me pass.

I am tired and my stomachache returns. Dull, nagging, insistent. As I reach our family camp in the attic, I find Szerén *néni* asleep, my mother and brother gone. Where are they? I lie down on the blanket next to Szerén *néni*.My palms on my stomach soothe the pain. The silence and dark gloom of the attic lull me to sleep.

It is hot and oppressively airless when I awake. In the darkness I see my mother asleep on my left and my brother on her left. Szerén *néni* sleeps to my right, snoring softly. The attic is full of sleeping bodies, all fully clothed. A strange experience, sleeping with your clothes on. I have never done it before. The heavy beams of the room loom at a slant, adding to my sense of claustrophobia. The heat seems unbearable.

I tiptoe to the window, a peephole among the shingles of the roof. In the faint glow of the moon, Dunaszerdahely slumbers under endless rows of rooftops. Directly below, the crowded yard is silent: Bodies on top of bodies rest in a jagged, sinister silhouette. In the sky the moon swims in a frilly sea of clouds. Oh, God, what's in store for us?

FOURTEEN

THE NEWS of deportation comes as a relief. We spent a week in the synagogue. A week crammed with people, stench, heat —beginnings of starvation. No room to move, no food, no toilet facilities, no hope. Children grew restless and sickly. Several people died. Fear melted into hopelessness. Oh, God, anything but this. Please, get us out of this!

Hope comes on the Sabbath with news of the arrival of the wagons. Somehow a rumor penetrates the synagogue compound from the outside—perhaps the members of the Hevra Kadisha, who buried the dead in the cemetery on Friday, brought it—that hundreds of cattle cars arrived at the train station, a sure sign of our departure.

It's God's will. He heard our voices and now will redeem us from this unbearable spot. Anything but this inconceivable confinement.

"It can get only better. Even if they take us to the camps. There at least we will live like human beings, and work. And if we work, they will feed us. They will not allow us to die of starvation."

Mother's logic. It is good to hear healthy, wholesome words. I am reassured.

During this past week I heard endless prophecies, feverish visions of utopia, promises of sudden redemption. Fantastic tales of divine delivery sprung up in the ghetto, daring plans of rescue. But daily they evaporated with the growing heat and diminishing food supplies.

We still have some food. The big loaf of bread Mommy baked in Nagymagyar is only half gone and the goose we roasted would be untouched had she not urged us to eat it. It would have gone bad in the sudden heat that descended upon us in these early days of June. But others start to run out of food. Families with small children would ask for food, and Mother is busy slicing bread from our big loaf. It is a pleasure to see the beautiful, bright smiles of lovely little children as they take the bread and shyly bite into the golden brown crust. What will happen when the bread is gone? Will "they" feed us? Would "they" give us kosher food?

"If not, we would have to eat it anyway," says one of the pious men in the attic. "Survival is a mitzvah."

Nonkosher food? I shudder.

But now the train wagons have arrived. We will be taken to camps somewhere in Germany, or perhaps, if we are lucky, in Austria. There are much nicer camps in Austria, some of them like vacation resorts. The rumors persist. We may be lucky. We may be sent to Austria.

Thursday morning the synagogue compound is astir with a thousand signs of preparation. Feverish packing of lifetimes into knapsacks to be carried into cattle cars. No more cribs, washbowls, baby carriages. Everything has to be reduced into a small parcel per family. All life's needs capsulated into a compact bundle. Nothing else is permitted, they tell us. Nothing else has room in the wagons. There is room only for bodies in the wagons, they tell us. We must economize with space, we must not take up precious space with unnecessary possessions. And so the packing becomes frantic. Once again, the question, what is most essential? What will we need the most? But now the sense of urgency is thousandfold. Now we know deprivation. Now our choices are narrowed even further.

Children cry in the semidarkness. Moans of the elderly and sick pierce the sounds of panicky preparation. In a daze we line up in the yard, a motley, dense humanity pressing all around in confused obedience. The march to the train station is unreal. The heavy shuffling, the dragging of loads, children, stretchers, the hazy, dust-speckled sun. Masses of people pressing on and on in an endless flow through silent streets.

At the station, the foreboding sight of rows and rows of cattle cars, drab, windowless boxes with doors agape, waiting in sinister silence. On the platform, a row of SS soldiers, stiff, sticklike figures snapping orders. Eighty-five people to a wagon! Move! Move! *In die Waggonen!* Into the wagons! The count. Eighty-five men, women, children, infants, elderly, crippled. No questions, no questions. Move on, move on— into the wagons.

The wagons fill up fast and the doors slide shut. One by one. Huge locks dangling on latches are snapped shut by important-looking officers with impassive faces. Remote, unapproachable, godlike. Now it is our turn. The wagon doors are high. There is a small metal landing precariously slanting to one side. Shoved, pressed, hoisted up, we are quickly loaded into the car. It is dark inside. Those who got in first are sitting alongside the walls. Others crouch in the middle of the wagon. My brother has a spot next to a wall. He is always the first everywhere. Now he gets up and offers the spot to Szerén *néni* and Mommy. Bubi and I crouch at their feet. Our knapsack serves as support. As the wagon fills, there is no room to move, not even to sit. Many sit on top of their knapsacks. Children are drawn into laps cradled by mothers in crouched positions. Now the doors slide shut plunging the car into total darkness. Panic grips my bowels. All at once I forget Mother's reassuring logic. I do not remember the rabbi's parting words: "God is going into exile with his people." I do not sense God in the cattle car. It is dark and chilly. And I tremble with fear.

Where is Daddy now? Are we leaving him behind in Hungary, or are we on our way toward him in Germany? Will we meet him there? Will we ever meet him?

"Shma Yisroel Hashem Elohenu Hashem Ehad!" Hear, oh Israel, the Lord our God, the Lord is One! A voice intones the timeless affirmation of faith. Groping in the dark, the men stand up and respond in prayer. As the low chant reverberates through the dark wagon, the train starts to move. Slowly, dim

light begins to filter through the gaps between the wooden
planks of the wagon wall. We are going fast now. Gusts of
cold air rush in through the gaps. A shiver runs through my
body. Oh, God, I do not want to die!

FIFTEEN

IT IS three days now since we have been locked in the wagons
which are clattering in the dark toward an unknown fate. We
are traveling east. As the train reaches the border towns of
Hungary, it becomes clear to us that we are not being taken to
Austria. Or to Germany. Where are we being transported?

We cross the border. Strange names of towns become visible through the cracks. What country do those names reveal?
My brother says Poland. Poland? Gina, the teacher, confirms
it: "We are in Poland now."

In Poland? There are no camps in Poland!

"There is Auschwitz."

"Auschwitz!"

"What is Auschwitz?"

"Auschwitz is a Polish death camp."

Sudden silence follows the words of the little, skinny man
from Galanta. He knows about camps. He had escaped from
Galicia to Slovakia and then from Slovakia to Hungary.

"But Auschwitz is for Polish Jews. Hungarian Jews are
taken to Germany or Austria. 'They' promised we will be
taken to Austria. They can't take Hungarian Jews to
Auschwitz."

"Mr. Stern is right. Auschwitz is for Polish Jews. The Germans do not treat Hungarian Jews the same as Galician or
Polish Jews. *Ostjuden* were singled out even in Hungary. They

were deported separately. They were taken to camps in Poland. But Hungarian Jews were promised special treatment."

"Gentlemen, we are in the Nazis' hands. They do as they please with us. Hungarian Jews are Jews. They are no exception."

"You are wrong. You'll see. We may still be going to Austria."

"How? We are in Poland already."

"We may be going a roundabout way. The tracks may be bombed out in western areas. This may be a roundabout route to Austria."

All agree with this piece of logic and the little skinny man from Galanta falls silent.

Right next to me sits Mrs. Bonyhádi with her two little children, Tommi and Suzie. Tommi is a well-behaved six year old and Suzie is a three year old, a very pretty little doll. Mrs. Bonyhádi, the reputed beauty of our town, came from another town to marry a local fellow. In Somorja she was widely admired for her tall, slim elegance and sense of fashion. I liked her because she once shared with me some poems she had written, and she thought highly of the poems I showed her. She begged to read all my poems and then became my fan.

Now in the wagon she tells stories to her two children in a melodious voice. The stories seem endless. Endless tales of beauty. Spring in the forest sunshine and bubbling brooks, wild little ponies cavorting among rocks, and little children riding them in the soft wind. She recites poems. Not nursery rhymes but short little verses from classic Hungarian poets, lovely lyric poems that sound like music. Her voice is music. It soothes my stomachache.

"Elli," she says now, "why don't you recite some of your poetry to us? Please, Elli. It would make us feel good and happy. Everyone would be so grateful. Elli writes beautiful poems, ladies and gentlemen. Truly marvelous poems."

My throat is dry and feels swollen. Ever since we entered

the wagons it feels as if I will choke any minute. I keep on swallowing hard to help the air flow through my throat. With thirst it is getting worse. Now I gulp again.

"I can't, Mrs. Bonyhádi, forgive me. I can't. I am sorry."

"Elli. It would be a great mitzvah."

It is Mr. Lunger's voice from somewhere in the far corner. Lunger *bácsi*. He was one of my favorite fans. He is a heavyset, generous man with a cigar constantly dangling from his mouth and bundles of paper sticking out of his pockets. Among those papers was one of my poems, and he would read it aloud to anyone who would stop long enough to listen. It was his favorite, "Our Beloved Nation."

"Lunger *bácsi*, I don't have my poems with me, as you know. And I don't know them by heart."

"You know 'My Beloved Nation.' You recited it many times. Even I remember some of it by heart."

I swallowed the dry lump in my throat and began to recite my poetry. I went on for over an hour, and the people crammed in the cattle car gave each one a thunderous applause.

"You have a captive audience," quips Bubi, and we all laugh.

"I am thirsty," says little Tommi.

Tommi has been complaining of thirst for the past forty-eight hours. Mrs. Bonyhádi's attempt at assuaging it by stories and poems is growing less successful.

"Tommi, you are a gentleman. Gentlemen do not drink before ladies. None of the ladies here has had anything to drink. You are not to complain. Soon we will get a drink and then you will offer it first to Suzie and me and only then will you drink. Okay?"

"I am thirsty now," says Tommi for the umpteenth time.

Mrs. Bonyhádi starts to sing. She has a pleasant singing voice and we, too, forget our thirst. At once she peeks through the cracks and exclaims with enthusiasm: "Look at those beautiful mountains! The Carpathians! See that lake? A small, blue, smiling lake surrounded by tall, proud pines! It's simply fabulous. We will have to come back here someday on a holiday. Let's make a vow that we will all come back here, a reunion."

She is a delight. In time we forget the darkness and discomfort, our thirst, and our destiny locked within the cattle car rushing into the belly of ominous Poland.

We even got used to the "communal pot."

Shortly after our incarceration in the wagon we became keenly aware of the problem of elimination. One of the elderly gentlemen offered to dedicate a cooking pot from his knapsack for the purpose and, together with his offering, delivered the most civilized speech I have ever heard.

"Ladies and gentlemen. We are confined in a small boxcar which does not afford us the opportunity to retire for our human needs. Let us remember that these needs are biological, God-given, and therefore not a cause of shame or embarrassment. Not one of us should restrain these vital functions. Yet, we shall retain our human dignity. This pot shall be used for the purpose. Whenever it is needed, one should simply call out, 'Communal pot, please,' and it will be passed to the required spot. It will then be passed to those who sit near the doors and they in turn will empty it outside. This can be done with dignity and minimal inconvenience to all concerned. By conducting ourselves with decorum, we shall prove our respect for each other."

It is inconceivable for me to use the pot in public. Yet, it is accomplished by others with a maximum of decorum and with a minimum of inconvenience. I have been unable to go through with the procedure and have refused to ask for the "communal pot." This has caused constant strife with Mother. Throughout the journey she would keep on urging me about the pot and I would refuse to discuss it.

Sometime during the fourth night, the train comes to a halt. We are suddenly awakened by the noise of sliding doors thrown open and cold night air rushing into the wagon.

"Heraus! Alles heraus! Alovanti!"

A rough voice. A figure clad in a striped uniform. Standing in the wide open doorway, his back illuminated by an eerie, diffused light, the man looks like a creature from another planet.

"Schnell! Heraus! Alles heraus!"

Two or three other striped figures leap into the wagon and begin shoving the drowsy men, women, and children out into the cold night.

A huge sign catches my eye: AUSCHWITZ

The pain in my stomach sends a violent wave of nausea up my gullet.

The night is chilly and damp. An other-worldly glow lights up tall watchtowers, high wire fences, an endless row of cattle cars, SS men, their dogs, a mass of people pouring out of the wagons.

"Heraus! Heraus! Los! Heraus!"

Metal buttons glisten on SS uniforms.

"My things! I left everything in the wagon!"

"On line! Everyone stand on line! By fives! Men over there! Women and children over here!"

"The diapers! I forgot the diapers in the wagon!" Young Mrs. Lunger starts for the wagon at a run, a child in each hand. Little Frumet is crying but Yingele is fast asleep on her shoulder. The man in the striped suit holds her back. "You won't need any diapers."

"But I do. Both children are in diapers. I brought a large bundle of diapers along. Let me get them, please . . . please!"

"You are not allowed to go back to the wagon. Stay on line right here! Where you are going, you won't need any diapers."

Mrs. Lunger's beautiful brown eyes open wide with astonishment. Uncomprehending, she hesitantly joins the others on the line. I stand behind her and her mother-in-law and the two Lunger girls. Lunger *bácsi* is on the other side of the tracks. Mommy and Szerén *néni* and I make only three. Two more women are shoved alongside us to make it five. My brother is hustled farther, on the other side of the tracks. He turns to say good-bye to us and trips on the wire flanking the tracks. Daddy's new gray hat rolls off his head. He reaches to pick it up. An SS man kicks him in the back sending him tumbling on the tracks. Mother gasps. Szerén *néni* gives a shriek and grasps Mommy's arm. I hold my mouth: A spasm of nausea hurls a charge of vomit up my throat.

"Marchieren! Los!"

The column of women, children, infants begins to move. Dogs snarl, SS men scream orders, children cry, women weep good-byes to departing men, and I struggle with my convulsing stomach. And I march on. Behind the lovely young Mrs. Lunger with her two little children on her arms and the oldest one hanging on to her skirt. Behind Mrs. Bonyhádi and her Tommi and Suzie docilely marching in the line before them. Next to me Mommy is silently supporting Aunt Szerén by the shoulder. I march and the sights and sounds of Auschwitz only dimly penetrate my consciousness. Daylight is slowly skirting the clouds, and it turns suddenly very cold. We left our coats in the wagons. We were ordered to leave our belongings behind. Everything. We will get them later, they told us. How will they find what belongs to whom? There was such wild confusion at the trains. Perhaps they will sort things out. The Germans must have a system. Leave it to them. The famous German order.

The marching column comes to a sudden halt.

An officer in gray SS uniform stands facing the lines of women and children. Dogs straining on short leashes held by SS soldiers flank him on both sides. He stops each line and regroups them. Some to his right and some to his left. Then he orders each group to march on. I tremble as I stand before him. He looks at me with a soft look in friendly eyes.

"Goldene Haar!" he exclaims as he takes one of my long braids into his hand. I am not certain I heard it right. Did he say "golden hair" about my braids?

"Bist du Jüdin?" Are you Jewish?

The question startles me. "Yes, I am Jewish."

"Wie alt bist du?" How old are you?

"I am thirteen."

"You are tall for your age. Is this your mother?" He touches Mommy lightly on the shoulder: "You go with your mother." With his riding stick he parts Szerén *néni* from my mother's embrace and gently shoves Mommy and me to the group moving to the right.

"Go, and remember, from now on you are sixteen."

Szerén *néni*'s eyes fill with terror. She runs to Mommy and grabs her arm.

"Don't leave me, Lórika! Don't leave me!"

Mother embraces her fragile, older sister and turns to the SS officer, her voice a shrieking plea:

"This is my sister, *Herr Offizier*, let me go with her! She is not feeling well. She needs me."

"You go with your daughter. She needs you more. March on! *Los!*" With an impatient move of his right hand he shoves Mother toward me. Then he glares angrily at my aunt: "Move on! *Los!* You go that way!" His stick points menacingly to the left.

Aunt Szerén, a forlorn, slight figure against the marching multitude, the huge German shepherd dogs, the husky SS men. A savage certainty slashes my bruised insides. I will never again see my darling aunt! I give an insane shriek: "Szerén *néni!* Szerén *néni!* I'll never see you again!"

A wild fear floods her large hazel eyes. She stretches out her arms to reach me. An SS soldier gives her a brutal thrust, hurling her into the line marching to the left. She turns again, mute fear lending her added fragility. She moves on.

The road to the left leads to the gas chambers.

SIXTEEN

OUR MARCH to the right slows to a halt. A tall, metal gate looms darkly ahead. Above it huge metal letters arch like a sinister crown:

ARBEIT MACHT FREI!

Work sets you free! Perhaps Mommy was right. We will work. And be treated like human beings. Fed and clothed. But *"frei"*? Free? What do they mean by that? Will they really let us move about freely if we work? Where?

The immense portals of the gate open and we march through them into an enclosure with tall wire fences. Several rows of wire. Plain wire fence flanked by barbed wire.

It's growing lighter rapidly. And colder. I wonder when we will get our things. I need my coat. The eerie light of the watchtowers grows dimmer. Rows of barracks, long, flat buildings, on both sides of the black pebble-strewn road enclosed in barbed wire. It's a road without an end. It stretches far into the fog. And we march.

Motorcycles. SS officers. Dogs. *"Marchieren. Los. Los!"*

It's cold. We march on.

Groups of people linger about the barracks on the other side of the fence. Are they men or women? Their heads are shorn but they wear gray, dresslike cloaks. They run to the fence as we pass. They stare at us. Blank stares. They must be insane. This must be an asylum for the mentally ill. Poor souls.

The road ends. Our silent, rapid march ends. By fives we file through the entrance of a long, flat gray building. A low-ceilinged room. Long and narrow. Noise. Shouts. Unintelligible.

"Ruhe!" Quiet!

A tall, husky blonde in SS uniform. *"Ruhe! Wer versteht deutsch? Deutsch? Austreten. Wer versteht deutsch!"* Who understands German? Step forward!

I step forward. A few other girls also step forward. We understand German.

"Tell them to keep quiet at once. If they won't listen they will be shot. Tell them."

I attempt to shout above the din and so do my fellow interpreters. To no avail. The low ceiling compresses the sounds. The noise like a tidal wave hurls back and forth.

"Ruhe!" The buxom SS woman begins to swing her whip above the heads, and the other SS soldiers in the room, as if on cue, begin cracking their whips, snapping into faces. A sharp pain slashes at my left cheekbone. I feel a firm welt rise across my face. Why? I am the interpreter. No one hears me. Quickly, I step back into the crowd. Perhaps it is safer there.

In seconds it becomes quiet.

"Sich auskleiden! Alles herunter!" Get undressed, everybody! Take off everything! *"Los!"*

The room is swarming with SS men. Get undressed, here? In front of the men? No one moves.

"Didn't you hear? Take off your clothes. All your clothes!"

I feel the slap of a whip on my shoulders and meet a young SS soldier's glaring eyes.

"Hurry! Strip fast. You will be shot. Those having any clothes on in five minutes will be shot!"

I look at Mommy. She nods. Let's get undressed. I stare directly ahead as I take off my clothes. I am afraid. By not looking at anyone I hope no one will see me. I have never seen my mother in the nude. How awful it must be for her. I hesitate before removing my bra. My breasts are two growing buds, taut and sensitive. I can't have anyone see them. I decide to leave my bra on.

Just then a shot rings out. The charge is ear-shattering. Some women begin to scream. Others weep. I quickly take my bra off.

It is chilly and frightening. Clothes lie in mounds on the cement floor. We are herded, over a thousand, shivering, humiliated nude bodies, into the next hall, even chillier. More foreboding. It is darker here. Barer.

"Los! Schneller, blöde Lumpen!" Faster. Move faster, idiotic whores.

We are lined up and several husky girls in gray cloaks begin shaving our hair—on our heads, under the arms, and on the pubic area. My long, thick braids remain braided and while the shaving machine shears my scalp, the hair remains hanging, tugging at the roots. The pain of the heavy braid tugging mercilessly at the yet unshaven roots brings tears to my eyes. I pray for the shaving to be done quickly. As my blonde tresses lie in a large heap on the ground, the indifferent hair butcher remarks: "A heap of gold." In a shudder I remember the scene at the selection—the SS officer's admiration of my "golden hair," the separation from Aunt Szerén. Where is she now? Is her hair shorn off and is she stripped of her clothes, too? Is she very frightened? Poor, darling, Szerén *néni*. If my hair were shorn before the selection, we would be together with her now. We would not have been separated. It's because of my blonde hair that Mommy and I were sent to the other side. Poor darling. If only we could have stayed together!

The haircut has a startling effect on every woman's appearance. Individuals become a mass of bodies. Height, stoutness, or slimness: There is no distinguishing factor—it is the absence of hair which transformed individual women into like bodies. Age and other personal differences melt away. Facial expressions disappear. Instead, a blank, senseless stare emerges on a thousand faces of one naked, unappealing body. In a matter of minutes even the physical aspect of our numbers seems reduced—there is less of a substance to our dimensions. We become a monolithic mass. Inconsequential.

From *blöde Lumpen*, "idiotic whores," we became *blöde Schweine*, "idiotic swine." Easier to despise. And the epithet changed only occasionally to *blöde Hunde*, "idiotic dogs." Easier to handle.

The shaving had a curious effect. A burden was lifted. The burden of individuality. Of associations. Of identity. Of the recent past. Girls who have continually wept at separation from parents, sisters and brothers now began to giggle at the strange appearance of their friends. Some shriek with laughter. Others begin calling out names of friends to see if they can recognize them shorn and stripped. When response to names comes forth from completely transformed bodies, recognition is loud, hysterical. Wild, noisy embraces. Shrieking, screaming disbelief. Some girls bury their faces in their palms and howl, rolling on the ground.

"Was ist los?" What's the matter? A few swings of the SS whip restores order.

I look for Mommy. I find her easily. The haircut has not changed her. I have been used to seeing her in kerchiefs, every bit of hair carefully tucked away. Avoiding a glance at her body, I marvel at the beauty of her face. With all accessories gone her perfect features are even more striking. Her high forehead, large blue eyes, classic nose, shapely lips and elegant cheekbones are more evident than ever.

She does not recognize me as I stand before her. Then a sudden smile of recognition: "Elli! It's you. You look just like Bubi. Strange, I have never seen the resemblance before. What a boyish face! They cut off your beautiful braids . . ."

"It's nothing. Hair can grow."

"With the will of God."

We are herded en masse into the next hall. Clutching a cake of claylike object handed to me at the door, the nude mass of bodies crushing about me, I shriek with sudden shock as a cold torrent gushes unexpectedly from openings in the ceiling. In a few minutes it is over, and once again we are rushed into another room. Gray dresses are handed to us and we are urged with shouts of *Los!* and *blöde Schweine* to pull them over wet, shivering bodies. Everyone has to pick a pair of shoes from an enormous shoe pile. *"Los! Los!"*

As we emerge, still wet, in gray sacks, with clean-shaven heads, from the other end of the building and line up, by now relatively quickly, in rows of five, the idea strikes me. The people we saw as we entered the camp, the shaved, gray-cloaked group which ran to stare at us through the barbed-wire fence, they were us! We look exactly like them. Same bodies, same dresses, same blank stares. We, too, look like an insane horde—soulless, misshapen figures. They, too, must have arrived from home quite recently: Their heads were freshly shaven. They were women just like us. They, too, were ripe mothers and young girls, bewildered and bruised. They, too, longed for dignity and compassion; and they, too, were transformed into figures of contempt instead.

The *Zehlappel* lasts almost three hours. This word, meaning "roll call," became the dread and the life style of Auschwitz. Twice daily we would be lined up with lightning speed by fives in order to be counted. Lined up at 3 A.M. We would stand three or four hours until the official SS staff showed up to count our heads. In the evening it lasted from five to nine. The lineup had to be accomplished in seconds in order to stand endless hours awaiting the roll call, *Zehlappel*.

It was inconceivable to me that the mad rush inside the showers would culminate in an endless wait outside. Wet bodies in a single loose cotton robe exposed to the chill morning, traumatized bodies hurled out to the cold wind to stand in a senseless, long wait.

The smartly stepping German staff appears briskly. With the tip of a stick lightly touching the head of the first girl in every row of five, we are counted and officially initiated into the camp. We become members of an exclusive club. Inmates of Auschwitz.

SEVENTEEN

NEWBORN CREATURES, we march out of the showers. Shorn and stripped, washed and uniformed, women and girls between sixteen to forty-five, separated from mothers, fathers, husbands, sisters, brothers, and from offspring—transformed into bodies marching uniformly toward the barracks of Auschwitz. An abyss separates us from the past: The rapid succession of events of this morning is an evolution of eons. Our parents and families belong to the prehistoric past. Our clothes, our hair—had they been real? The homes we left only recently are in a distant land, perhaps of make-believe. Our lives of yesterday belong to a bygone era.

We are new creatures. Marching expertly in fives at a rapid, deliberate rhythm, we are an army of impassive bodies animated by the hysterics of survival. We survived the entry into Auschwitz. Unknowingly, we survived the selection of the SS god Dr. Mengele, the tall, handsome, psychotic monster with the kind voice who gently stroked my "golden hair" and told me to lie about my age to his SS-machinery so as to save my life. We survived where our parents, little sisters and brothers, and grandparents did not. We, a few out of every hundred, survived the selection. While tens of thousands were sent to the gas chambers, we were sent to the showers. While we were shorn and soaped, our parents and grandparents, our younger sisters and brothers were suffocating in Zyklon B. And while we shivered on the *Zehlappel*, their bodies were turned into ashes in the crematoria.

Gone is Mrs. Bonyhádi and Tommi and little Suzie. No more thirst, no more poems. No hills and blue lakes. Tommi is not expected to act the gentleman anymore. Neither does young Mrs. Hédi Lunger need diapers for Yingele and Frumet. She is gone and so is her mother-in-law, holding on to her oldest little boy. Gone is the elderly gentleman with his communal pot. And Mr. Stern. And Mr. Lunger. Perhaps the little skinny man from Galanta survived the selection: He was no more than thirty-five. And Szerén *néni*? My darling, gentle, soft-spoken aunt!

As we march in a rhythmic, deliberate stance toward the future in Auschwitz, a heavy cloud of smoke rises from the stacks of a low, gray building to our left. It was only much later that we found out about the smoke. By then we had experienced enough to believe it. By then we knew all the faces of death.

As we march from the showers toward the camps we know only of survival. We sense its sinister significance. Survival is in every fiber of our muscles and with those muscles we march, not understanding, not even wishing. We march on, instinctively. We march, steadfastly avoiding German whips, German dogs, and poised German guns. With inexorable drive we march silently on. That quality, born in the showers, that new mystical compromise with death bids us to move on. Robotlike, our secret pact with death animates our march toward the camps.

When we reach C-Lager the sun is high. It scorches my freshly shaven scalp. My lips and throat are parched. The shoes I received are two sizes too small and now they are pressing on skinned toes and ankles. My own mystic march against death is turning into a graceless limp. Heat, dust, the monotonous, droning sound of marching feet. Unbearable thirst. God, let me faint.

Today is Sunday. We have had nothing to drink since we left Dunaszerdahely Thursday morning. I wet my lips in the shower but the whole thing was too rapid and ended too abruptly. I had no chance to drink. Now I am parched. The

sun is blinding. As I touch my smooth scalp it burns my palm.
The gun butts glisten blindingly. The motorcycle, what a spar-
kling, whizzing sight! It passes soundlessly as if in a dream.
Everything is flooded with brilliance. The dust, even the white
rising dust . . .

The camp is a huge, arid area surrounded by barbed-wire
fencing. Half-built barracks are scattered irregularly in the
distance. Large, deep holes mar the dry dusty ground, and we
are told to march around them toward the barracks.

Zehlappel. We are lined up by fives—rapidly, smoothly,
automatically. We are told this is our barrack. It is a long, flat
brick building without doors or windows. Without beds. Without plumbing. This is a camp under construction. Is there
water? No, there is no water in this camp.

After *Zehlappel* we are permitted to scatter. Large groups
of young women milling about the camp greet us. News of our
arrival spreads through the camp like wildfire. Soon we are
surrounded by a mass of faces, noisy, loud exclamations.
What are they all yelling? What's all this mad excitement?

They are inmates of the camp brought here days and weeks
earlier. All are anxious to meet relatives. Their eagerness is
like a mad hunger attacking us, about to devour us with a
passion like the scorching, blinding sun. I have not fainted yet.
I am standing in this mad, blinding place, in this white-hot
rising dust, this wild clamor. I am on my feet, by now bare-
footed. The ground is scorching. Is there water? Where is
water in this camp?

"Where are you from? What city? What town? Which
ghetto? Do you know if Budapest is liquidated yet? Have you
heard anything about Hajdúszoboszló?"

"We are from the ghetto of Dunaszerdahely. Csallóköz.
Upper Hungary. Slovakia. We do not know anything about
anybody. We were on the road for three days. And before that
under guard in the ghetto. We have no information about
other cities. . . . We know only of towns in our county, Csallóköz. . . . We arrived this morning. The men were taken. The

elderly. The children and their mothers . . . to the other side.
. . . That's all we know. Is there water in your camp? Where
can we get water to drink?"

The crowd grows. News of arrivals from Dunaszerdahely
brings fresh faces, eager, expectant faces, faces of those who
had relatives in the area of Dunaszerdahely. Instead of ran-
dom shouting, now names float in the air. Guta . . . Galanta . . .
Nagymagyar . . . Surány . . . the Weiss family, the Gutt-
manns, the Rosenbaums . . . do you know them? Did you see
them? Where are they?

"Bubi!"

The heat. The maddening crowd. The unbearable thirst. I
refuse to go insane, my God. I have not fainted. I refuse to go
mad.

A pair of brown eyes is peering into my face: "It's Elli!
Look Hindi, it's Elli. She looks like Bubi. Ellike!"

"But who are you?"

"Don't you recognize us? I am Suri, Suri Schreiber, your
cousin."

"Suri!" I scream. "And Hindi! My God, you are here, too!
When did you get here?"

"We came a few days ago. Who is with you?"

"Mommy. She is with me here. But everybody else was
taken away. Daddy, Bubi, Aunt Szerén . . . I don't know
where they are."

"We know. Only girls and young women are here. We were
separated from everybody. Our parents, Leah, Breindi, Aunt
Chava, and Grandmother went on the other side."

"How about Benzu? And Elyu?"

"Benzu was taken to the Russian front several months ago.
And Elyu is in a Hungarian labor camp. We two are together.
But now we found you. We will all be together from now on.
Where is Aunt Lóri? Let's look for her."

Suri and Hindi are my cousins from Sátoraljaulyhely,
daughters of my father's sister, Aunt Perl. Four years ago I
spent two weeks in their house during the summer. About the

happiest two weeks of my life. It was a large house with many
children and cats. Hindi is the oldest girl, about nineteen. Suri
is sixteen. Leah is my age and Breindi a year younger. The
two boys, Benzu and Elyu, are much older. Benzu is twenty-
one and Elyu, seventeen. But they treated me like an equal
and joined in whatever game I wished to play, Benzu the
handsome ladies' man and Elyu the Yeshiva student with
black hat, long *peyes*, and large blue eyes. My grandmother,
ignoring her lame leg, lorded it over the roost. My aunt, a
good-natured blonde, heavyset woman whose laughter rang
like bells through the house, and my uncle, a Hasid with a rich
brown beard and a generous disposition allowed Grandmother
to hold the reins of family and business. They looked to her
for advice and discipline.

Now they are all gone. On the other side. Only Suri and
Hindi are here.

We look for Mommy and find her lying on the ground. She
is half asleep, her lips cracked. A red blister has formed on her
nose, covering its whole length.

She is surprised to see my cousins but too exhausted to show
joy. Where do we get water to drink, do they know?

There is no water in this camp, they say. We get black
coffee in the morning and soup in the evening. During the day
we drink from the lake in the camp.

"Lake? Where is it?"

Mother wants to go there at once. Suri and Hindi lead us to
a puddle, a fairly large hollow in the ground filled with murky
water. It has an unpleasant odor.

"To drink from this? It's putrified! It's filthy! It stinks!" I
look at my cousins with horror.

"You drank from this?"

"We all did. There is nothing else. If you are thirsty enough
you don't care."

I am thirsty enough. My tongue is covered with a layer of
whitish stuff and my lips begin to crack. But I think I will
never drink filthy, smelly swamp.

Mommy bends down and takes a handful of water to her mouth.

"It is not so bad. Hold your nose. Then gulp. It is not that bad. Drink, Elli. I feel a little better already."

As I raise a palmful of swampy water to my lips, the smell makes my stomach heave. But I have no urge to vomit. My stomach has been empty for a long time.

I close my eyes and hold my nose with my other hand. Then quickly slurp. It was not bad at all. As a matter of fact, I like it. I delight in the touch of wetness on my lips, mouth, throat. I take another handful and drink it now greedily gulping without holding my nose. The smell does not matter. It is water. God-given, delightful, wet water. It quenches and revives.

"No more, Elli. Please, don't drink more. Some girls got very sick. They drank too much." Hindi forces me to spill the third handful.

The transport from Dunaszerdahely is a sprawling group when we get back from the "lake." Some sit on the ground, others stand, many are lying down with eyes closed, oblivious to the bustle about them. There is a lot of activity at the perimeter of the newly arrived transport. A steady stream of inmates passes, shouting and calling names, or directly addressing anyone milling about, searching faces for familiar features, hungrily peering into faces of those sitting or lying about. Sometimes an exclamation and wild embrace follow, then shrieks and exclamations, cries and embraces. Sometimes a lonely figure moves on, looking and searching, with every failure appearing more forlorn and dejected.

"No, I am not from Guta. Yes, I came from the Dunaszerdahely ghetto. . . . No, I do not know the Parsnitz family. . . . I am sorry. . . . Yes, I know the Taubers from Somorja . . . the Taubers . . . no, no one came on this side. . . . I am sorry. . . . Waldmann? Yes, I know the Waldmanns, Bobbi Waldmann is my best friend. . . . No, she is not here. She went to the other side. No one is here from the Waldmanns. I am sorry. The Stern family from Patony? Yes, I know them. The girls? They did not come with us to the ghetto. I do not know where they are. I am sorry. Yes, I am from Somorja. I don't know anyone from Komarom. Komarom was a different ghetto. We came from the Dunaszerdahely ghetto. . . . I am sorry. . . ."

With every No answer I feel the weight of the search. And it drones on, a continuous confrontation with young girls and occasional middle-aged women searching for families, friends, and security of contact. Every No brings visible despair. I begin to modify my style: I am from Somorja. The transport of Galanta is over there. Perhaps they know. . . . There are some girls from Megyer. They might know the Klein family. . . . From Surany? Yes, there are some girls from Surany among us. I'll show you where they are. . . .

Hindi and Suri come with me in search of girls from Surany. Mommy has long withdrawn from the crowd. Overcome by fatigue, she sits in one of the deep holes in the ground.

As we approach the group from Surany, I spot a tall figure wandering about in the crowd, shouting repeatedly: "Lórika! Lórika!"

"Aunt Cili!"

It is my youngest aunt, Mommy's sister from Miskolc. My beautiful, elegant aunt. Even now as she approaches in the loose, drab, gray dress, with shaven scalp, she looks distinguished.

"Aunt Cili!"

The vehemence of my embrace almost sweeps her off her feet. She grasps my shoulders and stares into my face. Her eyes wide with shock and disbelief: "Ellikém! My little Elli! Is it you? Here? . . . There are no children on this side. . . . How is this possible? Oh, my God. . . . Oh my darling. . . ."

She rocks me in a tight embrace. She is kissing my scalp. And we both begin to cry.

"You are here. My little darling. . . . Where is Mommy? Are you alone?"

"Mommy is here, too. Come, I'll take you to her."

We find Mommy asleep in her hole. As Cili *néni* kneels and strokes her face, Mommy opens her eyes wearily, as in a drunken daze. Suddenly she recognizes her sister's tear-stained face. She sits up with alarm. "Cilikém!"

Aunt Cili crouches in the dusty hole and the two sisters hold each other in a silent embrace. They have not seen each other for three years. And now, a reunion in the scorching dust of Auschwitz.

Still sobbing, Aunt Cili reaches into her bosom and takes out a piece of black substance tied on a string around her neck. She unties it and hands it to Mother. "Here. Eat it."

"What is it?"

"It's bread. My bread. My ration. Eat it. It's yours. I want you to have it. You must be very hungry."

"This is bread? It looks like a cake of mud. How can you eat this?"

"Eat it. You won't get anything to eat until the evening *Zehlappel*."

Mother takes a bite and tears spring into her eyes. "I can't eat this."

"You must. There is nothing else."

She takes another bite, swallows it, and throws it up promptly. Her tears flow on dusty cheeks. "I can't. I'd rather starve."

Aunt Cili cries, too. She bends down to wipe her tears with the edge of her dress. "Lóri, if you don't eat you will not live. You must."

I snatch the bread from her hand and begin to eat. The dry mudlike piece turns into wet mud and sand particles in my mouth. The others have eaten it. I swallow it. The first food in Auschwitz. To survive.

Hindi and Suri go back to their barrack, and Aunt Cili tells us about her husband and son. Uncle Martin was taken by the Hungarians to a labor camp several months ago, and Imre, my cousin, was arrested by the Arrowcross, the Hungarian Nazis, a few days before her deportation to Auschwitz. Imre is seventeen, a tall, dark and very handsome boy, a virtual copy of my aunt.

We vow never to be separated from each other. Hindi and Suri promise to return as soon as they have checked whether their absence from their barrack has been noticed. We decide to form a family of five. Suri says it is much easier to survive in Auschwitz if you are five. Bread and food is distributed on *Zehlappel,* the roll-call line. Every five get one portion of bread and a bowl of food, and then it is divided among them. If you don't know the others, you may end up without provisions. Those ahead of you on line take the larger portions of bread and you, especially if you are tall and placed last on the line, get the thinnest slice. And the bowl may be empty by the time it reaches you. Everyone gulps as large a gulp as she possibly can. Even though there are only four gulps to a person, if each takes too large gulps, the bowl may be empty by the time it reaches the end of the line. It happens all the time. But if you have family and friends on the line, you share the food equally. You may even pool your bread ration. Eat only half in the evening and leave some for the morning. It is better that way. Then you can carry a piece of bread hidden under your dress and nibble during the day. You don't get so hungry that way.

Hindi and Suri return and we all stand on *Zehlappel* together. But when the bowl of food is handed to me I am unable to take a gulp. It is a dark-green, thick mass in a battered wash bowl crusted with dirt. No spoons are given to us. Each girl tilts the bowl waiting for the green mass to slide to the edge and then gulps. The dark mush smells and looks repulsive. The edge of the bowl is rusty and cracked and uneven with dried-on dirt. My nausea returns in a flash. Despite nagging hunger pangs in my stomach, I feel like vomiting. I hand the bowl to Mommy. She takes a gulp and almòst throws up into the bowl. I try again. This time I take a mouthful but cannot swallow it. It has grains of sand in it just like the bread, and something else—pieces of glass . . . and wood . . . and cloth. I spit it out and start to vomit. My empty stomach feels as if it is rising through my gullet.

"Never mind. We all threw up at first. But then we swallowed it. It's food. You must eat it to live. Close your eyes, hold your nose. Gulp!"

Suri pats my head. "Go ahead, Elli."

I do it. And again. Four times.

The sun sets and it suddenly becomes very cold. Under the long, loose dress I feel every particle of my bare body. A slow shiver begins in the lines. The rhythmic shiver of thousands on *Zehlappel* in the dark, cold night of Auschwitz in time becomes a familiar sound. But now it is new to my ears. It is the conclusion of my first day in Auschwitz.

EIGHTEEN

AUNT CILI spends the night in our barrack. There are no beds. Each five receives two army blankets. They are to serve as mattress and cover. The unusual hardness of the floor, the close proximity of strange bodies, and the extreme exhaustion of the long, eventful day make sleep impossible. There are no windows in the barrack. From somewhere a cold wind keeps blowing under the blanket. There are muffled cries in the dark. Slowly, I drift off to sleep.

Suddenly, a shriek tears into the night. In seconds the barrack is agog with screams. A wave of panic sweeps the prone bodies, whipping them into a wild frenzy. Senseless shrieking and trampling on top of each other in the dark. Many surge for the door. Locked, they begin pounding on it.

Someone shrieks: "I smell gas! They are exterminating us!"

The screaming continues. Suddenly, a shot is heard under

the window. A second. A barrage of fire. The screaming stops. The German guards are shouting orders: "Back on the floor! Cover yourselves and don't move, or you'll be shot!"

In seconds it is quiet again, except for one girl. She keeps screaming: "Mommy! Mommy! They are killing her. They are killing my mother!"

Another shot rings out.

"*Ruhe!* Quiet or you'll be shot!"

But her shrieks grow louder: "Mommyyy! Where are you? Mommy. . . . They are killing my mother! Everybody, listen! Can't you hear? Oh, Mommy! Oh, God, they are killing my mother!"

The silhouette of a body sitting upright in the middle of the room. Someone places an arm on her shoulders, trying to soothe her: "Shh, quiet. You had a nightmare. Lie down here . . . quietly. Here." The arm is gently drawing her down on the blanket but the girl jerks her body away, springs up, and begins to scream again, her voice bloodcurdling.

"Let me go! Let me go to my mother!"

The doors open and two German guards come in, their guns drawn: "Who is shouting?"

Flashlights train on the lonely standing figure.

"*Komm mit!*" Come along. "*Los!*"

Each guard holds on to an arm, and the young girl, still screaming, is led out of the barrack. Seconds later a shot rings out.

I sit up with alarm. "They shot her?"

"Shh. . . . Please, for God's sake. Quiet everybody. We don't want another riot. It is dangerous." It is the voice of the woman who had tried to quiet the screaming girl.

Cili *néni* becomes frightened. She is afraid another such outburst in the night would create a general search for offenders and she will be discovered in the wrong barrack.

She sneaks out through the rear door. In the morning she will ask to be transferred to our barrack.

At dawn we are aroused for *Zehlappel*. It is still totally dark when we line up. The sky is studded with stars. It is cold. Some girls brought out their blankets and the whole row of five stands wrapped in one blanket. Why didn't we think of that? But soon a brisk girl appears and orders them to return the blankets. As the girls turn to run to the barrack, she strikes each on the head with her long narrow stick. She is our *Blockelteste*. As we come to know the word, we come to know arbitrary authority, cruelty, sadism. She is a Jew from Slovakia, in Auschwitz since 1942. She is one of the few who survived that first transport of young girls from Slovakia brought here to "entertain" the German troops. Two years in Auschwitz! Survival at incredible cost. She is eighteen now, thin but strong, a face set in a perpetual countenance of grim determination. Or defiance? It is a face of anger. Unapproachable. *Blockeltestes* are the commanders of the Block, the barrack. They have private rooms in the barracks and supervise their charges at all times. But in our barrack there are no beds, or rooms, or any other facility, so our *Blockelteste* sleeps elsewhere. But apparently she was told of the riot.

"You are lucky you were not all shot for what happened in your barrack during the night. Sabotage. If it happens again you will be sent to the gas. I am responsible for your behavior. If any of you makes sabotage anytime, I shall immediately report you. This is your warning."

Gas? What gas? What did she mean? "You will be sent to the gas. . . ." Can any of those horrible rumors we heard at home be actually true? What is sabotage? She did not explain and no one asks questions.

Cili *néni* and my cousins did not come to our *Zehlappel*. I see lines before every barrack, silent long lines. They must be there, with their own barracks.

It grows lighter gradually. The stars fade and a cold breeze begins to blow. How long will the *Zehlappel* last? My mother embraces my shoulders as my trembling grows fierce.

Quietly, I crouch. It is warmer this way. Mommy says she will poke me quickly when someone approaches so I can quickly stand up. Crouching, with my arms hugging my knees, I feel better.

All at once I notice that blood is flowing on the legs of the girl before me. A thick red stream of blood on the inner side of each leg. Oh, my God, she must have been shot! What should I do? Then, in a flash I realize. She is menstruating. Poor girl. Of course, we have no underwear . . . there are no pads . . . the blood simply flows. Down her legs. My God, but this is horrible. . . . Why doesn't she say something? Ask for a pad or something? But from whom? Whom can she say anything to? She might even be shot for reporting that she is bleeding. Does menstruating constitute sabotage?

How lucky for me that my last menstruation was just over when we got off the wagons. I would rather die than have blood flowing down my legs. In full view. Oh, my God! I would not bear it. . . . But what about next time? In less than three weeks! There will not be a next time. By then we will be free. The war will be over by then. It is drawing to its close now. It is a matter of days now. Everybody says so. Even Daddy said so before he was taken away: "The end of the war is near. . . ." In days we will be freed and go home. This cannot last longer anyway. It's impossible to survive this longer than a few days. . . .

NINETEEN

CILI *néni* was not permitted to transfer to our barrack. Neither was she allowed to visit us. So we met casually between *Zehlappels*, usually at the latrine. Hindi and Suri also did not show up. Two days later we met them also at the latrine.

"We were not allowed to leave the area near our barrack.

We could not come to see you. No more loitering is allowed."

We plan to meet regularly in the latrine. The latrine is a long, wide ditch behind the last barrack. We are allowed to go there in groups of fifty, under guard. Luckily, the German guard cannot bear the stench of the latrine and stands at a distance. This allows us a chance to talk and linger. Our meeting time is daily at noon. There is no way to tell time any other way. Noon we could tell by the sun.

At first I was frightened of the latrine. The ditch was wide and very deep and I had a nightmarish fear of falling into it. Mommy was holding my two hands while I was crouching above the smelly abyss, and I held hers while she was. But after the first few times we learned to balance at the precarious edge of the ditch. The fear is gone. Amazing how fast one learns. Everything. Even swallowing the dark daily mush became easy. Lying on the hard floor is much easier now, and the *Zehlappel* quite bearable. Getting used to thirst is the most difficult.

I am always thirsty. Mommy complains of hunger constantly. But for me thirst is much worse. The only liquid we get are the four gulps of black coffee at the morning *Zehlappel*. I think I am going insane, craving for water all day long. We, too, are forbidden to leave the area of our Block, and so the "lake" is out of bounds. No drinking during the day, and night, until the next morning. A long time. The sun is scorching most of the day. We loiter about the barrack aimlessly for hours. We are forbidden to sit or lie down, or to enter the barrack during the day. Secretly we do sit or lie, though. But when a German approaches we give a slight kick to those asleep on the ground, and in a flash all are on their feet. Mommy keeps on falling asleep and I keep guard. When I fall asleep and it is her turn to stand guard, she falls asleep, too. It is better that I lean against the wall of the barrack and sleep that way. I can keep alert when I sleep standing up.

We developed ugly and ridiculous blisters on our noses and earlobes. Our lips first cracked; then a brownish crust formed

on and about the lips. It must be from the brownish discharge
that keeps oozing from the cracks. It looks repulsive. Some
girls look like clowns, their mouths seem to reach almost up to
their ears. From a short distance they look as if wearing a
perpetual grin.

I look more ridiculous than most. Having an extremely fair
skin, I grew large blisters ringed with red on my cheekbones
and on the back of my neck. My ears look much larger because of the tall blisters at the edge of my earlobes. My scalp
turned fiery red. The hair began to grow, studding the bright-
red background with sharp-yellow thistles, like the needles of
a porcupine. During the night of the riot someone had torn my
left sleeve at the shoulder, and now it hangs down to my
elbow. On the exposed shoulder another blister popped up. I
walk barefoot since I cannot wear the shoes I received in the
showers. On my feet there are huge, silly blisters also and
another, very large one on the side of my right leg. Someone
kicked me in the wagons, and after festering for a while, the
bruise turned into an unsightly blister. So my ludicrous looks
are compounded by a strange limp. With blisters also on my
soles, I have not managed to devise a graceful manner to
navigate.

On the fourth day I saw myself for the first time in
Auschwitz. As we were approaching the last barrack on our
way to the latrine, our guard stopped to chat with another
guard. While we stood patiently waiting, I glanced at the window nearby and saw my reflection in the glass pane. I did not
recognize myself. My shorn hair was a shocking sight. How
could my mother and cousins claim that I looked like my
brother? Bubi is handsome with perfect features and a small
mouth. And I? My God! I am a disfigured scarecrow with a
mass of pus sores where my mouth had been. How is Bubi
now? Is he also disfigured by sun and thirst?

On the tenth day after our arrival we are ordered to start
marching straight from *Zehlappel*. Our march leads us past
the last barracks of the camp and through the gates. We are

leaving the camp. Where to? Mother begins to worry about Aunt Cili and my cousins. We are being separated from them without even saying farewell to them. What has become of our plans to form a unit of five? Daily we had been hoping to work out some way to get together. Daily we hoped for a relaxation of rules that would finally bring us together. Only yesterday Cili *néni* came with the happy news that a woman was willing to change places with her, a woman in our Block who had relatives in hers. She asked for a few days to think it over. But now we are marching out of the camp. Is this a final leave? Or perhaps they are taking us somewhere only temporarily. I thought it was only temporary, perhaps only for a few hours, and said so to Mother. But Mommy does not relax. Her worry over her sister is especially acute. She had been suffering from diarrhea for the last three days. Diarrhea was dangerous in Auschwitz, we were told. And Mother felt Aunt Cili's constitution could not stand up to additional hazards. She wanted to be with her. To help. To help, if there was any way one could help in Auschwitz.

Our march leads to the showers. With experienced speed we undress. The stares of the SS men do not matter. We feel no nakedness without clothes as we felt no clothedness in our uniforms. Our soul is naked, exposed, abused. Our bodies have lost dimension. The shower is a familiar experience. And so is the shivery, wet wait on the outside, the endless *Zehlappel*.

Finally, we are ordered to march again, past various camps beyond barbed-wire fences with gawking inmates, past tall watchtowers and the high, forbidding iron gate with its sign, ARBEIT MACHT FREI!—its irony now fully relevant. The train station. The wagons. But this time, away from Auschwitz!

I have a pair of shoes now. They fit and give me a new outlook on life. As the train begins to move out of the foggy morning of Auschwitz, I feel curiously elated.

"You'll see, Mommy. We are going to a better place. A much better place. Thank God, we have left Auschwitz behind."

But Mother's mind is not eased. She is worried about her sister left behind in Auschwitz.

All day the train rumbles along amid barren hills, stark landscape, and forlorn farms. At times we stop and stand still for hours. Toward the evening we enter a dense forest, and the train stops there for the night. It is only when light starts to sift through the cracks in the wagon walls that we start to move again. Barren fields and rain-soaked countryside pass slowly before the narrow gaps which afford a view from the wagon.

In the wagons it is quite pleasant. We are not too crowded, so that we even have space to lie down. The five Sternberg sisters from Dunaszerdahely are in our wagon, lovely girls with lovely singing voices. Their singing inspires others to join in, and soon the memory of Auschwitz dissipates in the birth of a new vigor. I am asked to recite poetry and several others respond in a chorus to the refrain of my most popular poem, "Our Beloved Nation. . . ."

The train stops again, this time at a station. The sign reads KRAKOW. I learned about Krakow at school. It is the capital of Galicia. A large and prominent Jewish community. My father's family originated from Galicia.

"Heraus! Alles heraus. Aussteigen!" Out! Everybody out! Off the train!

We disembark into a cold, dismal, rainy morning. Army trucks await us at the station. Through winding, hilly roads we are driven in the open trucks. Large raindrops hang on tree branches. The sky is heavily overcast. The narrow road leads through a small sleepy town then upward to the hills. The trucks stop before a wide gate. Above it the lettering in German and Polish: CAMP PLASZOW. As the gates open, we drive into a valley surrounded by high, steep hills. A circular clearing filled with neatly arranged rows of barracks around a central square. In the center of the square towers a flag pole on which the SS flag flutters high. On this spot the trucks discharge their cargo of one thousand shaven-headed women.

Almost instantly we are surrounded by dogs and a swarm of

SS guards. The *Zehlappel* is brief. We are assigned barracks to the left of the square and march there. These barracks are much smaller than the ones in Auschwitz. Each Block in Auschwitz accommodates a thousand inmates. Here we are about two hundred to a barrack.

There are beds in the barrack! Three-tiered beds covered with gray army blankets. Five people to a bed. There is straw under the blanket. We are to sleep on beds and straw. Not on the bare floor as in Auschwitz.

In the morning, the brief *Zehlappel* is followed by a work lineup. As we line up near the flagpole, *Kapos*, heads of work commandos, select workers for their commandos from among us. Several hundred for each commando for the day. There are many thousand inmates in this camp, men and women, and all have their work assigned each morning. Most of the women have their hair intact. And they wear civilian clothes. The men wear blue-and-white stripes with various arm bands. Most have yellow arm bands, with black Jewish stars at the center. Some, however, wear white arm bands with a black or a green triangle. Later we find out that these are not Jews. The black triangle arm band is for criminals who serve life sentences for murder. They are assigned supervisory positions in the camp. Most of them are *Kapos*. The green triangle is for political prisoners. They are Poles from the resistance movement. Their lot is as bad as that of the Jewish inmates.

The word *Kapo* means supreme authority over life and death. *Kapos* were delegated absolute power by the SS. Encouraged to exercise any method of control, including beatings and torture to death, the *Kapos* of Plaszow assume an aura of dread beyond normal human concept.

As if they had made a pact with the devil, the *Kapos* seem to revel in their cruelty. There is a devilish delight etched on their hard faces when they wield the whip. They seem to lack normal human responses. They do not communicate even with each other. They seem to seek no human contact. I glance with awe at the supreme figure of the *Kapo* standing

high on a rock or boulder, whip in hand, supervising our
work. Several younger assistants snap to his commands. If you
stop work for a moment, the *Kapo* would dispatch one of his
boys and the lash of his whip would send you back to your
routine. If the lad's strikes were tempered with a touch of
compassion, the *Kapo* would admonish from a distance.

"At her head, my *Junge*. Are you losing touch? Let her
have it in the head, *Liebling!*"

And the young "assistant" would repeat the lash, this time
aimed at the exposed head and neck, and the offender would
cry out in protest. In vain. Such outcries would cause additional hurt. It is better to endure in silence. It is better to
cooperate.

Once an older woman, working a few feet from me, stopped
to rest her arms, and the young assistant, instead of troubling
to walk over to her to administer the whip, picked up a piece
of rock and threw it at her. The rock struck her at the side of
the head slashing a deep, bloody gap. The woman collapsed,
unconscious. The boy, taken aback, ran over to the stricken
woman, and then in fright apologized to the *Kapo*.

"You missed, stupid *Junge*," the *Kapo* called to the contrite
boy with a chuckle. "As you see, she fainted. You should have
struck her dead."

The *Kapo*'s remark horrified me. For he was not one of the
criminals with the black triangle. He was a young Jew from
Krakow. His reputation as one of the cruelest *Kapos* had
aroused my sense of loyalty to him as a fellow Jew and I kept
rationalizing his acts. But this time I found no excuse. His
remark was beyond my ability to comprehend.

As we clustered about the unfortunate woman, attempting
to revive her, I expected Jacko, the *Kapo*, to order us all
whipped or to report us for sabotage. We had stopped working
without permission. But he stood there, aloof and erect, seemingly ignoring the activity. One girl rushed to bring water, and
several of us lifted the woman and carried her into the shade.

Jacko ignored it all. There was a heart beating somewhere under that sadistic exterior, after all. I was glad.

Our work consists of *Planierung*, straightening the hilltop with spades and shovels, in preparation for construction. Some of us work with spades straightening the ground, then shovel dirt into wheelbarrows. Other girls roll the wheelbarrows to parts where holes are filled with the dirt. In a matter of days we level large areas on the hilltop.

It was very difficult at first. As we arrived in the hills we were exhausted from the mountain-climbing alone. And that was at the start of a twelve-hour workday. We have half an hour rest at noon when we receive our cooked meal. It is a bowlful of food. Not as in Auschwitz where a bowlful was shared by five; in this camp everyone owns a small aluminum bowl tied about the waist, and the food is dished into it at mealtimes, noon and night. It is also much more edible than the fare of Auschwitz. It is either cabbage with some grain or other, less recognizable, pottage. But edible. Quite tasty, in fact.

Once, however, the food arrived at the mountains too early. While standing for hours in the sun, it became putrified and alive with long white worms. I noticed a worm wiggling in her food as my mother lifted the spoon to her mouth. I cried out and my mother looked at me with astonishment.

"What happened?"

"There is a worm in your spoon. Look, Mommy, there are hundreds of worms in your bowl. And in mine! Look!"

"Nonsense! These are not worms. Eat, and leave me alone."

"But Mommy, these are worms. Live worms. They crawl. Look."

I picked a worm out of my bowl and placed it on the ground. It began crawling. Then I picked out another. It too, began crawling.

Mother looked at me in despair. "What are you trying to do? What is your objective? Tell me, what do you want of me?"

I did not understand. I wanted to save Mommy from a

terrible thing. Disease. Or even death. Or, simply from the horrible feat of swallowing a worm. Worms. Instead, she was angry with me. Why?

"Do you want me to die of hunger? I can't leave this food. I am very hungry. And there are no worms in it! Say no more of it!"

As Mother turned away and continued eating, I turned my bowl over, spilling its contents on the ground and ran. I sat down on a boulder and began to cry. My God. My God. Is this all actually happening?

In the beginning our hands became bruised and blistery from the tools but soon hard callouses formed and that, too, made things easier. It took time for our backs to get used to bending without pain. We adjusted fast, and digging, shoveling, wheelbarrowing became endurable. After a while our *Arbeitführer*, our immediate work supervisors, allowed us to carry on a conversation while we worked, and we got to know each other, and looked forward to socializing. The talk is mostly about food. The women are trading recipes. They describe meals they cooked at home, in prehistoric times. They are also composing dishes, like shipwrecked musicians thinking musical notes out loud. Young girls tell of their first loves, dates, boyfriends. And as time, days and weeks, pass, the pain of remembering dulls, and we began to speak of our families. The memories are inexhaustible. The shared pain forges a strong bond. We work with the shovel but our souls indulge in dreams.

TWENTY

THREE WEEKS pass and I do not menstruate. Neither does anyone else. With amazement we all realize that menstruation ceased in the camps. The first week after our arrival there were many menstruant women, even in the wagon on our way to Plaszow there were several girls who bled profusely. Then, menstruation ceased abruptly. There is bromide in our food, we are told by old-timers. Bromide is supposed to sterilize women. The Germans are experimenting with mass sterilization.

The information causes panic among the inmates and at first many refuse to eat the cooked food, determined to survive on the bread ration alone. Soon hunger wins, and the food is consumed as before. The whole sterilization story may be just a rumor anyway.

I am secretly grateful for the bromide. Avoiding the fear, pain and embarrassment of menstruation is worth any sacrifice to me at the moment.

But the topic does not die. Married women keep wondering about the bromide in their food again and again. Will they bear children again? What will their husbands say when they find out? Perhaps less of the food will cause less of a damage. Some try to eat less and the conflict is painful. Rejection of a means of survival for the sake of a dubious gain.

No one can help. Rumors have no way of being checked. The old-timers, mostly Polish Jews who have been in the camps for over two years, bitterly resent us, Hungarian Jews. They are bitter about the fact that we arrived only recently. We lived in the security and comfort of our homes for the past two years while they were exposed to the torture of the camps. "You went to the theaters and resorts in Hungary, while our families were shot and burned, and we suffered in the camps," they would say to us. Then they would dramatize the dangers of the camp. They would tell us to forget our families, we will never see them again. Whoever was separated from us was promptly killed. They hinted darkly at the gas chambers and crematoriums. They told of torture of children. Of medical experiments. They told us we were fortunate our children were killed by gas and then burned. Their children were shot and often tortured or burned alive. Years ago there

were no gas chambers, only crematoriums, and whole families
were burned in them alive.

When I first heard some of these things I could not sleep.
Everyone of us believed they were untrue and told to us by the
Polish Jews in order to torture us, to avenge our "soft life."
But I wondered. I sensed an ominous, horrible ring of truth to
their words. Where would they get such cruel ideas? Where,
indeed, are the little children? And the elderly? And the invalids? Where was any provision for them in Auschwitz? I saw
our living conditions there, or here in Plaszow. No child, no
infirm person can survive under these circumstances. This
food, this exposure to cold and heat. The barracks, the facilities. Where are our families? Is it possible that they get "special treatment" as we were made to believe? Why would they
get special treatment? Why would the Germans give us sub-
animal treatment and to them . . . Is it possible that it is all
true? My God, is it true? Is it? What kind of "special treatment" did they receive?

Every night I used to cry myself to sleep. In the morning
Mommy would say it is all nonsense. Of course, they are all
lies. Incredible, cruel lies. The Polish Jews knew we were ig-
norant about the camps and were trying to frighten us. Everyone knew the things they said were lies. So was the rumor
about bromide in the food. We stopped menstruating because
we are near starvation. We lost weight and our organs are too
weak to function properly. Look what happened to our
breasts.

Mommy was right in that. The breasts began to sag at first
and then became virtual hanging sacks. Some very fat ladies
had the most ridiculously hanging empty sacks, like long, narrow, stretched-out empty balloons weighed down by a single
marble in each, reaching almost to the navel. Then the empty
sacks became shorter. Eventually the skin, too, was absorbed
and the breasts disappeared completely. We were all like men.
Flat. In time the bones began to protrude and shrunken skin
lay taut on every pointed bulge.

It is true. Even our stomachs slowed down in time. Hunger became less nagging, and the fullness of the stomach after the evening meal—less satisfying. The women stopped "cooking up" imaginary meals during work, and talk about food became less frequent.

Even talk about our families lessens. We think about them less frequently. We think less and talk less in general.

There remains only our daily routine—the *Zehlappel*, the work commandos, the evening meal. Dodging the more difficult commandos and making every effort to get into lighter ones.

In time we discover that there are less cruel *Kapos*, easier work, a longer lunch period. There are *Arbeitführers* who actually talk to you in polite tones, and get two cauldrons of food instead of one for their commando. There are ways to avoid the worst *Kapos* and to be picked by the nicer ones. In time we learn the game of the camp. This game is the stuff of our life. Beyond it things start to matter less and less.

The stone commando is the worst. We are lined up in a chain reaching the top of a steep hill. From the bottom of the hill large rocks have to be passed through the chain up to the top. The rocks are heavy and the *Kapo* of the stone commando, the most tyrannical. He murdered his father and would boast about it when administering some especially cruel punishment. He demands that the stones be passed quickly. If a stone is dropped, it hurtles against the women below. Work on the stone chain is the dread of the camp.

When Mother and I are picked up for the stone commando, she would order me to pass only the smaller stones, and the larger ones she would pass to the girl beyond me, skipping me. This would be dreadful. Mother would have to lean forward with the heavy rock, balancing it precariously, while the girl above me would have to lean down to receive it from her hand, causing additional burden to her. I would then insist on passing the large rocks and Mother would angrily ignore me. This caused me so much hurt and anxiety that my dread of the stone commando turned into perpetual nightmare. But Mother would not yield. She did not understand that it is easier to bear the heavy stones than her indulgence at the expense of her effort and that of another woman.

There are days when we managed to move a huge hill of rocks to the top of the mountain, and the following day we are ordered to move it down again to the foot of the mountain. With the same speed.

The next in line of hard work is the *Planierung*, the digging and leveling. This is a feared commando mostly because of the *Kapo*, Jacko, who makes it into a torture labor. There is no talking, no stopping for rest. And very little food.

One of the commandos is digging up graves in the nearby Krakow Jewish cemetery. It is being turned into a new concentration camp, an extension to the ground we are leveling for construction. Work in this commando is easier because the large monuments afford shade and hiding places for occasional rest. To me, however, this is the most difficult work. Sometimes you dig up small bones and skulls. The bones of children. Of infants. Despite lowered sensitivity, I am still pained by handling these bones. Despite a lack of contemplative powers, I think about the skeletons long after I am supposed to sleep.

Once I was picked for the cleaning commando, the favorite of commandos. It is a small commando in charge of cleaning the barracks of the Germans. We are given pails and washcloths and told to scrub the floors in about fifty barracks. At noon we are given scraps from the meals of the German soldiers. This makes it into a dream commando. But that day it was Tish'a B'Av, and I was fasting. With tears of regret I gave my lunch to another girl. This is my destiny. Two thousand years ago, the Romans picked the day when I was to taste real food to destroy the Temple in Jerusalem.

One hot day in July our lunch is interrupted by the arrival of large-covered trucks rolling into the square. We have been working in *Planierung* right above the camp and have our lunch on the shady slope directly opposite the center square of the camp. Men and women in civilian clothes descend from the trucks and are herded into the command barrack. They are well-dressed and have an air of independence about them. Like people. Not like camp inmates.

One of the men makes a defiant gesture as an SS man shoves him forward with the point of his gun. The civilian, a man in a light gray trench coat, turns and shoves the German soldier. A shot is heard and the civilian collapses. Then he stands up and begins to run. Another shot. He tumbles. A third shot levels him prone on the ground. He begins to crawl, drawing a line of red in the dust. The SS soldier goes wild. He discharges a barrage of bullets into the crawling figure, then starts kicking him uncontrollably. The others are herded into the barrack of the SS command and the single figure remains lying in the dust in the center of the square, a pool of blood ever widening about him.

We go on eating. There is no time to pause: This is Jacko's commando and the lunch hour is short.

TWENTY-ONE

FELICIA IS our *Blockelteste*. She is a short, black-haired, wiry woman of about thirty. Felicia's dislike of us sometimes turned to intense hatred. She would shout and threaten and snap her whip. She would wake us with loud curses in the morning and drive us to *Zehlappel* with kicks and shoves and slaps. She would refuse to look into our faces, allowing her hatred to flow above and about us.

Our Block is next to the SS-command barrack and we can see the civilians interrogated. One by one they are brought into the room and questioned. They are severely beaten in the course of questioning, their cries of pain keep us awake all night long.

Felicia's bed is opposite my bunk. As the shouts of the SS and the shrieks of the civilians penetrate our night, Felicia covers her ears and weeps. I can see her body shake with sobs. I do not understand.

In the morning her eyes are red and dark circles line her face. But her curses are as loud as ever and she swings her whip just as ferociously as before. She does not glance at anyone but drives us to *Zehlappel* like cattle.

The civilians are lined up in the square. A group of about sixty people. They look haggard and stand in a scraggly formation like doomed souls. They are obviously very frightened.

From our place on the mountain we can see them being marched to the barracks behind the square. Then about ten are lined up facing the wall of the barrack opposite the flagpole. One SS man does the shooting. Like target practice he fells the civilians, one by one.

The next row of ten is shot by another soldier. Against the same wall they are lined up, having to step over the bodies of the first victims. I see a young woman, also in a gray trench coat, fall on the body of a man she is about to step over and remain lying, draped over the body until a German soldier drags her to her feet and thrusts her against the wall of the barrack. He shoots her with the others.

The bodies remain scattered about the square as the Germans depart. Suddenly, one body, a man, begins to crawl in the direction of the departing Germans. One of the soldiers notices him and turns. Just then the man hurls himself on the soldier, throwing him to the ground. The other Germans rush to the soldier's aid and free him from the grip of the bleeding civilian. He is felled by bullets discharged from three German guns simultaneously.

Our indifference is shattered for a while. For the rest of the afternoon we keep glancing at the prone bodies in the main square of the camp. It is my first direct encounter with death.

Or is it? The heap of dead bodies, the large pool of blood . . . is this death? Is this something more inexplicable? Something far more beyond comprehension than death?

As we approach the camp toward the evening, my throat tightens. I am apprehensive about having to pass the heap of blood-soaked bodies on our way to *Zehlappel*. Will there be a smell? I have heard that corpses decompose fast in the heat. These bodies lay in the sun for many hours.

To my great relief, by the time we reach the camp the corpses have been cleared away. The square is empty, except for large pools of dried blood. After *Zehlappel* we are ordered to carry pails of water from the well beyond the last barrack and sweep away the blood.

Touching the blood with my broom creates a curious bond with the fallen victims. Grief, compassion, and fear, which have been successfully repressed on the mountain, well up in an overwhelming wave. I can once again barely control my nausea.

My nausea lasts during the evening meal and all night long. In the morning I am dizzy and can barely stand at *Zehlappel*. I am unable to swallow the black coffee, and as we march past the sight of yesterday's shooting, I am about to faint. But Mommy holds on to my arm and keeps encouraging me to breathe deeply and walk erect. By the time we reach the mountain, I feel a little better. Work is difficult and the day passes slowly. Back in camp I have violent abdominal cramps. The pain is unbearable. During the night I am seized by diarrhea and vomiting. I crouch behind the barrack, vomiting and eliminating blood simultaneously. It goes on and on and I am convinced I will not live until the morning. Mother stands guard. Being sick behind the barrack is sabotage. My fear of being discovered by the Germans vies with my fear of dying.

The diarrhea epidemic sweeps the whole camp. In a few days it reduces us to raglike dolls barely able to walk. The routine continues, however. *Zehlappel*, march to work, twelve-hour workday. On the verge of collapse we carry on.

Until one day. It is a cold, rainy day, and by early afternoon we are drenched to the bone, digging the heavy, soggy
ground with heavy, wet shovels. A sudden downpour sends us
scampering for cover under nearby barracks on stilts. While
we huddle under the dripping planks, a team of SS officers
arrives to survey our work. Their indignation fills the air with
shrill tones and the barking of dogs. The *Kapo*'s henchboys
wield the whip under the barracks, and in moments we are
back on the job. Shivering miserably, we fail to comprehend.
We committed sabotage. Sabotage witnessed by the SS staff.

At the evening *Zehlappel* the dreaded news is announced.
We shall be decimated at dawn. The punishment for sabotage.

We have heard of decimation. The Polish inmates have
mentioned the word frequently enough. In earlier years, the
entire camp or a barrack or a commando would be decimated
for every minor infraction. The inmates of the guilty group
would be lined up at dawn, face a firing squad, and at the
count of an SS soldier every tenth would be shot. No one ever
knew where the count would start and who the tenth would be
until the moment the shot rang out. No one knew until the
moment. One, two, three, four, five, six, seven, eight, nine,
and ten . . . shoot. Sometimes they would start counting in the
middle of the row. Sometimes at one end, then switch directions. You never knew if you would be the tenth. Not until the
moment of shooting.

Now it is our turn. Our commando will be lined up at dawn
and . . . It cannot be true.

"It is true all right," said Felicia. "You have committed
sabotage. For sabotage they used to shoot the entire commando. You got off easy. Decimation."

Decimation, my God. I may be the tenth. Or Mother. My
God, what if Mother?

I am unable to swallow even a spoonful of the evening
meal. I have not eaten more than a spoonful or two for the
past several days. The diarrhea depleted my appetite. I have

been thirsty constantly. Now I cannot swallow at all. Mother pleads, "Eat, you won't be able to go on without eating."

Go on? We are to be decimated in the morning. One of us will surely turn out to be the tenth. Go on? Where? If Mother dies, I die. Oh, God, let me rather be tenth!

I weep hysterically. When I have to go to the latrine, I insist that Mother come along with me, and when she has to go, I go with her, so that we should be together every moment of the night. Every moment left to us. We spend the night holding each other in bed or walking to the latrine. The diarrhea epidemic is still going strong.

This is a new experience in terror. I insist that we both stay awake all night to be aware of every moment left to us. I am terrified of dying, apprehensive of the sensation of the bullet penetrating my body, of blood. I keep seeing visions of my bullet-ridden body in the dust. I actually feel the pain, taste blood and dust. Yet I am even more terrified of seeing my mother shot. The thought of her falling into a red pool of blood convulses my insides. A pounding in my temples. A sense of strangulation in my throat, my chest. A slow pain creeping from the intestines.

There is a soft murmur from the bed above. The girls from Guta are reciting the Psalms. The chant of the doomed. They have received a small prayerbook from somewhere and manage to say evening prayers daily. Sometimes they lend it to Mother and she also says the prayers.

Mother whispers to them: "Please, say it a little louder. So we can follow, too."

The murmur is louder now and Mother and I are able to repeat the verses in Hebrew after them. The pounding in my temples subsides.

In a pause between passages I can hear muffled sobs. Almost all our barrack belongs to the *Planierung* commando and is involved in the sabotage. In time we realize that the entire barrack is awake. One by one the girls join in reciting the Psalms. And the sobs grow silent.

Furtively, I keep glancing at the window. It is still dark. Thank God.

As the first light of dawn filters slowly into the barrack, there is a sudden silence.

"Read on," someone calls. "Read on until they come for us." And the little, skinny blonde from Guta and her sister read on while the light turns ever brighter. The cool breeze of the morning sends shivers through the bunk beds.

It is bright morning now and no one has called for us. What time can it be? Perhaps they decided to shoot us at the regular-morning *Zehlappel*.

"It's six-thirty. Time for *Zehlappel*," calls Felicia, the *Blockelteste*. But her voice is not savage. It is tired and sad. She must know something. No one dares to ask questions.

Slowly we file out of the barrack.

The morning glare is blinding. A strange brightness envelopes the barracks, the square. I tremble with the terror the cool breeze stirs on my skin. We huddle, Mother and I, in an embrace of rhythmic shivers on *Zehlappel*. Soon the SS will arrive.

The sun rises and the glare becomes unbearable. We stand for over two hours, our trembling numbed into a faint echo. I am very tired. A recurring dull ache keeps jostling me into reality. The reality of the shooting to come. Impending, bloody, dusty death. Mother's, perhaps. But it keeps sliding away from me. It keeps receding. Now I think of it all in a soft daze. It is vague, unreal. I am very tired.

The SS does not come. All the camp stands wearily for hours and the SS does not show. Felicia bites her lip nervously. What has happened? The *Lagerelteste*, the head of camp, a tall, thirtyish inmate with the immobile face of an Indian chief, keeps walking away from his post near the flag pole. The tension is unbearable.

Then, suddenly, the *Kapos* come. Hurriedly, they select their commandos. Our *Kapo*, Jacko, detaches our commando without a word and with a jerk of his head indicates that we follow him. Follow him, just like that. Today like every other day. Simply march in formation behind Jacko out of the square, through the gates toward the mountain. Up the mountain to the spot where we interrupted our *Planierung* yesterday. Yesterday. Only yesterday I held this shovel. It was still wet. The ground is still soggy from yesterday's rain. Only yesterday.

Today is just another day. We start working. No one speaks. We are alive. The sun is shining and the wet grass is brilliant. The sky is azure. A soft breeze. My tiredness turns into drowsy fatigue. In a dreamlike trance I dig into the soft earth. It is July 1944, and I am alive. Thirteen and a half and alive. It is a clear, beautiful day.

What is happening? Why don't they shoot us? Did they for some reason forgive us for yesterday's sabotage and simply decide against decimation, or are they only postponing it until tomorrow? The conversation starts slowly. Most are of the opinion that the decimation will be tonight or tomorrow morning. Some even know of other instances, in the earlier days, when such things occurred. Quite often. The Germans would do this in order to torture the guilty even more. They would do this daily for a week sometimes. Every evening the decimation would be announced for the following dawn then postponed, unannounced, for another day.

But I have stopped worrying. To me a miracle has happened. I knew with all my heart that Mother or I would be dead today at dawn. I felt the pain of the entering bullet, tasted the blood. I saw my bloody corpse strewn in the dust among many others. I experienced death. And now I am alive. I saw the sun rise. I am touching the earth, the grass. I am here on the mountain. It is so simple, to be alive. You move, you breathe, you touch. You feel the air about you. You can see, see far about you. The mountain, the people, the barracks. The sky. I have stopped being afraid.

In the meantime, there is feverish activity down below. Large trucks roll into the camp, discharging a great number of civilians. This time there are hundreds, and the SS is surrounding them with guns drawn. They are taken into the command barrack, a few at a time, and then hustled back into the trucks and driven away. Other trucks come with more prisoners. Some in dark-green overalls, or uniforms, in handcuffs. All are interrogated inside the SS-command barrack, then driven away in trucks. This goes on all day.

Back in camp, we are totally ignored by the SS. The roll call is done by the *Lagerelteste*, and we are herded into our barracks and told to remain indoors. From our windows we can see trucks with prisoners coming and going all night long. We can hear prisoners interrogated in the command barrack.

The next day all is quiet again. All is routine. The decimation is never mentioned again. Apparently more important events replaced it on the SS agenda. Rumors have it that an entire factory staged an uprising, management and workers, and the SS was busy with that. Others say the green-uniformed prisoners were partisans, underground fighters, from the hills, and now an offensive is being mounted against them.

Soon more rumors circulate about the partisans. It is believed that they came into the nearby hills in order to stage an attack on our camp and free the inmates. The attempt was unsuccessful, however. It was discovered just before the actual attack, and now the Germans are cracking down on the whole countryside. Some inside contacts were discovered in camp, and now they are used to track down partisans in the hills.

What if the partisan liberation attempt had worked! The night we spent in terror of death by decimation would have been the night of our delivery. Just like the story of Purim. But it failed, and we continued as slaves of Germany.

Yet a miracle did occur. The incident of the factory uprising or partisan attack discovered during the predawn hours of our scheduled decimation saved our lives. Thank you, God, for this miracle.

TWENTY-TWO

THE DECIMATION incident changed Felicia. She has become friendly and communicative. She has told us all about herself, sharing every tragic detail of her road to the position she now holds.

She was married and lived with her husband and her eighteen-month-old infant in Krakow. When the Germans came, her parents moved in with them. They were afraid to live alone in their small village.

Soon after the occupation, the Germans came to her house. There were four of them. Four soldiers with guns. It was Friday night, and the family sat around the dinner table. One of the soldiers put his gun in her hand and ordered her to shoot her family, all of them—her baby, her husband, father, and mother. Horrified, Felicia shrieked and gave the gun back to the soldier.

The soldier repeated his order, this time adding his condition: "If you don't do it, I will kill them. But not so simply. They will die in slow agony."

"The Germans looked at each other and grinned," said Felicia in tormented whisper. "I shrieked like a madwoman, 'No, I will never do that!' The soldier, a tall, husky man in his late twenties, stepped over to the highchair where the baby sat. 'Is this your baby?' he asked. When I nodded he took the baby by the shoulders and said, 'If you don't do as I say, I will kill your baby.' One of the soldiers then gave me a gun. 'Shoot,' said the first soldier. As I stood transfixed, immobile, he swung the little boy upside down and called to one of his men to hold on to one of the baby's feet. And then, each holding a foot they tore my child in two . . . my child, my own little baby boy

. . . right before my eyes. . . ." Felicia's sobs are the howls of
an animal. Hiding her face in her hands, she goes on: " 'This
is what we will do to your family if you don't shoot them. Tear
them to pieces. Bit by bit. Do you hear? Now, shoot!' " I
screamed and screamed, and began to shoot. I shot everyone,
everyone. When I finished, they quickly got the gun away
from me. I wanted to kill myself last. But they did not let me!
They did not let me! Do you hear? They did not . . ." She falls
on her face and screams like a crazed beast. "They did not let
me . . ." She is beating her head with her fists. "They did not
let me die . . ."

We stand in stunned silence. My God, what unearthly horror. But she continues relentlessly: "They took me away with
them and put me in a building together with other Jewish
women who were all separated from their families. I don't
know where their families were. No one spoke."

"We stayed there for several days or weeks, I don't remember. Then they brought us here, into this camp. I was assigned
a barrack as *Blockelteste*. The Germans said I deserved the
position, I was a brave woman. I earned this position. Now
you know."

Felicia's sobs continue all night. No one can ease her pain.
We are silent in the face of her agony. But now I understand
her earlier hatred of us. Her bitter resentment of our "lack of
experience." And the resentment of the other Jews from Poland. The Jews who faced Hitler's hordes unprepared, in the
early months of German victory. They all had stories to tell.
Of ditches dug by entire families. Of shooting at the edge of
the ditch. Of last-minute embraces, of prayer. Of surviving
under a heap of bodies. Of crawling, bloody and exhausted, all
night long, only to be arrested in the morning and put into a
concentration camp. Here in Plaszow, or elsewhere in the
numerous camps throughout Poland. Gradually, we understand. Slowly, painfully we begin to believe the stories. The
experience of the decimation threat has sharpened our awareness. Our illusions have vanished. We, too, have become part

of the pattern. For the first time we are truly integrated into the concentration camp. As if to prepare us for the spectacle we are to witness soon.

TWENTY-THREE

It happened on the mountain at work. One of the older foremen, a Jew of about thirty-five, has been in charge of our commando for several days. Jacko is ill. Quickly we realize that this new man is much kinder, and the pace of work slows. We stop for long breathers, stretching our limbs, straightening our backs. Some girls even sit on the ground resting during work.

Suddenly, out of nowhere, an SS officer materializes. Like a stone statue, he stands on the embankment, arms folded and legs apart, surveying the scene. Our new foreman freezes in fear. Then he begins to curse and shout wildly. His efforts at restoring order are frantic. We perceive the situation at once, and in a matter of seconds are at work digging and shoveling at a rapid pace.

Except an elderly woman, Mrs. Zinner. Ever since the onset of the diarrhea epidemic, she has been getting weaker and taking ever longer rests during work. Now she is the only one who does not resume work. She sits, her face buried in her lap. The foreman runs to her and screams at her. When she does not move, he begins poking her with his stick.

The German flies into a rage.

"Whip her!" he roars, "whip her bloody! Here, take my whip. And make sure she is dead before you are through with her!"

He hands the whip to the bewildered foreman. He takes it

slowly, hesitantly. But does not move. He stands motionless, rooted to the ground.

The SS glares at him: "Whip her, you dirty dog! Kill her or I will kill you, you Jew dog!" As if unaware of what is happening about him, the foreman stands with eyes riveted on the German, both hands gripping the whip.

The German swings around. With a short whistle he summons his dog and barks something at the eager beast. In a flash, the huge German shepherd is on top of the startled man, throwing him to the ground. In a savage fury, the animal grips an arm and is ferociously ripping clothes and flesh.

I dare not look. My body shakes violently. With all my might I clutch the shovel and keep on working. My eyes fastened to the ground I hear the whimpering cries of the foreman and the blood-curdling snarls of the animal.

Then, after what seem like endless moments of agony, the SS man emits a shrill whistle and the dog springs to follow him. He is marching off now with brisk, measured steps, striking his highly polished boots with his whip. Without a word, he is gone.

The foreman stands up, dazed, bleeding profusely. To our horror, his right arm is dangling limply within his torn coat sleeve, attached only by a shred of blood-soaked fabric. At the shoulder, a bloody stump protrudes from the wide-open gap in the striped uniform.

TWENTY-FOUR

THE APPROACH of August brings a slew of rumors. Evacuation. Advance of Russian troops. An assassination plot against Hitler. Unrest in Berlin and on the fronts. Things converging to end the war.

One morning the flag is at half mast. It is whispered that Hitler is dead. Days pass and nothing happens, and we realize it all has been a mistake. Nothing but rumors to keep up prisoner morale. To help survive.

But rumors about evacuation prove right.

On an oppressively hot morning in early August we are loaded on trucks and driven through winding roads among the now-familiar hills. An endless caravan of trucks. The entire camp is evacuated.

Once again the train station of Krakow comes into view. It, too, is familiar. We saw it seven weeks ago, when we arrived. Only seven weeks. Yet long ago. It was before I became part of death and blood and naked horror. Before I experienced decimation, tasted death itself. It was before I saw men tortured and mangled. It was before I knew that there are no limits to human cruelty.

In these seven weeks I changed. I grew into a concentration camp inmate. I learned to live with fear and hunger and abuse. I learned to swallow dirt and live worms. I learned to endure cold, pain, and long hours of hard physical labor. I learned to live with waning hope and to cling to reality born of pretenses. I learned to wait . . . and wait . . . and wait.

I have become thin and tall. My neck is long. My hair has grown, and now it stands erect, about an inch high, like a crown of yellow bristles about my head. Other girls have boy-ish hairdos. Some have curls framing their faces. But I have a crown of thorns like a porcupine. My cheekbones protrude so sharply that sun blisters have formed on each because of their extreme exposure to the sun. Sun blisters have blown my lips up like those of a clown.

The sun is scorching as we stand on the platform. At long last the loading into the wagons begins.

"One hundred to a wagon!" the *Kapo* shouts.

One hundred, my God. There will not be room even to sit. I hope we will get sitting space for at least one of us. Mother is tired, overcome by the heat.

We are shoved up into the cars. Mother gets a spot near the wall and I sit on her legs. But soon she is compelled to draw up her legs as more and more people are pressed into the wagon and begin to complain that she is taking up too much room with her legs partially stretched out. She starts to explain that I am sitting on them, saving space. She is kicked and told to draw up her legs. She does. I stand up but am unable to stay on my feet. I am pushed and shoved and keep falling on top of others sitting. Mother screams: "Leave her alone!" She tries to get up to give me her place, but as she scrambles to her feet others press into her place and she tumbles.

More and more people are pressed into the wagon, increasing the heat and the stench. Air is steadily drained from the wagon. Breathing is becoming difficult.

The train stands for hours. More trucks arrive. Dogs bark. More shouts. Then we hear a *Kapo*: "Thirty more into every wagon!"

Thirty more? That is impossible. We are on the verge of fainting from crowding, heat, and lack of air. Thirty more and we will suffocate.

The inmates from Poland, the old-timers, assure us that it is possible. There have been precedents. Incidents in which more than half of a transport suffocated before they arrived at their destination.

Soon we discover it is possible to absorb thirty more. Noise subsides as the sweating bodies are pressed closer together. It is barely possible to breathe, almost impossible to speak. The lack of air imposes its own dominion. You simply comply. You sit or stand with your mouth open, eyes half closed, limp. You do not breathe but draw in air, in short gasps. You do not sit or stand upright but lean against the thing or body next to you. You do not think. You let your mind go limp.

Mother keeps sweating profusely but is unable to wipe her brow. Someone is sitting on her shoulder. I keep mopping her face with the hem of my uniform until she closes her eyes. She has fallen asleep, I think. But then with alarm I realize she has fainted. What should I do? Many others have fainted. They are white, their eyes closed and their mouths open. They are piled one on top of the other in silent heaps. The woman Mommy is now lying on has fainted also and is leaning against the wall patiently tolerating Mommy's inert body on top of her. Earlier she grumbled every time Mommy moved, poking her with a knee or an elbow. Now they are both still, their breathing belabored, plaintive.

As the evening bears down the heat grows more oppressive. Loud wheezing and hoarse moaning break the density of the darkness. I am lying drenched in sweat, on a pile of bodies. Someone is lying on top of me, lifeless, wet, and heavy. I cannot move. I do not know where Mommy is. She must be nearby. Perhaps in the same pile. I do not know.

Sometime during the night the train begins to move. The rattling of the rapidly moving train drowns out the sound of moaning and I feel better. The movement, the sensation of going ahead, inspires confidence. There is life in movement. Hope. Standing still is terrifying.

The train moves all night and all day. The second evening we reach an area where the air is somewhat cooler. We must be traveling north. Most people are revived. Breathing is somewhat easier. The moving train sucks in air through cracks in the wagon walls.

Mother also revives. She insists that I sit in her place while she stands. But she is still unable to stand up. I stand and crouch alternatively throughout the day and the following night.

On the morning of the third day the train comes to a halt. The doors open and chill air rushes into the wagon. Dazed by the light and air, we scramble slowly to our feet. Some are unable to get up. I have to pull Mommy to her feet. Men in striped uniforms drag us off the train. For over two days we have had no food and drink and little air. Our limbs are cramped, our lungs and brains compressed. The freedom of space and movement is now overwhelming.

As I stagger out of the wagon, my glance falls upon the sign of the station: AUSCHWITZ

TWENTY-FIVE

THE MOTORCYCLE stirs up dust as it roars past us. Mother has barely enough strength to walk. The train ride from Krakow has drained her of energy. And of determination. She has lost her will to live. As we staggered into marching formation on the platform, she seemed unable to grasp the mechanics of survival. She wanted to stay in the wagons with those unable to walk. Indifferent as to its implication, she kept insisting that she was unable to march and asked to be left behind.

In my alarm, I grabbed her arm and shook her violently: "Stop! Do not say that! You can walk. Come, walk!"

I pulled and dragged her along. Like a puppet on a string, she started to move her legs involuntarily and keep pace. When the selection officer appeared on his motorcycle alongside our rows on the road to the camp, and asked straggling women whether they can work, Mother whispered to me: "I cannot work. I cannot even walk. I will not even reach the camp."

"Yes, you can walk. In camp we will get food. And water. And you will feel better," I hissed between my teeth.

Now the motorcycle is coming back again. It comes to a sudden halt. The tall, heavyset SS officer in gray uniform approaches our row. My throat tightens. My heart pounds so loudly I am certain he can hear it. God, let him pass us! Let him drive on! God, save us! But I can feel his gaze. We march on, stoically dragging our feet in a desperate effort at speed, not even glancing in his direction. His scrutinizing stare pierces my awareness. He keeps pace with our row. There is no mistake about it. He is watching someone on our row.

Suddenly his stick reaches into the middle of our row and taps Mother on the shoulder: "Hey, Grandma, can you still work?" To my astonishment, he speaks Hungarian. A *Volksdeutsche* from Hungary! A Hungarian volunteer in the SS army. They are worse than the Germans.

Mother crashes on, ignoring the question. As Mother's silence confirms his suspicion, the SS officer is about to reach for her arm and pull her out of the marching column. I poke her sharply in the rib and whisper under my breath: "Say yes. Say it, for God's sake!"

She turns to the SS officer. Her voice is a thin, high-pitched screech of a bird, barely audible: "If I must, I will. I will work."

For one awful moment time stands still. Then the officer swings back on his motorcycle and drives on. My legs tremble. Thank God. My dear God!

Mommy marches on like an automaton.

In camp we are handed numbers on slips of paper and lined up to have them tattooed on our arms. The lines are long, the sun scorching. Through veils of fatigue persistent thirst penetrates. But Mother bears it silently, indifferently.

I notice the tattoos of one line are smaller and neater than the rest, and once again drag poor Mommy to that line, a much longer one.

After languishing hour after hour on the line, A–17360 is tattooed slowly, painfully on my left arm.

During *Zehlappel* there is a sudden downpour. We eagerly suck in the drops from our lips, hands, and arms. Finally, wet, chilled to the bone, we are herded into our barrack.

These barracks are different. Different from the partially constructed barracks in the last camp in Auschwitz or the ones in Plaszow. These Blocks are long, narrow buildings with huge portals on each end. When you enter you are overwhelmed by its length, its height, by the endless rows of bunk beds reaching the ceiling on either side. A forbidding gabled roof looms darkly above a curious brick structure running through the entire length, slicing the Block into two equal parts. A chilly, dark dread hangs in the air.

We are permitted to get on the beds, twelve women to each bed. A square area of wooden planks covered with an army blanket, in tiers so low that when sitting upright my head touches the tier above.

I am glad to get under covers after the chilling rain. I am shivering with exhaustion. Ignoring the din all about me, I crawl on the bed on the lowest tier next to Mother. She is lying with her eyes closed, motionless.

A sudden crackling sound. One of the planks in the tier above breaks, sending the women on the bed into shrieking peals of laughter. Mother's still body right below the dangling plank is oblivious to it all. The other women in our bed move aside. Only Mommy remains, lying motionless, inches below the broken plank.

I attempt to arouse her, but she refuses to move. In a frenzy I get up and plead with the women on the broken tier to get off so as not to crack the other planks also. But they laugh at my alarm. Food is being distributed, and each is eagerly expecting her turn. Not one of them pays attention to my frantic pleas.

I decide to get help from our *Blockelteste*. She is a very young, pretty, robust brunette, a girl from Slovakia who addressed us in flawless Hungarian when we came into the Block. We were told her name was Elsa Friedmann, and that she was sixteen, the daughter of a shoemaker from Presov. I have no other choice but ask her help. I am going to explain to her that I do not wish to get the women into trouble, I only want her to tell them to get off the bed until it is repaired. I am sure Elsa will understand that and not punish them for having refused to get off at my request.

I find Elsa at the entrance of her room. She is giving orders to her aide about the distribution of the food. As neither of them pay any attention to me, I apologize and tell Elsa my request is urgent. Elsa glares at me: "Go back to your place immediately!"

"You don't understand, please. The bed is broken above my mother and she is too weak to move away. Please, tell the women to get off the cracked plank before it breaks completely and falls on my mother. Please, they will listen to you ..."

My voice chokes with anxiety. Elsa looks at me incredulously: "You, you dare come here and interrupt. Get out of here, you little bitch!"

The epithet is delivered with the accompaniment of a fierce blow to my right cheekbone. My head reels from the impact of the slap. My eyes fill with tears. I run back to the bunk. The plank is hanging precariously and the women are sitting on it unconcerned, absorbed in their food. Perhaps I was wrong after all. Perhaps the plank is not going to break. Perhaps it is sheer hysteria on my part. I am too young and too scared and excessively concerned about my mother because I am still a child. I thought I had grown and matured in the camp, but I still behave like a baby.

I am hurt and very tired. I lie down next to Mother, determined to stop worrying about the broken plank. After all, if it breaks, the women above are liable to get hurt, too, and they do not seem to worry. Why am I alone such a coward?

The food is now distributed to our tier. I manage to raise Mother to a sitting position and she begins to eat. But when I reach for my portion, the cauldron is empty and I am told to wait for the next batch. I lie down again, supporting Mother's back with one hand.

Suddenly, a loud crash, and the entire upper bunk comes tearing down. I am aware of sharp pain on my forehead, as a plank is pinning me to the bed. There is broken wood all about me. Women's screams. Naked bodies. A cloud of dust.

Slowly I move my head to the right to see if Mommy is all right. I do not see anything as another broken plank presses against my right cheek blocking my view. But I hear a thin, high wail from the other side of the plank. Again: "Yaaaaay . . . yaaaaay . . ."

It sounds as if it is coming from far away. Yet I can hear it amid the noise. All at once I realize it is my mother's voice. Right next to me. My God, she must be badly hurt.

I begin to move my shoulders and realize that I am entirely free, except for my forehead. Pressing against the plank with one hand, I manage to free my forehead also. Sliding on my back, I begin to crawl out from under the debris.

When I get out, I see that Mommy is pinned under a huge pile of wood in a most peculiar position. She is lying on her back but her head is bent forward in such a way that her face stares at me in a vertical position. It is terrifying. Her eyes are wide open. But she does not appear to see me. She keeps on emitting that high-pitched, barely audible wail: "Yaaaaay . . . yaaaaay . . ."

The women still sit on top of the broken planks, some shrieking in pain. I yell hysterically: "Get off, get off this instant! There is someone right under you. You are crushing her to death!"

Like madwomen they keep on screaming, ignoring my pleas. I begin to pull them by their arms, savagely pummeling those who pull back. I cry and yell and pound at their flesh.

"Ellike, what is the matter?"

It is Mrs. Grünwald. "What happened?" I am unable to speak; I point at Mommy's body under the rubble. Mrs. Grünwald shouts at the women, and several of them get off the bed. Others refuse. They are simply beyond caring.

With the help of Mrs. Grünwald and Ilse I lift the plank which presses Mommy's head against her chest, and start to pull her out by the legs.

"Leave that white thing alone and help me!" cries Mommy. "What is that white thing you are pulling there?"

I am shocked. "It is your leg. I am pulling you out by your leg. Don't you feel it?"

She does not feel her legs. We manage to pull her out and carry her onto the brick divider. The *Blockelteste* has heard of the accident and now orders everyone on the two lower tiers to find sleeping places elsewhere. She permits Mother to stay on top of the low brick wall, and me to stay with her.

Mother does not feel any part of her body and cannot move. Soon she falls into a stupor and does not respond to my voice or touch.

I find Juliska Tauber, a young doctor from Somorja. Juliska follows me. When she sees Mother, she decides we need a sharp object. A pin, for instance. Someone has a needle, and Juliska sticks it into Mommy's body in several places but elicits no response. Her face grows grim as she pokes Mother's soles, and the lifeless body does not stir.

She puts her arm about my shoulders.

"Ellike, you are a big girl now. You will understand what I am trying to tell you. You see, your mother is unconscious. And she is totally paralyzed. She has lost sensation in her entire body. I think her spinal column is broken. Ellike, you see . . . you see, it is a matter of a short time. Hours. She will never regain consciousness. . . ."

I do not answer.

Juliska holds my shoulder.

"I am sorry I had to tell you this. But it is better that you know. You will not be alone. There are quite a few of us from Somorja. You will not be alone. We will take care of you."

It is cold in the Block. The rain has been seeping in and cold puddles line the brick divider on which Mommy is lying. I stand next to her. I am chilled and very hungry. I have not received my portion. The accident occurred before the full cauldron of food arrived. And I am very tired.

I climb up on the brick structure next to Mommy. Sitting at her head, I am able to wipe the rainwater from her head. There is a leak in the roof right above.

Mommy must be cold, too. Her feet feel like ice. But I have

nothing to cover her with. All I can do is rub her legs with my hands to warm them.

As I crouch on my brick perch I doze off several times during the night. Each time I awake I bend above her mouth, touching her lips with my cheek. She is breathing. Thank God.

At dawn I can see that Mommy's eyes are partially open. At times they flutter wide open and stay open for several moments. Please, please, I implore you, let her live! If she will not, I will simply die, too. I cannot go on . . .

The *Blockelteste* tells me to take Mother to the *Revier* after *Zehlappel*. The *Revier* is an infimary where minor ailments are treated. Once a month there is a selection at the Revier for those who do not recover in a month's time.

Mrs. Grünwald, Juliska, and Yitu Singer, the rabbi's daughter from Somorja, help me carry Mother on a stretcher to the *Revier*. A few days later Juliska is assigned to work as physician there, and she brings me daily reports about Mommy's condition.

I am not permitted to visit Mother. But I speak to her through a knothole in the wooden wall of the *Revier* quite near her bed. On the third day after her admittance, Mother begins to talk, and now she can answer me through the hole. She tells me she can lift her head. Then her right hand. Then she begins to sit up in bed. Food is minimal in the *Revier*. Sick people do no work, deserve no food. She complains of hunger. That is a good sign.

I discovered the hole one day as I was on my routine lingering session about the *Revier*. Every day, after *Zehlappel*, I would sneak to the barracks which held the infirmary and try to get news about Mommy from the staff. Juliska comes to our Block only in the evening, and I am anxious about Mommy's condition all day. Most of the time I have had to hide behind the *Revier* so as not to be discovered by the SS. I would then rap lightly on the wall and call Mommy's name. Some of the patients would answer and tell me that my mother's bed was farther on.

Soon I found the exact spot where Mother's bed stood. Rapping on the wall and repeatedly calling to her, I hoped to raise Mother from her stupor and stimulate her to speak. Just then, on the third day, when I first heard Mommy's voice, I noticed a loose knot in the wood. As I began to poke it, it gave way and fell in. I peeked inside and could see the top of Mommy's head close by.

"Mommy," I called in ecstasy, "Mommy, I can see your head."

Mother's voice was tired but distinct. "Ellikém! My little Elli. How are you?"

I could not answer. Tears choked me. This was Mother as I had known her. Not only has she recovered her speech but her old self. She was going to live.

Mrs. Grünwald, Ali's mother, adopted me during Mother's absence. We would stand *Zehlappel* together—tall, slim Mrs. Grünwald, her lovely daughter Ilse, and I. Ilse is my age, one of the very few younger girls in Auschwitz, tall and dark. I had not known Mrs. Grünwald and Ilse before Auschwitz. I knew only the two boys, Yossi and Ali. They used to stay in our house while taking the examinations at our high school.

I used to daydream about my meeting Mrs. Grünwald, the mother of the boy of my secret dreams. Ali spoke often of his mother. She is very beautiful, he used to say. I had imagined meeting her in my favorite blue dress, my hair braided in a basket—the hairdo most becoming to me. I met her instead in Auschwitz, wearing an oversized gray uniform, my head shaved, large blisters covering my cheekbones, and pus-filled sores obliterating my lips. But she liked me. She told me she had also been eager to meet me: Ali had spoken about me, the only girl he had ever taken notice of. And Ilse treated me like a sister. She looked like her brother. I had liked her instantly. Amid the uncaring madness of Auschwitz, I had found a pocket of love.

During the second week in Auschwitz, Mrs. Grünwald has fever. Her body is practically glowing with heat. During the

morning *Zehlappel* when it is very cold, and when the roll call
begins while it is still dark and ends only in midmorning, Ilse
and I huddle close to the burning body of Mrs. Grünwald to
keep warm. Ilse stands before and I behind her on line, both
of us embracing her. Like an oven, her body radiates heat day
after day. As the week passes and her fever does not subside, I
begin to worry. I am glad to see that Ilse does not seem worried. Neither does Mrs. Grünwald make much of her fever. On
the contrary, she is happy to be able to keep us, her "two little
girls," warm during the long cold dawns of Auschwitz.

Mrs. Grünwald's fever keeps increasing during the second
week. Her lovely face grows yellowish and her eyes burn with
a reddish glow. But she refuses to report her condition.

The following week she becomes uncomfortably warm. I
can barely tolerate the heat pumping from her every pore,
buffeting my body locked in her embrace. She grows listless
and her voice is barely audible. Now even Ilse starts worrying.

"Mommy, we have to report to a doctor. We must get some
help."

She waves her hand: "No, dear. If they take me into the
Revier, who will take care of my little girls?" She manages a
faint smile. "I will wait until Mrs. Friedmann gets out. Then I
will report. Okay?"

Mommy is able to sit and lift one leg. I tell her about Mrs.
Grünwald's fever through the hole in the wall. She says Mrs.
Grünwald should stay out of the *Revier* by all means. Every
three days the feverish patients are taken away. It is more
risky than injury.

As the days draw closer to September, the mornings become ever colder. Ilse and I are the envy of the *Zehlappel*.
People envy Mrs. Grünwald as well: She too suffers less from
the cold because of her fever.

Many others begin to have fever. They are happy. They are
all grateful for their built-in heater.

One day I was caught loitering about the *Revier*. The SS

soldier brought me to the command barrack and I was convinced I would be executed. Instead, I received a punishment. I was ordered to kneel on the gravel in front of the command barrack without food or drink for twenty-four hours.

The command barrack is near the entrance of the camp at a distance from the other barracks. The sharp, black gravel upon which I have to kneel is strewn alongside the barrack stretching until the barbed-wire fence. I am kneeling facing the fence.

Beyond the fence there is a road flanked with barbed wire on its other side. Beyond that fence I could see endless rows of barracks identical to the ones in our camp. In fact, from the spot where I kneel I can look down the road both ways and see infinite rows of barracks like ours in every direction.

The immense proportion of Auschwitz strikes me for the first time. Never before have I had a chance to see this. An array of identical low, gray buildings neatly stretching wherever the eye can see. Beyond the horizon. A world of barracks and barbed wire.

Groups march on the road. Men in striped uniform accompanied by SS guards and dogs. Trucks and military cars. Women drawing carts with large cauldrons, others carrying cauldrons on wooden bars across their shoulders. Women and men in varying degrees of malnutrition.

There are some who can barely walk, and it seems as if they will collapse any moment. Others seem nothing more than darkened skeletons yet they walk without faltering. No one looks to the side. Not one of them notices me. They move as if animated by a magnet of a single direction, straight ahead.

Suddenly a marching column appears on the road. Men and women and—children! Marching on and on. They are marching in rows of five. Women with their hair, with colorful clothes, some with hats on. Men and young boys and little children. A little girl clutching a doll. Their faces white, without blisters and sores. They walk fast, breathless, afraid. But they walk like people, nervous and alert. They are not robots animated by an unseen force. They are people moved by a force within.

They must be a transport, just arrived! They still wear the facial expression of the free. They have not yet acquired the inmate posture. How different they are!

Some glance at the barbed-wire fence as they walk. Several look at me. A young woman even smiles at me. I take a chance. I call out to her, in German: "Where are you from?"

"From the ghetto of Lodz."

"Did you say Lodz?"

"Yes. Lodz."

"You came now from Lodz?"

"Yes. We have just arrived."

The last words she shouts from a distance. She is marching on. A little boy drops his clown. It is dirty yellow. As he is about to pick it up, the roar of a motorcycle approaches. An older boy gives a tug, and the little boy marches on without his clown. The clown remains at the dusty roadside.

The column marches on and on. Row after row after row. Now they are gone and all is quiet again. The dust settles. The clown lies still in the sunshine.

My dear God. Have mercy. The little children. The little girl with the doll, and all the others. All the others. The little children in our transport not more than three months ago. A lifetime ago. Oh, where are they all? Where did they march? And where are these men, women, and children marching? Can it be true about the smoke? About the crematorium? The older inmates say our camp is adjacent to the crematorium, and the smoke smarting our eyes, our throats, our lungs is the smoke of the crematorium.

Is it true, my dear God? Is it true that little children are trampled underfoot in the gas chamber? Is it true that the stronger grown-ups struggle like wild animals to reach pockets of air higher up, and they trample on little children? Some mothers hold their children, lift them high up, to save them from being trampled to death, holding them up until they, too, fall and suffocate. Older people, too, are trampled by younger and stronger ones. They told us. They told us again and again so we should believe it. Those who work in the gas chamber and crematorium told them, and they told us. And I heard and screamed. It was easier to scream and scream than to think. To think of Yingele and Frumet and Tommi and Suzie. And Aunt Szerén. And now the little children from Lodz. Oh, no. No!

I am getting dizzy from the heat. The sun is high and strikes my scalp with relentless fury. I am very hot and very hungry. The sun's glare is blinding. My throat is dry. The sun is so hot.

TWENTY-SIX

ON A hot, sunny afternoon two days later I am dozing, crouched in a corner next to our Block. Suddenly I am awakened by a great commotion.

I look up in a daze and see a bunch of girls, most of them from Somorja, led by Elsa Grünwald (no relation to Ilse) approach me in a flurry of excitement.

"Elli! Elli Friedmann!"

In the midst of the excited crowd walks a tall smiling young man in an immaculate, new, striped uniform. His smile broadens as he comes nearer.

"Bubi!"

My brother stands before me, tall, erect, handsome. He has changed. He is a man with wide shoulders, a strong face; he is healthy-looking. Smiling. Is it a mirage?

It is not a mirage. It is a miracle. It is my brother in the flesh come to visit Mommy and me. But how? How is this possible?

As we sit in the shade of the barrack hidden from the view of SS guards, Bubi tells me the incredible story. Soon after his arrival he was picked by the SS camp commander as his personal interpreter. Bubi, blond and tall, in command of fluent German, was given a private room, the food of the SS, and a new uniform. His cap, a flat, round sailor hat instead of the regular-striped prison cap, bore a special tag with the word: *Tolmätscher*. Interpreter. A green arm band spelling the same word in white letters added to his distinguished appearance.

He accompanied the commander into different camps in Auschwitz. Everywhere he went he was looking for us until a small, crumpled scrap of paper came to his hand. There were many names scrawled on the paper and among them were Mommy's and mine. He recognized my handwriting. The paper said we were in B-Lager. This was yesterday. Today he had himself assigned on an errand to our camp. And here he was.

I had written our name on that piece of paper four weeks ago. Some girls got the idea of writing names and messages on scraps of paper salvaged from garbage cans, tying the paper around a small rock and throwing it over the fence into the next camp when the guard was at the far end of his patrol. The bundle, we hoped, would be found by someone in the next camp, read, and thrown into the adjacent camp until it came into the hands of relatives. It was like a message of the shipwrecked tossed into the sea. Daily we waited for a reply with a hope at once naïve and desperate. In less than a week a reply came. A bundle of scraps of paper tied around a rock was thrown into our camp at sunset, and we found it. There were names and messages. Many strange names, and also messages from relatives in response to our names. But no message for me. I had hoped to hear from my father or Bubi or from our many aunts, uncles, cousins. But I received no message, even though I made it a daily ritual to go to the fence at dusk and wait for the flying package. Now, four weeks later, my note actually reached my brother. The mysterious hand of the worker of miracles.

Bubi embraces me and I begin to cry. He is embarrassed.

"Are you still a cry baby? Where is Mommy?"

I tell him what has happened to Mommy. He wants to see her right away. I tell him of my predicament. "I am not allowed to go there. Two days ago I was caught near the *Revier* and had to kneel on pebbles in front of the SS command for twenty-four hours. And I was told if I will be found once again near the Revier, I will be sent to the gas. Do you know about the gas?"

"Of course. Many in our camp work in the *Sonderkommando.*"

"What is the *Sonderkommando*?"

"It is the commando whose job it is to clear bodies from the gas chamber and put them into the ovens. They have to remove all valuables from the bodies. They have to search ears, noses, mouths, and elsewhere where jewels may be hidden. It is their job to pull out gold teeth and even teeth with gold fillings. They are a very special commando."

He lowers his eyes as he speaks. I shudder. I remember the transport from Lodz.

And the *Sonderkommando*, who are they? They are young men just like himself, Bubi tells me. Some of his friends are among them. Sometimes they recognize the bodies of their relatives. They get special privileges, as much food as they want. Even so, the suicide rate is very high among them.

Mommy thought she was hallucinating when the nurse brought Bubi to her bed. She could not believe she was actually seeing him even after Bubi was sitting on her bed and kissing her face. Poor Mommy! She was so shaken that later she could hardly remember his face or even what he had said to her. But she had the pocketknife and handkerchief with Daddy's initials Bubi gave her. He had managed to save these by hiding them in his shoes during the showers. He still had his shoes from home. They were in perfect condition, he said, because he used part of his daily butter ration to polish them.

"Good shoes are essential to survival," he tells me after his visit with Mommy. "I prefer to eat a little less butter as long as it helps maintain my shoes."

Butter? Who gets butter in Auschwitz? But I say nothing about it.

"My shoes were taken away in the showers," I tell him instead.

Bubi promises to come again soon. Now that he knows for sure where we are, he will get to our camp on some pretext. Every week, perhaps. He promises that next time he will try to bring Mommy some food. He tells Mrs. Grünwald Ali is in the same camp and looks well. He has a special job with the SS and is well-fed and clothed. Bubi promises to take his mother's regards to Ali and when he comes again, bring a message from him.

Mrs. Grünwald is delirious with joy. The good news about Ali fills her with a brilliant glow. Her color changes. Her yellowish complexion is flushed with pink.

"Can you bring him along next time you come?" The thought makes my heart leap.

"I don't think I can, Mrs. Grünwald. He has a different assignment." Then Bubi confides to me in a whisper: "I could not tell her Ali is in the *Sonderkommando*. Members of the *Sonderkommando* are under heavy guard."

He also did not tell me members of the *Sonderkommando* are executed every four weeks.

The two SS men with whom he came are leaving and Bubi gives me a quick embrace. At the gate, he turns to wave to me once more. Then he motions to indicate two braids. "Where are your braids?" he mouths. I shrug my shoulders, and we both laugh.

Despondency replaces exhilaration after Bubi leaves. Will I ever see him again? Will we all be together again?

TWENTY-SEVEN

HAD SHE known her son was in the *Sonderkommando* and that members of the *Sonderkommando* are executed every four weeks, Mrs. Grünwald might be alive today.

Three days after Bubi's visit Juliska Tauber tells Mommy she must leave immediately. Tomorrow there is to be a general selection in the *Revier*. Every patient laid up over three weeks will be taken to the gas. Mommy has been there for over four weeks.

She cannot walk. She can stand for a few minutes but is not able to walk yet even with support. Yet she has to get out of the *Revier*. Yitu comes bearing Juliska's message. I am to come immediately and take Mother from the *Revier* before the German supervisor arrives to check the patients.

I run to several of our friends to ask them to come along to help me carry Mother to the Block. It is a risky undertaking, and I know I can ask only the closest of friends.

Mrs. Grünwald, Yituka, and Ilse immediately volunteer and we go to the *Revier* walking casually and praying we do not meet an SS. Even to the latrine it is forbidden to walk alone. One has to wait until a group of fifty gather and an SS guard comes along for the thirty- or forty-yard walk from our Block to the latrine. Sometimes it take hours until a guard is found to accompany us, and we have to wait, controlling nature.

Now we are walking alone, four women, without permission and without an SS escort.

We make it. As soon as we get to the *Revier*, three nurses carry Mother through the door and hand her to us. Only two of us can carry her at a time. We chain-lock our hands and have her sit on them. A few steps later, another two take over. None of us is strong enough to carry her for a longer stretch. Walking as fast as possible, we reach the Block undetected. Thank God. The block is already lined up for *Zehlappel*. We sneak into the lines one by one. Mrs. Grünwald and I are carrying Mommy behind the lines. We put her on the ground in a crouching position in the back of the row until the SS will arrive for the roll call. But she is unable to crouch long. She can only sit or lie with her legs stretched out. We have to take a chance. Mommy sits on the ground, and as the SS approaches, several girls help me pull her up. I stand behind her to support her during the roll call.

It works. Thank God. But how long can this be kept up? Two days? Three days? Sooner or later we will be discovered, and what then? Mother cannot walk to the Block after *Zehlappel*. She has to be carried, and that, too, has to be accomplished without the *Blockelteste*'s notice. If she sees her, she will report her as an invalid. She will not take chances harboring an invalid in the Block. That is unquestionable sabotage. Something has to be worked out. Perhaps Bubi will come soon and he will help. But who knows when he will come? What will happen till then?

A sudden commotion at the front end of the Block interrupts my musing. It must be at least eleven, lights are out. What is all the noise about? The news spreads rapidly. Five hundred women from our Block will be selected for transport tomorrow morning. To work in factories. In Germany.

Thank God. This is the answer. We will get away from here to a place far from the gas chambers. Mommy will be saved. Selection! How will she pass selection?

Mrs. Grünwald comes over to our bed. She whispers: "We will hide somewhere. I don't want to leave Auschwitz."

"But why?"

"Ali is here. We may meet one day if Ilse and I manage to hide while the selection is on. If we stay in Auschwitz we may somehow meet Ali. But if we go far away into Germany, we will be separated from him. You must hide as well. So you should not be separated from Bubi."

Indeed, there will be only five hundred taken for the transport. And there are one thousand women in the Block. If the count begins at the front end of the *Zehlappel*, all those at the other end will remain here. All one has to do is stand at the far end of *Zehlappel*.

"All you have to do is stand at the far end of the *Zehlappel*, and you will be among the five hundred who will be counted out. You don't have to hide," I whisper.

"I won't take any chances. The count may begin at the other end. Ilse and I will hide. Won't you?"

Mommy is silent. She is overwhelmed by all this. But I know we must leave for her sake. Somehow she must pass selection. But we will not be near Bubi if we leave.

Mrs. Grünwald turns to tiptoe away in silence as she came. Then she turns back.

"If you decide not to hide, then . . . good-bye. God bless you. I will tell Bubi you were taken to Germany."

"Good-bye, Mrs. Grünwald. Tell Ilse good-bye for us."

The darkness of the Block swallows her slim, tall figure. That is the last I see of her. And of Ilse.

We decide not to hide from the selection in the morning. Leaving Auschwitz is the only chance of survival for Mommy. She may pass selection somehow if I support her from the back while the SS is passing. Then we will be far from Auschwitz. Far from selections. Staying here would subject her to danger every moment. We have to leave Auschwitz even if it means being separated from Bubi.

The count begins at the front end of the *Zehlappel*, and Mommy and I are in the five hundred. We are ordered to take off our dresses and line up single file for selection.

It begins to rain. It is a cold, heavy downpour. An inexorable winter rain, heavy like lead.

The selection committee of three SS officers, two dogs, one

Lagerelteste, one *Blockelteste*, and an interpreter hurry indoors. We, too, are ordered into the Block. Amid snarls of
Los! Los! and angry barking of dogs, we are lined up alongside the brick divider in the middle of the Block and ordered
to move toward the selection committee at the open leaf of the
gate. Those who pass the selection go through the gate and are
told to dress outside. Those who do not are sent back into the
Block, dropping their dresses in a pile at the gate. They remain naked, awaiting their fate.

By the time Mommy and I reach the gate, there is a small
heap of sopping wet dresses on the ground, and there are
about thirty shivering bodies huddled together on the other
side of the brick divider. As we approach the commission I
hold onto Mommy as if I were huddling against her for
warmth. The first SS grasps her arm and jerks her out of my
grip, looks over her body, and shoves her impatiently through
the open gate into the fog and rain. Then he looks me over.
Suddenly he notices a wound on my leg. It is the bruise I got
in the wagon on our way from the ghetto to Auschwitz and
has been festering ever since. Now it is a wide-open hole,
oozing with a dark brown liquid and an awful stench. The leg
is swollen and reddish all about the hole. It has been quite
painful lately.

The SS pokes his friend. "Look at this." He points to the
wound on my leg. "What do you think it is?"

"I don't know, but it looks bad. She won't be able to work
with this. I don't give her a week, and she will be dead."

"Drop your dress and join the others on the other side."

"But officer, please. That was my mother right before me.
Let me go with her. Please . . . please, I must go with her!"

"Shut up, swine! Get to the other side!"

I must go after Mommy. She is out in the pouring rain. She
cannot stand without support. She cannot put on her dress.
Out there alone. She might have fallen by now. In the cold,
pouring rain. Naked.

I turn to the other SS. He is younger. Perhaps he will listen.

"Officer, please. I can work. I am very strong. This wound is really nothing. Nothing. I've had it for over three months now and I was working in the mountains, heavy work. *Planierung.* Officer, I promise I will work hard. Please, please . . . let me go with my mother!"

The officer looks at me with disgust. He lifts his stick and jabs me in the chest with its point so that I stagger backward. Then, without a word, he turns to continue the job of selection. And I am to join the naked group in the back.

I begin to tremble violently. This is impossible. This cannot be. Mother passed the selection and I am held back. One ironic quirk and we both perish. Mommy cannot survive a day without help. I must get to her.

The others begin to comfort me. It is not so bad. We may not be sent to the gas. We are simply held back here in Auschwitz. There will be other transports later. Then we will leave Auschwitz. You will see.

I am not listening. I have to get to Mother. I have to follow her before it is too late. Before she collapses. Before they discover she is an invalid.

My head is spinning. My trembling grows more violent.

Mrs. Huebsch from Somorja is in the group of naked, shivering women. She had put a piece of rag around her throat so that she should not be placed in the transport. She wants to remain in Auschwitz because yesterday she got a note from one of her sons through the bundle "mail." He is in Auschwitz, so she does not want to leave Auschwitz.

"Ellike." She is embracing me. "You are very cold. I will hold you. You will be a little warmer that way. Don't worry, I will be your mother from now on. I always wanted a little girl. You will be my little girl. I will take care of you."

"You don't understand. I have to get to Mommy. She needs me. She cannot even stand without me. She cannot do anything."

Mrs. Huebsch is surprised. She had not heard of Mother's accident.

Now I recognize a girl I had worked with at *Planierung* in Plaszow. She is the youngest of three sisters. The two older ones were sent on the transport, and now she is standing in the group visibly shivering and crying. I go over to her and whisper in her ear: "Come with me. Let's sneak out of here and join the transport. My mother and your sisters are there. We can sneak out through the hind gate and join them. No one will know."

She continues crying. "I am afraid. They will shoot us."

I look around. No one is paying any attention to us. I run to the hind gate. It is locked.

The selection is drawing to an end. Now there is only a short line on the other side of the divider. The last ones on the line are disappearing through the open gate. The only means of escape is through that gate.

The *Blockelteste* steps over to us. She holds a bundle of dresses. "Here. You can put these on. Dress quickly, you will be taken from here."

Under her watchful eye I put on a dress. But when she turns, I quickly climb over the brick divider, pull off the dress, and run to the end of the line.

There are only three or four girls ahead of me. I clutch the dress to my left leg covering the wound. The SS are in a hurry now. The selection has taken too long.

I am last on the line. I hold my breath.

After a quick glance at my body, the first officer shoves me through the gate into the rain.

It is dark outside. I quickly put on the dress. I look around and I see no one. Like a sheet of lead, the rain bars my vision. Where did everybody go? The *Blockelteste* is closing the gates. The SS men and their dogs, with the *Lagerelteste* and the interpreter in tow, are marching toward the SS command barrack. But the transport is nowhere.

I run to the next Block. It is dark and silent. But the third Block is lit and noisy. I run there.

In the midst of a large crowd, on top of a table stands a

stout woman in a uniform calling out numbers from a long yellow sheet in her hand. Women whose numbers are called line up at the far end of this enormous barrack so different from our own.

I join the crowd trying to find familiar faces. No one. I am afraid to ask whether this is the transport. I am worried about Mother. Afraid to be discovered. I wait.

As the numbers are called one by one, the crowd lessens. I still do not see Mother. Where is she? Where is someone I know?

The roll call ends and I am the only person left in the middle of the Block. Quickly I step behind one of the rows. Where is the transport? And Mother? What kind of group have I just joined? I see no familiar face.

The lines stand noisily for hours. Finally the SS arrives and begins the count. When he approaches our line and discovers we stand six to the row, he angrily snatches the first girl on line and shoves her aside. Then goes on counting. The little skinny girl begins to cry. Two others on our line are crying. The three are sisters.

At the conclusion of the count I decide to give myself up. But one of the sisters steps out before me and pleads with the SS that she, too, be left back in Auschwitz together with her youngest sister.

A tall brunette steps out from another row. "I will stay in her place."

The SS looks at her. Then silently he motions the two sisters to get back on line. I sigh with relief.

It is late evening by the time we are given the order to march. A cold, wet evening.

We march through the gate out into the road which I saw several days earlier while kneeling on the pebbles. It is the same road the transport from Lodz marched on. I look for the yellow clown. It is not there.

Our march ends at the showers. We stand in formation outside the showers for over an hour. I still do not know where Mother is. I do not know whether I have joined the right transport. All I know is that I am in a transport, that I am being taken away from Auschwitz. But I still do not know into what transport I have forced my way. Perhaps Mommy's transport was lined up in another Block while I in my agitation ran into another. Perhaps right now Mommy's transport is loaded on trains and shipped who knows where. Perhaps at this very moment she is being showered inside while we are awaiting our turn. What if she leaves through the other exit while we are entering from this side?

I begin to tremble again. All the agonized effort has been in vain. And somewhere my mother is in trouble while I am stuck in a transport heading for a different destination. Perhaps soon after she was shoved out of our Block into the rain, it was discovered she is an invalid and sent to another barrack. Perhaps she was held back in Auschwitz. And I am on my way to a distant camp. Perhaps she told the SS immediately that she could not stand on her feet, and they pulled her out of the transport. My God, what should I do now?

The doors of the showers open and we march inside. There is no way out. No escape from here. And even if I could, where would I go?

"Auskleiden! Los!"

In the great tumult of hurried undressing in the crowded room, I notice a motionless figure helplessly huddled against the wall. It is Mother!

I cannot believe my eyes. My good fortune. It really is Mother. I have found her! After all the panic and tension of the day, such perfect bliss. I have found her! Mommy is actually here! We are together and on our way together somewhere far from Auschwitz. Mommy is safe. Oh, God, You are good to me. Thank you, thank you, thank you. I rush to her: "Mommy! Oh, Mommy!"

She does not seem surprised to see me. She seems desperately ill. How did she get dressed? How did she walk? Who helped her? She does not remember.

Now I help her get undressed. Sitting on the floor, Mommy carefully tucks the pocketknife and the handkerchief she received from Bubi into her shoes. We are to leave our dresses in this room. We will get disinfected uniforms at the other end of the shower block. Our shoes we carry along into the shower. It is in shoes one conceals possessions.

We are driven through the shower and ordered to put on shoes fast—*Los! Los! Blöde Hunde!* Fast! Move on! Idiotic bitches!—I quickly put on my shoes and by the time I am ready to help Mommy with hers the room is almost empty. The tall, husky SS woman supervisor is standing in the doorway driving the last few girls into the other room. Mommy is sitting on the wet floor, clumsily trying to wrap the handkerchief around her foot. The SS woman notices her and shouts at her to hurry and get to the other room. But Mommy does not hear. Concentrating on the impossible task of maneuvering the handkerchief around her foot with paralyzed hands, she is oblivious to everything. The SS woman leaps at her, grabs her arm, and begins to twist it.

I lose my head. I forget everything. I remember only that Mother's arm is paralyzed, that she is weak and ill, and that the SS woman is going to break her arm. I jump at the tall, husky woman and shove her against the wall. "Leave my mother alone! Don't you see you are going to break her arm?"

The towering, buxom figure in the dreaded SS uniform swings around. The punch on my cheek sends me reeling. A second punch knocks me to the slippery floor. Then she is on top of me, kicking me in the face, in the chest, in the abdomen. The black boots gleam and my blood splashes thinly on the wet floor. A final kick sends me rolling across the floor toward the exit. Then the door slams and I am lying numb on the cold, slippery floor. From somewhere cold drops keep falling on my face. Then a thought formulates somehow—I am alive! I taste blood. I am unable to lift my head. My body feels totally numb. But I am alive. She did not trample me to death. She could have shot me. But she did not. I have committed the inexcusable. I attacked an SS officer. The gravest possible form of sabotage . . . yet I am alive. Brutally bruised, but alive.

The noise in the adjacent room has subsided. Then I hear Mother's low, tired voice: "Elli . . . Ellikém. Try to get up. The others are out of the showers. Try to get up. Ellikém. Do you hear me? I can't help you. You must get up. Now, by yourself."

I roll on my abdomen and slowly pull myself up. My head reels. Blood is trickling from my nose and I cannot open my left eye. There is a sharp pain in my left side, but my legs are not broken. I can stand.

I limp slowly out of the damp room. I see the handkerchief soaking in a small puddle on the floor.

"Mommy, wait." I stagger over to the dismal-looking little cloth and pick it up.

"Leave it there," Mommy's voice is a painful sigh. "I don't want it anymore."

"But *I* want it."

In the next room I manage to put on a dress and a pair of shoes I receive. Then I help Mommy put on hers. We join the others standing in lines of five in the dark, cold night of late September.

We stand outside the showers until morning. We stand there with freshly shaven heads, wet bodies, in thin, gray cotton dresses throughout the night. We think we cannot bear this. The exposure to the cold. The hunger. The fatigue.

Many begin to sob aloud. Others whisper in barely audible tones. And some recite phrases remembered from Psalms. The cold autumn wind is relentless. We have no means of protection against it. The brick wall of the barrack does not have nooks and crevices for a haven. The cold is inexorable, like the wind.

The pain in my side grows sharper. My left cheek is swollen. The blood on the cut above my lip has dried, making it difficult to speak. The wound on my leg is throbbing viciously.

I am unable to stand on that leg. There is a painful bump on the back of my head. Mommy says I fell to the stone floor of the shower room with a frightful bang. But my head did not crack. Solid material, Daddy used to tease. Solid, like rock. Stubborn and willful.

"You are insane," several girls accost me. "Totally insane. Didn't you know what you were doing? You jumped on an SS woman! And she did not kill you!"

I crouch against the wall. After the SS guards retire to a nearby barrack and we are left on our own, everyone begins to crouch. The dark night seems endless and forbidding. The sky is starless and our exposure to the wind seems to hold an ominous message.

Mommy is slumped against the wall of the barrack. Eyes closed. I drape one arm about her skeletal shoulders and huddle close to keep us warm. She is asleep. Her open mouth is a dark hollow. Sounds of weeping muffle the audible chatter of teeth. I grapple with a thousand questions. Why? Why rush us through showering, shaving, dressing—to drive us out into an endless night? Why disinfect us and then—wet and almost bare—expose us to certain death by pneumonia? Why suffer so pointlessly? Is this really a transport or simply another exercise in torture? Are they taking us to the trains or, perhaps, to the gas chambers? Why didn't that SS woman kill me? Because we are designated for the gas? Will this night never end?

Eventually it is dawn, and the brighter rays of the morning bring our German masters. With reassuring familiarity they bark us into straight lines of five. The roll call brings the reality of our existence into focus. We have survived the night.

We march for hours, it seems. Wagons are at the station. As we board them, I feel I have won the first triumph of my life. I help Mother slowly, painfully up into the boxcar. Then I climb up, smothering a cry of pain between clenched teeth. But a sense of triumph overwhelms the pain. As does a sense of gratitude. And fatigue.

TWENTY-EIGHT

MOMMY WAKES me by gently shaking my shoulder. Sun streaks into the wagon through open doors. The train stands still. My head is heavy. I cannot open my left eye.

"You slept for over twenty-four hours," Mommy says. We have arrived in Augsburg.

Augsburg. The Battle of Augsburg. When was it? Augsburg is somewhere in southeastern Germany.

The curious faces of a staff, men and women officers, greet us. Incredulous, astonished glances. Puzzled, somewhat embarrassed looks are exchanged.

"We expected women. Five hundred women. Who is in charge?"

The tall officer at the head of the group speaks, addressing us directly. Our guard escort delivered us and returned with the departing train. These are our new masters, these puzzled, awkward men and women in immaculate gray uniforms of the Wehrmacht.

"Do any of you speak German?"

Several girls volunteer.

"We expected a transport of women from Auschwitz. Are you from Auschwitz? Were you sent instead of the women?"

"We are women."

A wave of disbelief runs through the assembled army personnel. Women? Our freshly shaven heads, gray prison garb, and sticklike bodies are not very convincing proof.

We quickly line up in rows of five, ready to march. Our new masters stand, waiting. We stand at attention, awaiting the order to march. As the last wagon pulls out of the station, the commandant speaks again. *"Aber wo sind euere Packete?"* But where is your luggage?

Laughter rings from all directions. Our luggage?

"We have no luggage, *Herr Offizier*." The interpreter suppresses her giggles. "We have nothing."

"Tell him our valets are bringing our luggage on another train." General laughter greets the wisecrack in Hungarian.

"Mine is sent special delivery!" And: "Oh, I forgot my golf clubs in Auschwitz!" Laughter is breaking up the lines.

"You have no luggage at all? No personal belongings? How can that be?" The officer is incredulous.

"No," repeats the interpreter now in a low voice. "We have nothing."

We march through the clean, provincial streets. Houses, neat little gardens, cobblestoned sidewalks. People gawking at us from windows. The few passersby on the street turn around with surprise.

Houses, people, streetcars. My God. Life still goes on. Despite Auschwitz. Despite the gas chambers.

Mommy drags her feet. She is unable to keep up with the pace of the march. A short, blonde woman officer approaches her timidly.

"What is your name?"

"My name? My number is A–17361."

"But what is your name?"

"My name? Laura Friedmann."

"Frau Friedmann, can you walk a little faster?"

Mrs. Friedmann? She actually called Mother by her name, and with a title—Mrs. Friedmann. First the questions about luggage. Now this. Is this a dream?

"No, I am unable to walk faster. Even this is a great effort. I received an injury in Auschwitz. I am partially paralyzed."

I hope it is safe to say all this to a German.

"Do not worry," she replies. "Here you will get better. We will take care of you."

We arrive at the central streetcar station. We are put on streetcars reserved for us. Through slow city traffic we travel to the factory quarter. We disembark in front of a large factory complex and march through the gates of a tall brick building. MICHELWERKE. Large black lettering above the gate.

Michelwerke is an airplane factory manufacturing parts for the Luftwaffe. To increase production, they have requested five hundred female inmates from a concentration camp. And here we are.

Our quarters are set up in one of the buildings on the sixth floor. But first we are led to the basement shower rooms. Real, metal shower heads, not just holes in the ceiling as in Auschwitz; wooden mats on the floor; and taps marked "warm" and "cold!" We are handed a clean towel and a piece of soap each! Towels and soap! Girls, my soap is perfumed! Mine, too! Girls, this is a dream. Paradise. This cannot be true! We are making this up.

Warm water comes from the shower when you turn on the tap marked "warm." And you turn it off when you are through. At your leisure. It does not start and stop by some unseen arbitrary hand. You are your own master in this shower!

And the towel! It is soft and clean, and it rubs you gently dry. As we get out of the showers, a secret spark of self-esteem is nurtured deep within. It is a message from God. A divine promise of redemption. A message of faith. Of hope.

The sun shines warmly in the yard. We are told to sit on wooden benches set up around long tables. We are served soup in porcelain bowls. Golden yellow soup with long noodles in white, clean porcelain bowls! Real food.

Several girls begin to weep, silently. They weep and slurp the warm soup. Parched, eager lips, trembling fingers. The next course is dumplings with sauerkraut. The flavor surpasses anything I have ever eaten. But it is not enough to satisfy my hunger. I feel elated but hungry when the meal is over.

After the meal we are lined up in the yard, and a tall, heavyset, red-headed man in white overcoat approaches us with a grave, unsmiling face. He is the manager of the entire division and it is his task to assign work for us. One by one, each of us is ordered to step out of the line to be inspected by Herr Zerkübel. He scrutinizes each face, peers into eyes, fingers the cheekbones. Tall, blonde, fair-skinned girls with blue or green eyes are to step aside. There are eight of us. Then he adds shorter ones with blonde hair, fair skins, blue or green eyes. He needs thirty-five in this group, he says. So he adds redheads and girls with light-brown hair. But all have to have fair skin and blue eys.

This group is to work in the *Montage*. The work in the *Montage* requires superior intelligence and Herr Zerkübel determines high intellect by the color of hair, skin, and eyes. The colors of the Aryan. The superior race.

The second group consists of girls with brown hair and eyes, but of fair skin. They are assigned work in the *Dreherei*, less complex, more routine metal work. The black-eyed, black-haired women, among them a noted physicist, a doctor, and a college professor are assigned polishing of metal parts in the *Lakiererei*, the most primitive work.

Our quarters consist of three large rooms with individual double-tiered bunk beds. Each bed has a straw sack and a sheet. A white sheet!

We are in heaven.

The elite of the camp, the workers of *Montage*, receive the smallest and brightest of the three rooms. Our beds stand farther apart lending the room an air of spaciousness. The two other rooms are more crowded, and their windows open on a narrow alley, making them somewhat gloomier.

The next day our food consists of a bowlful of nondescript mush served in metal army bowls. It is clean and much more edible than the fare of Auschwitz, and the bowls are our own. Yet, the glow of utopia sparked by yesterday's reception receives a chill blow.

We are roused at dawn for *Zehlappel* and breakfast—black coffee and a piece of brown bread. Then we line up for work in three groups—the *Montage*, the *Dreherei*, and the *Lakiererei*.

Mother is assigned to the *Putzkommando*. Her task of

cleaning floors and windows allows for gradual recuperation. No one supervises the *Putzkommando*. And so, in lieu of medical attention, Mother has the opportunity of rest. With this single deference to her condition, she begins to improve. Gradually, she starts to regain the use of her hands. Her left arm however remains partially paralyzed for over a year, three fingers of the left hand, permanently. Her walk also begins to improve. Soon she recovers her sense of balance and begins to walk unaided. Slowly, very slowly, she starts to actually work in the *Putzkommando*—to wash floors on her knees and carry pails of water.

But her posture remains permanently altered. Her head is bent forward almost as sharply as when the accident occurred; her upper back is curved. Some numbness in her limbs remains. But she is able to function. And we are free of fear of the gas chamber.

Augsburg is not a concentration camp in the conventional sense. It is a camp for inmates who labor twelve hours a day and live on rations below minimum, who are escorted to and from the toilet by SS guards, and are not permitted any contact with the outside world or with the other workers at the factory. But we are not subject to the standard abuses of Auschwitz—beating, maiming, exposure to the elements—and the selection.

As time went on, the German staff changed its friendly attitude. A new SS officer arrived. He brought the change. He came from Dachau and instituted radical innovations. Twice daily, *Zehlappel*. Then a change in the quality of the food and the removal of the white sheets! The table and benches are taken away, and we have to eat our food crouched on our beds or sitting on the floors of the corridor. But the most painful thing for us is the change of attitude of the German staff. Their friendly posture turned to curtness and, in some, to outright animosity. Two days after the new SS officer's arrival one of the guards called us *blöde Hunde*, idiotic bitches, and we shuddered with the familiarity of the term. Guards began to avert their eyes instead of looking straight at us. They began to shout orders. And several began carrying whips.

The commandant of the camp, the *Oberscharführer*, remained fair and, at times, even kindly. He is not an SS, but an officer of the Wehrmacht, the regular army.

Soon after our arrival, he ordered clothes for us. We had arrived in the regulation gray dresses with the large red KL— KONZENTRATIONSLAGER—painted on our backs, unfit for cold autumn weather.

The clothes arrived—dresses, coats, even sweaters. They were colorful civilian clothes and, unlike the sacklike gray uniforms of Auschwitz, these were meant for women.

Our joy knows no bounds. I have received a pink woolen dress and a brown tweed coat with a brown fur collar. As I try it on, I feel luxuriously pampered. It is soft and warm and makes me look like a young woman. It hugs and comforts my thin, bony body and makes it feel and look well-nourished.

I can barely sleep from excitement. I keep touching the soft fabric of the coat and brushing the fur collar against my cheek. In the morning I wear the pink dress to work. The old German who works next to me lifts his face from his work desk with astonishment when I sit down at my customary seat. He does not recognize me at first. The surprise in his eyes reveals the extent of the change in my appearance.

My outlook on life is changed. In my pink dress I am a person. Even old Herr Scheidel has noticed it. And his reaction, a free civilian, is of paramount importance. His look of recognition changes my self-image, my world.

But Herr Zerkübel, the supreme master of the *Montage*, remains impassive. On the morning of our transformation we all sit self-consciously and secretly giggling at our workbenches in anticipation of his reaction. At ten o'clock every morning, like clockwork, Herr Zerkübel comes out of his glass enclosures in the center of the *Montage* to inspect our work. Like Zeus from Mount Olympus, Herr Zerkübel would descend with measured steps and erect posture in an aura of awe and strut past each inmate in silent observation of her every move. Not a muscle moves in his face. Not a flicker of an eye would betray his emotion. He gives no indication whatsoever whether he even notices our presence. Not ever since the first day when he selected us does he once acknowledge that he is aware of our existence.

When he is displeased he would, after he has again ensconced himself in the glass office, summon our guard and have him escort the culprit into his terrible and exalted presence for a reprimand. The reprimand would be delivered to a point above the inmate's head, in seeming negation of her very being.

But now, in our new clothes, he has to take notice. Some of the girls brush their budding hair with wet fingers into neat shapes, pinch their cheeks to achieve surprisingly becoming complexions, and assume graceful postures. The effect is quite startling.

Herr Zerkübel remains aloof. His stony face and posture continue to hold immutable disregard of our being. Our new clothes do not render us visible to him.

It does not dampen my enthusiasm. I feel the change in my old partner, Herr Scheidel, and that is enough.

Back in our camp in the evening, I try on my coat again. It is beautiful!

Suddenly I notice white stitching at the hem of the lining. As I look closer I see the stitches form letters. LEAH KOHN—DÉS. It is a name and a place. A town in Hungary. And the name of a girl. A Jewish girl. These clothes were taken away from Jews, Jewish women, and given to us! This coat belonged to Leah Kohn from Dés. She was tall and slim, just like me. And she liked this coat very much. That's why she embroidered her name into it before they took it from her. Is she alive? Is she shivering in a gray cotton prison sack, while I delight in her coat? Or was she taken to the gas chamber after having been stripped of it?

Leah Kohn's coat becomes an agonizing burden. And so

does the pretty pink dress of a nameless owner. I have become an accomplice to SS brutality and robbery by wearing these clothes. By benefiting from pillage and perhaps murder, I have become a participant in the crime. How dare I wear this coat? This dress? Leah Kohn, forgive me. Please . . . !

TWENTY-NINE

Work in the *Montage* is interesting. I have three small machines. Each, a sort of soldering machine, attaches another small part to the gadget we are assembling. The parts were cut out in the *Dreherei*, finished and polished in the *Lackiererei*, and then brought to us in the *Montage* to be assembled into a compact gadget. This gadget was the final product of the entire division. It is some kind of precision instrument which controls the distance and direction of the bomb ejected by a fighter plane.

The complete gadget is like a medium-sized camera with colorful wires and screws in an intricate pattern. We work in an assembly line, all thirty-five of us, each adding one or two small parts to the growing gadget. Only four or five German civilians work in *Montage*. Their job is to test the more complex parts of the assembly before the gadget gets any farther. Herr Scheidel, for instance, operates a small machine into which he inserts the part after I attach and solder several screws and wires on my machines. His machine checks the accuracy of my work. If I make a mistake, the entire part up to that point has to be discarded. An inexcusable waste. Inexcusable. Mistakes are chalked up as deliberate negligence. Or worse. Sabotage. We were forewarned.

The completed gadget reaches the glass office of Herr Zerkübel after it has been tested by two German workers. He then inserts it into his checking apparatus and all the small parts on the gadget begin moving in harmonious complexity, sending a fine set of whirring, ticking, and rattling sounds like discreet bells through the entire *Montage*. It is a proud sound, a happy sound. The instrument is working perfectly, and we made it. We created something intricate and complex and difficult.

It is also a tragic sound. The success of our work contributes to the success of the German war effort. We are toiling against ourselves.

During October several of us from *Montage* are transferred to *Dreherei*. There is need for extra workers in *Dreherei*, and those inmates who have a German partner are spared in *Montage*. Their work is taken over by German civilians.

Herr Scheidel is sorry to see me go, he says. He started to talk to me the third week after our arrival, whenever the guard turned his back and Herr Zerkübel was not looking. He spoke with a peculiar dialect and at first I did not understand him very well, but soon I got used to his nasal tones, and we managed to snatch some conversation when opportunity presented itself. He lived with his wife, he said. His only son was in the army. On the Russian front. He said "Russian front" with a certain emphasis and lowered his voice. I did not understand why. There were certain things he emphasized in this rather secretive manner, things that did not seem particularly confidential to me. On the other hand, he asked me openly about conditions in the camp, about how much food we were getting, how late we worked—the civilians left at five and we worked until seven-thirty—and whether we were treated fairly by our guards. I did not answer his questions. His naïve openness seemed to indicate an ignorance of the severity of our status. I could not be sure of his intentions. I told him we were not allowed to discuss our lives in the camp with anyone. In fact, we were not allowed to talk to anyone. He had been instructed not to speak to us either, he said. I told him instead about my past, my family, and the home I left behind.

One day he brought me a small brown paper bag. He put it on the desk when no one was looking and indicated with his eye that I take it. There were rinds of bread in it. Thin, somewhat dry rinds, but edible. He was panicky when I tried to thank him, averting his face in fright and acting feverishly preoccupied with his work. I brought the rinds back to camp and shared them with Mommy. They made a delightful snack. Mommy had received bits of food from German workers in parts of the factory where she cleaned floors. Herr Scheidel's sudden generosity astounded us. It came after weeks of association, long after I despaired of ever receiving any food scraps from him.

At about this time I had asked Herr Scheidel if he would bring me some paper. I knew it was risky but had not expected the extent of his astonishment.

"Paper? Did you say paper? What do you need paper for? What kind of paper?"

"Just a small piece. A few small pieces. Any paper. For writing. Any paper at all."

"Writing what? What do you want to write?"

"A poem. I want to write a poem. I . . . some time ago I used to write poems."

"Ah, a poem. You are a poet, ha? A poet!"

His laughter was rasping. I began to regret my request. But the next day Herr Scheidel surreptitiously placed a small parcel on my lap under the workbench. In crumpled brown paper a few yellowish slips of paper were carefully wrapped. This was the beginning of a clandestine paper smuggling operation by Herr Scheidel.

My transfer to *Dreherei* has changed all that. On my first day here I am befriended by a French POW who hands me a roll under the workbench. A fresh, white roll! And when he sees I am putting it away, he tells me to eat it and promises to

give me food again. The next day he brings me a small cake of
soap. Every morning he brings me some food—a piece of
bread, a carrot, a raw potato.

Dreherei is a very large place with very large machines.
Several French POWs work here. They wear civilian clothes
with an arm band—GEFANGENE. They are not undernour-
ished. And they are permitted to speak to each other and go to
the toilet unescorted. Their workday begins at eight in the
morning and ends at six in the evening. We work from 6:30
A.M. until 7:30 P.M. We are not allowed to leave the machine
for any reason or to go anywhere without the guard.

Jacques, my POW, laughed when he saw the SS guard take
us to the toilet, two or three girls at a time. The POWs are
guarded by the regular army, not the SS. Their guards leave
after depositing them at the factory and come to fetch them
after work.

Jacques is a balding, jovial, heavyset fellow. He cannot
speak German, so our conversation is limited to his pointing
to objects and pronouncing their equivalent in French and my
repeating the French words. He taught me to say pretty girl in
French and then pointed at me. I blushed deeply. I think I
would have fallen in love with him out of gratitude for his
unexpected compliment had I had the chance. But I had not.

The next day I was assigned to the night shift. I never saw
Jacques again.

My assignment to the night shift coincided with Yom Kippur. Before we leave for work in the evening we are served
our breakfast and at twelve midnight, the lunch—a bowl of
soup. Our supper is served back in camp after our return from
work, in the morning. On the night of Yom Kippur I could not
have my breakfast before leaving for work because it is served
too late, almost half an hour after sunset and thus after the
beginning of the fast. The midnight meal, naturally, I have to
forego. And the supper in the morning. I am unable to fall
asleep. I am ravenous after twenty-four hours of fasting. My
last meal was supper the morning before. In the evening, be-

fore leaving for work again, I cannot have my breakfast. It is served before the conclusion of the fast day which ends an hour after sunset. So I start my second night of work without food, by now having fasted thirty-six hours. I will eat in six more hours at midnight.

But I did not last that long. At eleven o'clock I fainted. I dropped unconscious to the floor next to my huge machine. I came to in the medical office of the factory. An hour later I was brought back to work. Long after the midnight meal had been served.

In the morning, when I held the hot cup of coffee in my trembling hands, I was not hungry anymore. I was very tired. I had gone without food and sleep for forty-eight hours, twenty-four of them doing hard labor.

The next day I was transferred back to the *Montage*. Herr Scheidel seemed very glad to see me. His long, wrinkled face was contorted into a strange grimace: He was smiling.

As he sat down next to me, he exclaimed, "*Heil* Hitler!" It was his favorite expression, the equivalent of "thank God!" Every evening at five, when the bell rang to signal the end of the workday for the German civilians, Herr Scheidel would shout "*Heil* Hitler!" and happily scamper off his stool to get his bag and overcoat and hurry on skinny, bowed legs out of the factory.

Now, for the first time I do not mind the exclamation. Strangely, it warms me. Is it possible to forget the words and remember only the intention?

The winter begins early. During the first week of November a heavy blanket of snow descends on the courtyard of the factory. Our windows are covered with ice-flowers and in the *Montage* it is getting chillier. Herr Scheidel comes, bundled up in two sweaters under his winter coat. My pink dress has short sleeves, and I am cold. I had not received a sweater in September. There were not enough sweaters to go around.

"Are you cold?"

"A little."

"Tomorrow put on a warmer dress. Or wear a sweater."

Herr Scheidel's voice is paternal. I do not reply. The next day he is annoyed as I shiver audibly.

"Why didn't you put on something warmer?"

My silence does not make him understand. He keeps on grumbling *"Donnerwetter,"* and shoots angry glances in my direction.

In the camp a heavy gloom descends with the snow. Our relatives are somewhere out in the cold, freezing. They are standing long hours on *Zehlappel* or working without warm clothing. The barracks are made of thin wood and the cold penetrates day and night. Who knows how many will freeze this winter?

Our comfort in the protection of the factory building, even during *Zehlappel*, is the source of much guilt. Soon, evenings after work are spent in collective reminiscing. Instead of the regular program of singing and poetry recital which had become routine in the *Montage* room after the second week, we sit in groups on our beds and tell stories about parents, sisters, and brothers. The recollections are sad, and they end in despair. The onset of winter drains our resources of hope.

Groups are ordered to clear the snow in the courtyard and on the paths of the nearby vegetable field. It is soon discovered that in the mounds alongside the paths potatoes are stored for the winter. While others shovel snow, one or two girls dig up potatoes and hide them under their coats. Little by little enough potatoes are smuggled into the camp to allow at least one potato to a person almost every evening. We wash these potatoes in the toilet and eat them raw with the skin. Only after lights out do we dare consume these concealed delicacies. With one eye at the entrance in apprehension, each girl bites with care into the hard, delightful surface of the fresh, moist potato. The guard would often step into the room on his patrol, and the slightest noise would cause him to snap on the lights. The potatoes have to be eaten with utmost caution.

Several Orthodox girls save their potatoes for Hanukkah. It is decided that Hanukkah lights will be lit in oil smuggled in from the factory. The potato find solves the problem. Cut in half and carved hollow, the potatoes are to serve as containers for the oil and threads from the blanket as wicks. There are eight days of Hanukkah; four potatoes are sufficient for lights.

Mommy also saves a potato. For Sabbath lights. The following Friday night at sunset she lights the oil a friend smuggles in from *Dreherei* in the carved-out potato halves on the windowsill. But moments after she pronounces the benediction of Sabbath over the faintly flickering lights, the *Oberscharführer* enters the room. The room is dark, only the light from the windowsill illuminates the tall bunk beds and the frightened faces of the young girls who have gathered to hear Mommy's blessing for the holy day.

"What is this?"

His tone is unusually gruff. He steps over to the window and turns to face the assembled young women frozen in fright.

"Whose is this?"

No one speaks. Mother calls out in a low voice. "They are mine, Herr *Oberscharführer*. I lit these lights. For Sabbath."

He stands looking at us. He is angry. "Do you know what you have done? Lights in the window! Ach, you would not understand! You," he turns to Mother, "take these lights!"

Mother slowly goes to the window and picks up the burning potato halves. The *Oberscharführer* leads the way. Mother follows him. At the door he turns. His face is not angry anymore.

"This should never happen again."

He orders Mother to put out the lights in the toilet and dump the potatoes into the refuse can. We were going to eat the potatoes after Sabbath.

The *Oberscharführer* does not punish us. He does not ask where did the oil or the potatoes come from. We are very lucky.

The incident does not deter us from planning a Hanukkah celebration with lights. Instead, we decide to be extra cautious.

When Hanukkah came and the first light was lit, a girl was posted at the door as a lookout. The Hanukkah lights have to burn only for half an hour. This makes the task easier. Every night, during the half hour the lights are burning, another lookout stands at the entrance watching the corridor, while someone stands at the window in readiness to put the lights out at a signal and hide the potato halves in the straw sack of a nearby bed. The rest are singing Hanukkah songs. A modern-day Hanukkah miracle occurs. Our plans work, and we are not discovered.

There are some girls who remember Christmas. With nostalgia they recall happy memories of Christmas trees and presents. To them the concentration camp is an especially bleak place. They cannot identify with the hope the historical Jewish holiday Hanukkah offers, commemorating liberation from foreign oppression. Or later, Tu BeShvat, which commemorates the blossoming of trees in the Holy Land. Or Purim, which marks the downfall of the enemy and Jewry's escape from annihilation. Or Passover, the holiday of freedom from slavery, the commemoration of redemption. To these forlorn Jewish girls, deprived of the comfort of Jewish tradition because their parents had wished to assimilate into Gentile culture, the concentration camp is even more inexplicable, less endurable.

Purim was a sad day for us. During early spring, some young girls were taken to work in another part of the city. On one occasion one of the girls attempted to escape. She was caught and put in solitary confinement. On the day of Purim, her head was shaved and we were assembled to face her as she stood in handcuffs to be taken to Dachau. She had to stand on a chair in full view of the whole camp while her sentence was pronounced. She was to be hanged in the public square of Camp Dachau.

We cried unashamedly. But Eva, the eighteen-year-old girl with gentle brown eyes, just stood there quietly, somewhat embarrassed. She was aware that her action might have endangered the entire camp, and it was this that caused her embarrassment.

I had not known her well. She had worked in *Dreherei* and lived in the other room. She was a quiet, unassuming girl. No one knew why she decided to escape. She had not confided in anyone. It was a desperate move.

As she was led away she averted her eyes. We attempted to touch her as she passed and whispered silly, inane phrases of encouragement and farewell. I had the feeling she did not hear us. She was wrapped in a cloak of apathy.

Now we were only four hundred and ninety-eight.

In December another one of us had been taken away. She was Bella, the young bride of twenty, who had discovered in Auschwitz that she was pregnant. In December she was due to deliver her baby and she was taken to the hospital of another camp, we were told. No one knew what became of her. We were afraid to inquire from even the kindest of our supervisors about her fate. Even though the *Oberscharführer* was not an SS, and several of our guards seemed to have some sympathy for us, we never attempted to breach the enormous gap that existed between us by approaching them with any request. Neither did they attempt to approach us with any remark that went beyond the business of inmate–guard relationship. Their kindness consisted of a lack of brutality. They avoided humiliating epithets and other verbal abuse when speaking to us. And their looks did not hold unconcealed hatred.

But not all.

THIRTY

ONE DAY in January an attractive, tall SS woman with large green eyes and long, dark blonde hair arrived in our camp in Augsburg. She caused a stir among the SS officers. They all seemed to have an instant crush on her. She was followed about by two or three men wherever she moved. The other SS girls eyed her jealously as she was courted by all the SS men from the *Oberscharführer* down to the silly youngster we call "the Goat" because of his bad posture and bleating voice.

The blonde beauty was a high-ranking officer. She was addressed as Frau *Oberscharführerin*. And she walked with the air of a sex goddess combined with the command of a queen. The role truly fitted her. She was indeed a proud beauty.

Even we inmates derived pleasure from looking at her. I admired her elegant appearance and her winning smile.

"She must be kind-hearted," I remarked to one of my friends, "no one with a face like that can be anything but good."

Within two days I found out, quite bitterly, how wrong I was. The morning after her arrival, Frau *Oberscharführerin* conducted the morning *Zehlappel*. She arrived, in high, polished boots, her immaculate pale gray blouse collar folded open over the trim officer's uniform, her arms folded over a whip, marching at the head of a delegation of SS men. When she reached our lines, the haughtily amused glance on her beautiful face hardened. Her features became steel. With the point of her whip she counted the rows of five. Suddenly, her face becomes distorted with open hatred.

"You!" she shouts. "You in the back! Wipe that smirk off your face!"

I turn to my right-hand neighbor. The angry glance seems directed at her. But she is not smiling.

"You! It is you I meant. The tall *Mistvieh* in the last row!" She leans forward slightly and snaps the whip at my head.

"Wipe that smirk off your face, or I will do it with my whip!"

With an awful certainty I realize she is talking to me. But I have not been smirking or grinning or even smiling. There must be a terrible mistake.

There is no mistake. She means me. Now she is glaring at me.

"That's better."

She moves on and the count continues.

I freeze with incomprehension and deep hurt.

I know I have not smirked. Then why did she single me out for humiliation? There must have been a mistake.

During the evening *Zehlappel* I fear a repetition of the morning incident. The whole day I cringe with the memory of it, and as the evening approaches my stomachache grows sharper.

But she does not appear. The *Zehlappel* is conducted by the *Oberscharführer* himself, and it passes without incident.

The next morning I stand transformed into a statue of impassivity as the *Oberscharführerin* passes our row. Again she casts a special look of contempt toward me, but says nothing. Was I imagining that special glance for me? Perhaps it is my own sensitivity which colored her appearance in my eyes. She may not even remember yesterday's incident at all. Certainly she does not remember me.

Again, I am wrong. Again, I am to find out soon, to my sorrow.

As we stand on line for supper, she passes in the corridor, chatting with two SS men. Suddenly, she spots me in the line. She comes over to me and whispers in half tones, *"Du Mistvieh!"* You misfit!

I look at her. Her face has a look of uncontrollable rage as she returns my glance. Then she turns to her companions and continues her lively chatter.

The *Oberscharführerin* is consistent in her hatred of me. Whenever she passes me anywhere—in the corridor, at *Zehlappel*, or in our room—she does not forego the opportunity to remind me of our special relationship. Never does she allow our meeting to go unremarked. It is invariably, *"Du Mistvieh"* and then an additional epithet, a threat, or a demand. *"Du hesslicher Mistvieh,"* you ugly misfit, or "beast, stop talking so loud, stop your idiotic grin," or "stand at attention when you see me pass" or "you will see, I'll take care of you one day" or "don't worry, you won't live too long as long as I am around." The remarks are always whispered in half tones between clenched teeth. Always with deliberate malice directed at me accompanied by a look of frustrated rage.

The whole camp notices it and wonders about it. While she acts with cold contempt toward every inmate and on occasion with deliberate cruelty, she has no other pet who earns her special hatred. Her relationship toward me is startling. Her live hatred and unrelenting persecution of me is incomprehensible. Why? For God's sake why?

In time I begin to wonder whether my porcupinelike hair, my inordinate height and skinniness, and my protruding bones are so repulsive as to arouse such hatred. Perhaps her sensitivity to beauty rendered her fiercely impatient with a creature so strikingly ugly. Her intolerance of my ugliness must be causing such hatred. Just as I had been struck and fascinated by her beauty, she is struck and repulsed by my ugliness.

In time I become convinced of this. And I am miserable.

Once she passed me in the hall and gave me a kick: "Get out of my way, *Mistvieh*!"

This started a new cycle of fear. I started to believe she will fulfill her threats of killing me. What if in a fit of anger she were to shoot me? There is no barrier to her wishes. My life is exposed to her whims. I live in fear. Daily I dread meeting her. The shock of total abuse, of humiliation, of fear is debilitating.

And there is no one to turn to. No superior officer would defend me against her even if I were not a Jewish inmate. Even if I were a German. She is the darling of the SS staff, and the favorite of the *Oberscharführer*. I cannot convey my fears to Mommy. I do not want to frighten her. Instead, I comfort her whenever she is saddened and pained because of this abuse. I insist it does not matter while my fear and apprehension deepen.

As time went on, this too became another aspect of our condition. I learned to live with this painful humiliation and fear. My dread of meeting her and my anxiety about the possibility of actual harm at her hands became part of everyday routine. It was to be borne with a positive attitude. "It, too, shall pass . . ." "It, too, shall turn for the good . . ." The resources of the Jew. The secret of survival of the "eternal people."

THIRTY-ONE

TANGIBLE SOURCES of consolation as the winter bears on are the frequent bombardments by the Allies. The air raids grow in length and frequency during January and February, and toward the end of that month, they become daily affairs. February 28, my fourteenth birthday, the entire population of Michelwerke spends the workday in the air raid shelter.

Except for us. We are not permitted to go to the shelter. We, too, are ordered to leave the premises of the factory and march to the basement level, while our German captors go to the fortified shelter, one flight below.

The air raids are our happiest hours. From our "basement," which was actually a ground-level lounging room for the workers, we could hear the bombs falling in the vicinity. We are able to tell from the shrill sounds which are direct hits, and rejoice. Unsupervised we spend hours in the comfortable surroundings of this basement, telling stories, jokes, and singing. When an explosion sounds particularly near, we cheer loudly. I do not think there was even one among us who in these early months of the bombings was ever afraid.

Incidents of fear occur only during early March when the frequency and length of the bombings ripen our conviction that the end is near. The war is drawing to its end and the Allies have the upper hand. The taste of liberation becomes ever more tangible. And with the growing belief in its possibility the fear of death grows.

As we return to work we see smoke rising in many places in the city. The *Montage* is on the sixth floor, and from my window I can see great distances. The damage is extensive and it leaves a marked impact on the morale of the Germans. They are silent and solemn after each raid, listlessly going about their work.

"I hope my house was not hit," Herr Scheidel would say and glance at his watch. "Well, in an hour and a half I shall find out."

Then at the ringing of the five o'clock bell he would exclaim with relief, "*Heil*, Hitler!" and hurry with doubled effort out of the *Montage*.

Once the factory received a direct hit. The windows were shattered and the electric circuit was knocked out. But the bomb did not explode. It fell in the courtyard and was later taken away by the demolition squad. It was a large bomb. Had it exploded it would have wrecked the entire factory.

On a Sunday morning in early April the bombing started early. Bombs fell relentlessly from the dark hours of dawn. The entire offensive must have been directed against our quarter of the city, the factory district, because the shrill whistling preceding every explosion sounded very loud and clear. The explosions followed each other in close succession. The building trembled and objects began to fall. Some girls prayed, others sang. Some sat alone, afraid.

I was very excited. It is the end. Germany is being virtually demolished by the English and the Americans. Our delivery is very, very near. Maybe tomorrow. Perhaps even today. Who knows what the next hour will bring?

For hours the bombing lasted. In midmorning, as we got back to our rooms, smoke and burning fires rose from every direction.

As we stand on *Zehlappel* the Goat, who is very nervous today, announces that he needs forty girls to clear the rubble in the yard. The entrance to the factory yard and the passage to the building are blocked. From one end of the line he separates eight rows and orders them to march. I am among them. We are heading for our rooms to get coats. It is a brutally cold, windy morning. The snow is drifting in the air. In patches it is frozen to the ground. But the Goat is in a frantic hurry as always when he receives an order. This time he received an immediate order and he is not going to waste a moment:

"*Los!*" he shouts nervously. "Follow me. March!"

This is insane. It is bitter cold, and we have only dresses and shoes on. We have no stockings or underwear. It is certain death to go out and work in that weather without our coats.

The cauldron of the coffee arrived, but Goat does not allow us to get even the coffee. He is in a hurry.

"But our coats. *Bitte, Herr Offizier*, let us quickly get our coats. It will take only a minute."

"*Los!*" he shouts, beside himself. "March after me this instant!"

He heads for the staircase and the rows march at his heels. As we pass the toilet, several girls duck through its doors. I follow them. We quickly hide behind the tall trash cans in the toilet, and the others march on.

But when he reached ground level, the Goat counted his

charges. It was his habit to count us every few steps even on the way to work. He discovered that eight were missing. In a panic he ordered the column back to the camp. The *Oberscharführer* was notified and a campwide search commenced for the missing girls.

All this time we crouch behind the trash cans. From sounds filtering into the toilet we realize what is happening and hold our breath. But soon someone comes in and says: "Come out, girls. The *Oberscharführer* is very mad. He ordered the entire camp to go without rations for three days if you do not show up immediately."

We file out of the toilet. The *Oberscharführer* orders us to line up against the wall in the corridor and there we stand until night without food.

It is bad news but not as bad as it could have been. I expected to be punished by having to work all day outdoors without coats on. As it turned out, we were excused from cleaning the rubble in the yard altogether. While we were hiding, the rest of our group was taken downstairs by the Goat to do the work, after the *Oberscharführer* allowed them to put on sweaters and coats.

I am terribly hungry. This is the fifth day of Passover. Mommy and I had decided that one of us would observe Passover by not eating the bread ration and the other one would compensate for the bread by sharing her ration of the cooked meals at noon and in the evening. I had volunteered to give up the bread ration. Mommy had agreed because she was in far worse physical shape than I. So I had only black coffee in the morning, and one and a half bowls of soup at noon and in the evenings. All that liquid without the morning and evening ration of bread made me ravenously hungry, and by the third day I felt quite weak. Now, on the fifth day, having foregone the coffee in the morning, I am feeling faint. I find it difficult to stand, but I am afraid to crouch even when the Germans are not looking. I do not dare attempt a second violation in one day.

So I stand alongside the wall among the others. In a couple of hours we are all sorely fatigued and our campmates cast compassionate glances at us. They are not permitted to speak to us. Poor Mommy keeps walking back and forth, passing me every few minutes, her face a mask of pity. I make an effort to encourage her but as the hours pass, it proves increasingly difficult.

The cauldron of soup is distributed in the hall right before our noses. So is the evening meal and bread. But we stand there and believe the day will never end. My legs feel wooden and the length of my spine is a stripe of pain. My stomach feels heavy and numb. There is a light trembling in my whole body. I am very cold.

At 10 P.M., after the camp had gone to bed, the *Oberscharführer* comes to us.

"Are you tired? Are you hungry? Did you learn your lesson?"

We begin to cry. We are beyond fatigue. Beyond hunger.

"Go to your Blocks!"

We are barely able to move. Slowly, we trudge to our respective rooms.

In my room it is dark and quiet. Noiselessly, I approach my bed. Mommy stirs. She sits up abruptly and embraces me: "Thank God, it's over! Come, sit here for a moment." From under her blanket she takes out a bowl of cold soup. It is her supper. She has been saving it for me.

"Eat it, you must be faint with hunger."

"It is your supper. You have not eaten from it. I will eat half. Take out your spoon and let's eat together."

"No, I will not eat. You have to eat it all, you have not eaten all day."

"Look, Mommy. I am very hungry, it is true. And I will eat half of the soup. But you must eat the other half because you have become very weak and very thin and every drop of food you deny yourself may prove disastrous. Take your spoon and let's eat together."

Mother gets very angry. She whispers: "Stop talking and eat!"

She takes the spoon and thrusts it into the soup. Then raises it to my mouth.

I shake my head with lips shut tight. Mommy looks at me, her face aflame. But I am adamant.

"I will not eat if you will not share it with me."

Mommy's anger and despair charge the air. "If you will not eat the soup I will empty the bowl on top of the bed!"

I shake my head. "I will eat only if you will also eat."

Mommy takes the bowl of soup and turns it over. In a splash, the contents land on top of her gray blanket. Pieces of potato scatter in every direction. The liquid is being sucked up by the bedding.

I cannot believe my eyes.

The soup. There is no soup! Mommy deliberately spilled it. And on the bed! Oh, my God, what has happened? What has happened to her? My God, what is happening to us?

"Mommy, why did you do this? For God's sake, why did you do it?!"

Mommy begins to cry. She hugs me and we lie down on my side of the narrow bed. I begin to cry, too. For the soup, for Mommy, for all of the unhappy, miserable, cold, and hungry prisoners of the world.

We cried until dawn. Our weeping was uncomforting, heavy and hopeless. Bitterness burned my throat. Unrelieved, oppressive, desperate. The sky seemed to darken with the coming of dawn. Our grief was total, and for the first time, uncontrollable.

Much later we found out that was the night Daddy died—on the fifth day of Passover.

THIRTY-TWO

DURING THE last days of March rumors had circulated about our evacuation. The enemy was near. We will be taken to Dachau or to another camp.

The German workers at the factory did not seem aware of the coming changes. Herr Scheidel did not indicate he knew anything about our leaving. We had become friends. He would have expressed covert remarks of regret about not seeing me anymore. Nothing. His *Heil*, Hitler! at the end of his working day was as cheerful as ever, and his leaving was just as dogmatically uneventful. Perhaps the rumors are empty speculations, nothing more.

April came and nothing happened. The *Oberscharführer* was as stern as before, Herr Zerkübel as stoic and superior in his aloofness, the Goat just as ludicrously punctilious, and the *Oberscharführerin* as unfathomably cold in her general conduct and as vehement in her persecution of me.

Then, one morning at *Zehlappel*, during the first week of April, the *Oberscharführer* read the order. The next day we were to be taken to Dachau. Our guards were to accompany us to our new destination.

The journey through Augsburg was the high point of our trip. The Gothic buildings lining the cobblestoned streets were enveloped in a fine spring mist and our streetcar wound around them in snakelike motion. Good-bye, Augsburg. I had hoped you would be the scene of our liberation. I had dreamed countless dreams of Allied troops marching down your cobblestones toward us, bringing liberty with the rattle of armored trucks and tanks. I had had a mysterious sweet premonition of freedom when I first took sight of your reassuring civilized air eight months ago. Eight months of dogged hope. Of dreams. Of prayer. Now I am leaving you, still a prisoner. Heading for what future? Dachau.

At the streetcar terminal we disembark and continue our trip on foot. Our road leads through bombed-out streets, devastated neighborhoods. The past eight months have not left the city unscathed. A large portion of it lay in ruins.

The train station is also in ruins. Our wagons stand at some distance. In order to reach them, we have to wade through heaps of rubble.

The train takes off immediately. By nightfall we arrive at a huge, sprawling camp a short distance from the railroad tracks.

The road to the camp is a rocky path through a stark landscape of boulders, barren trees, and an endless row of telephone poles. In the gathering dusk flocks of crows sitting on the telephone wire are strikingly etched against a metallic sky. Their shrill cries accompany us on our road like ominous threats.

It is Camp Landsberg we are approaching, one of the subsidiary camps of Dachau. But when we arrive at the austere gates of the camp, our leaders are told there is no room for us at Landsberg. The evacuation of many smaller camps in the vicinity has filled Landsberg beyond capacity.

We stand on line near the fence far into the night while our guards telephone for orders concerning our fate. During the early hours of dawn the order reaches us. Back to the wagons. We will move on to another camp.

I sigh with relief. While the crows overhead are screeching their dire message, we are leaving this forbidding place. Elsewhere there may be a latent promise in the air. Here there is only threat.

It is late afternoon when we arrive at Mühldorf. Here there are trucks waiting for us at the station. Through several miles of tended fields the road stretches toward a small, crowded camp.

In the camp we are surrounded by flocks of inmates. Eager to find out what camp we came from, what had we been doing there, and where are we from originally, they talk rapidly and animatedly. Mühldorf had been wracked by typhus throughout the winter. Between thirty and fifty people died daily. The survivors, the anxious women who now surround us, are emaciated beyond anything we have seen. Compared to them we looked definitely well nourished. Even the inmates we saw at Landsberg were less skeletal, although we had been struck by their appearance when we saw them. Mühldorf fared no worse than other camps, we are told. The death rate at Dachau was even higher.

The inmates at Mühldorf tell us we look very well and are incredulous when we tell them that during the winter no one died at Augsburg. Out of the five hundred of the original transport from Auschwitz there are four hundred ninety-eight of us: Two had been taken to Dachau. One of those two may even be alive, together with her baby. No, that is impossible, they tell us, not in Dachau.

We see male inmates behind the barbed wire fences. Since it is a small camp, men and women at Mühldorf are in close proximity, separated only by a fence.

In less than an hour we find out that there are men from Somorja on the other side of the fence. And that Bubi is also in this camp, except not right here but a few kilometers away in the twin camp called Waldlager, a forest camp. It is deep in the nearby forest.

Mommy and I become very excited at the prospect of meeting Bubi. But how to get to Waldlager? We find out that trucks with provisions go to Waldlager every day and if we are lucky we will be assigned work at unloading. We should persistently volunteer and eventually we may be selected to go along with the trucks.

Our lucky turn comes sooner than expected. The next morning about one hundred women are selected for transfer to Waldlager, Mommy and I among them. We are put on trucks immediately after *Zehlappel* and driven through green woods to the other camp.

We are in ecstasy. The sun shines, and I feel happiness tremble within me. Everything is turning out beautifully. Oh, my dear God! Thank you, my dear God!

In Waldlager the inmates live in bunkers dug into the ground. Only a small mound indicates that underneath is a deep, long hole in which fifty people live. The opening is also cleverly camouflaged with tall grass, and the entire camp looks like a forest of outsized mushrooms.

In our excitement we can only think of Bubi. As soon as we arrive we inquire about the men's camp and find it directly adjacent to the women's camp. It is possible to meet men at the fence and even talk to them when the guards are not looking. Both men and women go to work and the meetings take place after the evening *Zehlappel*. Mommy and I spend the day anxiously awaiting the evening.

It is raining during *Zehlappel*, and we are worried that the men will not come to the fence. Indeed, the fence area is deserted for a long time, and we are just about going to give up hope when two men slowly approach the fence. They are even more skeletal than the women.

When they see us they ask us in Yiddish: "Are you from the new transport?"

"Yes, we came today."

"From which camp?"

"From an airplane factory in Augsburg."

"You must have been well off there. You look strong. Where are you from?"

"We are from Czechoslovakia, Hungarian territory. Somorja. Somorja is the town's name. In Csallokoz."

"I know," says the older man. He has been speaking all along. "I know. There are a few men here from Somorja."

"Yes, we heard. That's why we are here. We heard that my

son, Bubi Friedmann is there. Do you know him? Bubi Friedmann. Tall and blond. He was an interpreter in Auschwitz.
Perhaps he is an interpreter here, too. Do you know him?"

"Yes, we know him. From Somorja. He is in a bunker with
other men from Somorja. We will tell him to come here. Wait
right here."

The two leave with slow shuffling motion and disappear
into the thickening dusk.

We wait. The drizzle becomes heavier and we are chilled.
In the hazy wetness the barbed wire fence looms like a strange
net webbing with hanging raindrops forever uniting and dripping to the muddy ground. The piece of bread Lina gave
Mommy for Bubi was becoming soggy.

Lina worked in the kitchen and had said to Mommy after
Zehlappel: "Give this to your son when you see him. The men
get very little food here. He may be hungry."

At first Mommy declined the bread. Bubi was not under-
nourished at all. On the contrary, he was strong and healthy.
He had an excellent position in Auschwitz. And if he did so
well in Auschwitz where thousands were dying, he must be
even better off in Waldlager.

But Lina said: "Mrs. Friedmann, just take the bread. And
give it to him when you see him."

Out of the foggy grayness a tall, thin figure is now approaching with a slow, hesitant gait. It must be Bubi! But as
he comes nearer we see that he is a mere skeleton with tattered
prison garb hanging in shreds from his emaciated frame. He
comes with a painful limp and loud clatter. A tin can is hanging about his waist which makes a frightful din everytime the
figure takes another lame step. He seems headed for the fence.
Toward us. When he reaches the fence, he stops a few feet
from us. From such close proximity we can see his face clearly.
It is the face of a skeleton with the skin bruised on the high
cheekbones. Elsewhere scabs and a light fuzz cover the skin,
obscuring features and facial expression. He is unlike anyone I

have ever seen. He resembles those creatures in science fiction magazines my brother used to read. But as he stands there silently staring at us, a horrible certainty grips me.

"Bubi!" It is he, I know it.

He does not answer.

Mommy opens her eyes wide with horror: "This is not Bubi. This is not he."

He sees the bread in Mommy's hand. His voice is low, rasping: "You may throw the bread over the fence, Mommy. The guard does not mind."

Mommy shrieks. "Bubi! It's you? Oh God, is it really you?"

"Mommy, throw the bread over the fence."

Mommy swallows hard. She swings her arm and the soggy piece of bread flies to the other side of the barbed wire, landing in a small puddle at Bubi's feet. With the deliberate effort and the jerky motion of a robot, Bubi bends down to pick it up. He tumbles and with an awful clatter rolls into the puddle. Mommy gasps. I grasp her shoulder but cannot control my trembling. Bubi struggles to his feet and, bread in hand, trudges away without turning around. In seconds his figure is swallowed by twilight, but the clatter of his tin can continues to echo in the fog.

THIRTY-THREE

MOMMY AND I cannot sleep. What has happened to Bubi? Our reassuring memory of him from Auschwitz has turned into a nightmare. It is obvious that he will not be able to survive long. He is barely alive now, even his mind seems affected. At meeting us he barely spoke. Asked only for the bread. What has happened to him?

"We will give him one bread ration and we will share the

other one among ourselves. He must be very hungry. That's why he spoke only about the bread when he saw us. Perhaps if we give him a ration every day he will survive until liberation."

Liberation. When will that be? Will it ever be? The wild hopes of the days of bombardment in Augsburg started to dim in the wagons and continued to evaporate in the stark reality of another concentration camp. How much longer? How much longer before we, too, contract typhus? The death toll is even higher in Waldlager.

Tomorrow. We will see, perhaps we will think of something tomorrow.

Then we started to speak of Bubi's looks. Mommy could not understand how I was able to recognize him. He looked so horrible. So . . . unlike a human being. I had not recognized him. There was no clue in his appearance to connect him with Bubi. It was something else. Some terrible intuition. The same chilling knowledge which made me tell Aunt Szerén that I would never see her again. And which operated through that awful dream, the dream about the hovering bird and Daddy. . . . The premonition of tragedy.

The next day Bubi came again. We had the bread ration ready for him, and Mommy hurled it over the fence. Today, too, he picked it up and left. Without speaking to us. His limp and inordinate clatter, his shuffling walk remained long in my mind. Long after he left. Long into the night.

Mommy is assigned to work in the kitchen of the camp. In a long barrack she sits with many other women and peels potatoes. The workers in the kitchen are permitted to eat from the potatoes. Sometimes they peel carrots, and they can eat them, too. But they are not permitted to take out anything. They are frisked as they are leaving the barrack. A few days after our arrival, a young girl was hanged in Waldlager because they found a carrot and two potatoes on her at frisking time. Mommy did not dare hide any vegetables on her body and I was glad.

The workers in the kitchen do not get any bread ration to

compensate for the vegetables they eat during peeling. This meant that we had only one bread ration, and this had to be given to Bubi. Mommy could not come to the meeting with Bubi after her assignment to vegetable peeling. They worked there until long after *Zehlappel*. Without her bread ration to be shared between the two of us, Mommy told me to give only half of my ration to Bubi. Here in Waldlager the bowl of soup is smaller than in Augsburg, and the bread ration is much smaller. Mommy felt I could not afford to give up my portion of bread every day. But I felt I could. Mommy then began to shout and ordered me to obey her. To give only half of my bread ration to my brother. Then she began to cry and plead with me to obey her. In tears she made me promise not to give away the entire ration. She said she could not bear it if I came down with a disease. We must stay alive for Bubi's sake. Without us he cannot make it.

In the evening Bubi asked me where Mommy was. This was the first time he had spoken since our first meeting, when he told Mommy to throw the bread over the fence. When I told him Mommy worked with vegetables he said that was good, this way she could eat. But then I told him I had only half a ration for him because of that. He said I should not give him even that much from my own. I need it to survive. He said he had thought we were getting the bread we had been giving him from someone. He would not have accepted it otherwise. Every drop of food is needed to survive here. But then he told me in the last few days ever since we arrived he has been feeling much stronger. The extra piece of bread made a great difference.

I was practically bubbling with joy when I reported to Mommy about my meeting with Bubi. I told her that he spoke to me at length and that he is feeling much better. Thank God! He was not affected mentally at all, neither did he lose his speaking ability. And he knows who we are. All this has been troubling us up to now. But now we knew our fears were unfounded. Bubi was okay. He only had been too weak to speak. It seemed his walk was somewhat improved also. Mommy was very happy. Our hopes were intact once again.

My meetings with Bubi have become the highlight of my day. Mommy is away the whole day and I am ordered to work about the camp, raking and picking up refuse. There are days when I work in the forest, digging. New bunkers are being built. The digging is hard, as the ground is still half frozen. But I enjoy working in the forest in my newfound happiness. The young new blades of grass, the wet earth, the soft brown trees are a fitting milieu for my new optimism. Bubi is getting stronger and I decide to contribute to it as much as I can. I decide to give him my entire bread ration. I am going to tell him I got it from someone. That way he will accept it. And he will get all well soon.

Bubi was happy to get a large piece of bread, and when I told him I got it from someone, he began to eat it immediately. He said he was getting hungrier. It seemed he was beginning to take interest in getting better. He spoke more and asked questions. Only now did I tell him about Augsburg, and he in turn told me about the events which led to his present state. He told me he had volunteered for transport from Auschwitz because he knew of the mass-scale extermination that was going on there. He was placed in a transport that was to work in a cement factory at Waldlager. Soon after his arrival he injured his leg at work, and the cement dust infected the wound. The leg swelled up to an enormous size and he could barely stand on it. Yet he worked for three months with the infected leg until finally he was operated on. The operation took place on an ordinary kitchen table, with an ordinary pocketknife, without anesthesia. Six times he was operated on, as the leg continued to blow up with pus. In the Revier the rations were reduced, and it was there that he grew into a skeleton. For weeks he lay in the Revier unable to move from fever and pain and unable to swallow even the meager bread ration allotted to the sick. Once the patient who shared his bed and blanket died of typhus, and it was two days before the corpse was removed.

He spoke slowly, without emotion. His tale could have been the description of an experiment in physics. It was told in dry, matter-of-fact tones. He walked slowly up and down alongside the fence as he spoke, limping and clattering with the tin can. He could not stand long on the injured leg, it was still not healed. He told me he had slashed the leg of his trousers wide open to fit the swollen leg into it. And now it hung in tatters, partially exposing the filthy bandage over the injured right leg.

On the third week of our stay in Mühldorf, a sudden change occurred. News spread that the Americans are approaching and the Germans decided to give up the territory without a fight. After Mommy left for work I decided to send a message to Bubi. As I was heading for the fence I saw a man next to our barrack. A man! A male inmate from the other side of the fence. What has happened? He said the gates between the camps are open and there are no guards. There are guards stationed only at the gate leading to the outside.

I begin to run. I am going to the men's camp to see Bubi. But before I reach the gate I see Bubi approaching. He is in our camp, coming to see me. As we meet I embrace him, and he too puts his arms around me. We stand there silently, in a tight embrace. I close my eyes. Freedom. It has come. This is it.

Bubi comes with me to our bunker and we sit on its roof, a small hill. The sun shines weakly and there is a soft breeze.

"So this is it," I said. "Freedom. It has come. This is it."

"Not yet. These are only rumors. We are not liberated yet."

"But where are the guards? You can see we are together. Where are the guards? They allow us to meet. This is the beginning. Soon the Americans will be here, and then we will be liberated. This is the beginning."

"One never can tell. One never can tell what the Germans

will do next. There may be a battle. The Americans are not here yet. These are only rumors."

As we sit on the slope of the bunker hill, Bubi removes the dirty gray towel that has been wound around his neck. There are large pale brown patches on the towel. He begins to poke at one of the patches with his forefinger and it begins to move. A swarming activity is initiated in the patch. I look closer in bewilderment. The patch consists of thousands of tiny insects now crawling in every direction.

"What are those?" I am horror struck.

"What do you mean?"

"These tiny insects. What are they?"

"What do you mean? Tiny insects? You never saw lice?"

"No. Never. In our camp there were no lice. No one had lice."

"But now they do. All those who are at Mühldorf or here in Waldlager. This camp is full. And so is Dachau. So is every concentration camp. You were lucky. Yours was not a concentration camp. The lice gave us typhus. And they suck our blood. I have rashes all over my body from the lice."

"You have lice on your body?"

"Of course. All over my body. They like the folds of the towel, so I keep the towel about my neck and when they crawl on it I shake them off. I do this several times a day. It is called *Entlausung*, delousing. Everybody has another system of delousing. This is mine."

"Except me. I do not have lice."

While we spoke Bubi kept delousing himself. He put the towel around his neck and a few minutes later took it off with thousands of lice crawling on it. He was expertly crushing the lice that stuck to the towel after he had vigorously shaken it. I trampled those that fell like a louse shower to the ground after each shake. Bubi then put the louse-free towel back around his neck, and the sequence was repeated again and again.

I spoke about the future. After liberation I wanted to travel all over Germany to find all our relatives in the different con-

centration camps. Especially Auschwitz. Most of them had
been in Auschwitz. We had no idea about Daddy. He was
taken to a Hungarian labor camp earlier. He must be in Hungary. Maybe we should go home first. Perhaps we will find
everybody home. Everybody will be heading home after liberation. Perhaps that's the best idea. To go straight home and
not waste time searching here in Germany when everybody is
going to head home anyway. . . ."

Bubi interrupts. "Whom do you expect to find after the liberation?"

"Why, everybody. Daddy, Aunt Szerén, Aunt Cili, Uncle
Márton, Imre, Uncle Samuel, Aunt Regina, Suri, Hindi . . ."

He touches my hand. "Look at me, Elli. You will find no
one. No one survived the death camps. We are here. We are
the survivors. The others we did not meet because they did not
survive."

"But there are many other camps. Maybe they are there.
Daddy and Aunt Szerén and the others."

"Daddy is different. He may be alive. He is a young man, he
may have been taken to a labor camp and there survived. He
is strong and athletic. He has a chance. But not the others.
Don't expect to ever meet the others again."

"You mean Aunt Szerén? . . . She was taken to the camp
for older people."

"There was no such camp. She was taken to the gas chamber."

"How do you know? That's a lie! A lie they were telling us
in Plaszow. They told you a lie!"

"You know it is not a lie. I told you about the *Sonderkommando* in Auschwitz. I had friends who worked in the
Sonderkommando. I knew all the details."

"But Uncle Samuel and the others?"

"They all went to the gas chambers. They were above forty-
five."

"My God! It can't be true. . . . Cili *néni*. We met her in Auschwitz. And Hindi and Suri. We met them when we first came to Auschwitz."

"If you met them in Auschwitz they may be alive. But since then so many have died. Do you know how many died here in the winter? And how many are dying daily? Every morning at *Zehlappel* you find out who is missing. Then the *Blockelteste* orders two men to go into the bunker and carry them out. The corpses are counted in the *Zehlappel* until they are officially reported dead to the authorities."

I am shattered. Freedom. We are the survivors. Perhaps there is no one else. Only us.

I had known about the gas chamber all along. Its shadow followed us even when we left Auschwitz driven by its fear. But I had stubbornly clung to the myth of the camp for the elderly and children. Some children must have survived.

"No. No children survived. They were all gassed."

"And the mothers? Mothers went to the other side with their children. What happened to the mothers?"

"Mothers were gassed together with their children."

"No, Bubi. Do not say that!"

We sat silently for a long time. Freedom. The lice crawl slowly on the towel. And Bubi keeps crushing them with his fingers.

THIRTY-FOUR

THREE DAYS later orders arrive for our evacuation. On a Tuesday morning during the last week of April we are loaded into boxcars once again. I was supposed to see Bubi that morning at ten. This has become our custom in these last few days since the gates between the camps have opened. We are loaded on trucks right after *Zehlappel*, and I have no chance to even send him a message.

The train station of Mühldorf. Endless rows of boxcars. Endless columns of inmates. Tens of thousands. Truckloads from every direction, from every camp in the area of Dachau. Striped uniforms, gray women's garb pours from trucks onto wagons. One hundred to a wagon. Crowding. But we have experienced worse.

The pain is to be moving away from the advancing army. From liberation. The Germans do not want us to fall into American hands. There are rumors. We are to be taken to a deep tunnel and blown up. The Germans do not want to have live witnesses to atrocities in the concentration camps. We are to be liquidated in the trains.

Rumors. Pay no attention to them. We survived until now despite rumors. The Americans are near, soon we will be liberated. In two or three weeks, perhaps. The Germans would not dare kill us now. It is too close to the end. God, do not let the rumors win.

By nightfall the loading ends and the train begins to roll. There is a small window with metal bars at one end of the wagon and the cool April breeze pleasantly rushes through the anxious ranks of crouching figures. I crouch in the vicinity of the small window, and from my place I can see the lovely woods we are leaving. Then the train comes to a curve and I can see the engine and the cars ahead of us. Incredible! There are at least a hundred boxcars between us and the engine! As I turn to look the other way, I estimate at least a hundred wagons more to the end of the chain of cars. About two hundred cars filled with concentration camp inmates. Where are they taking us? Where will they have a place for us all? The circle is getting smaller. Where are they taking us? God, help us. Do not let the rumors be true.

The train rolls slowly all night and all day the next day. No food or drink. How can they feed this multitude? Tens of thousands. On Thursday we stand near a small forest for hours. During that afternoon of waiting near the forest I see a dog fight involving three airplanes. One of them is hit and I see it fall, careening in a wide arc behind the trees, carrying its flaming hulk to a sudden noisy end somewhere beyond my vision.

We move on through forests and hills and tunnels. Slowly and haltingly, we roll past fields and villages, farms, and towns. We roll into stations and out again, sometimes without pause. Sometimes standing for hours, and then moving slowly on.

By Friday morning I am not hungry anymore. The violent hunger pangs have mellowed into a dull, persistent ache, and a pleasant lightheadedness sends me into a daze. Mommy also begins to sleep for longer periods. Her nagging hunger must have also subsided somewhat. A bright sunshine is filtering through the cracks. The train is standing.

We must have been standing for a long time now. My recollection of movement is quite distant; it must have been as long ago as the middle of the night when we last moved. We are standing here for hours.

I prop myself up with great effort. My companions are sprawling on top of each other in a stupor. Mommy is also in a deep sleep, her head rolled on my left shoulder. I ease it gently aside and stand up to get a view through the small window.

We are standing on a high embankment. There is a gently sloping valley below, a green cornfield, houses in the distance, a small hamlet. Tall hills loom on the horizon, dark and beautiful and forbidding.

The entire scene is flushed with bright sunshine. Brilliant rays of early spring dance in the valley. In the wagon it is dark and airless and smells of apathy.

I sink back into my corner and place Mommy's drooping head back on my shoulder. Who knows how long we will stand in this place?

It is Friday noon. The sun stands high. Since Tuesday

morning we have been locked in this boxcar. Without food. Or drink. Four days. How long can one go without food? I do not remember having learned anything about it in school. How much longer will we stand in one place? Who knows? It is easier when we are moving. There is hope in movement. Life. Just to stand aimlessly, endlessly, locked in a boxcar, crowded and thirsty. . . . Why are we standing here so long?

My shoulder is getting tired. I shift Mommy's head to my lower arm. It prickles. Her hair is short and stiff and it prickles my arm. She opens her eyes.

"Why don't you sleep a little, Elli? Come, put your head on my shoulder and sleep. I will sit upright and you rest a little."

At that moment the wagon doors open with a sudden jerk. Two men in striped uniform jump up on the wagon steps and shout: "We are free! We are free! Get out of the wagons!"

Cold air rushes in. The two men disappear and the occupants of the wagon awake from a lethargic daze.

"What? What happened?"

All surge toward the wide-open doors. Drunk with the sudden onrush of fresh air, one by one we lumber as quickly as we can down the metal step. The boxcar is empty within minutes.

Outside, the cold fresh air is filled with the noise of thousands pouring out of the wagons, scampering down the high embankment, shouting, shouting, embracing. The entire valley is filled with the swarming multitude of striped prison uniforms, of gray women's dresses. Others crowd on the tracks, between the wagons. Many are simply milling about, embracing everyone they meet: "We are free! We are free!"

Most inmates head for the cornfield, and you can see hundreds breaking off young green husks and eating them. Others are headed for the village to get food. But where are the Americans? Or the Germans? Only inmates are to be seen everywhere. Inmates wherever the eye can see.

"Mommy, let's go to the cornfield. We will pick some corn. Or to the village to get food. Everyone is going."

"I am not going from here until we find Bubi. He is in this transport and we must find him."

"How can we find him? That's impossible. There are thousands here, everywhere. We don't know where he is. Maybe he, too, went to the fields or to the village. We will never find him here at the train."

"I am not going anywhere until we find him. He could not go to the field. How could he get off this steep embankment with his injured leg? He has no strength to walk even. He must be here somewhere among the cars."

We start to walk along the endless row of wagons. Mommy suggests that we look into each wagon. Perhaps Bubi fainted or was too weak to get off, and he is in one of them.

There are quite a few women and men in some of the wagons unable or unwilling to get off. Some are asleep, or, perhaps, dead. They do not answer when we call to them. None of them is Bubi.

There are some who, like us, are simply walking along the tracks. But they do not seem to be looking for anyone. They are walking about in a daze. When we address them, inquiring about Bubi, they do not answer. There are a few who sit or lie on the ground, unaware of what is happening. But the multitude has left the train area. They are down in the valley or in the village. The green field is covered with prisoners.

"Mommy, there is no point in hanging about here. This train is endless. We cannot look in every wagon. We must hurry and get some food."

"I am not leaving until we find Bubi. I am not leaving until we find Bubi. I am not leaving until we . . . Bubi!"

He is walking toward us with slow, limping steps, dragging his tattered, injured leg.

"Bubi!"

I cannot believe my eyes. This cannot be. Among the thousands . . . He, too, was looking for us. Near the wagons.

He is in poor condition. He is barely breathing. His wound

has opened and is bleeding slightly. His face is bruised. Someone in the wagon had kicked him in the face.

We sit down on the pebbles lining the tracks. What should we do next? Bubi is not strong enough to go anywhere. We have to get food. I am going down to the village and get food. Mommy and Bubi will stay near the train until I return.

"You will go nowhere. We will not be separated. We will stay together."

Just then a young man passes, carrying a large piece of bread. Several inmates found the Germans' food-storage wagon and raided it. When the young man sees us, he breaks off a piece of bread and offers it to me.

I point to my brother. "Give it to him, he needs it worse than I."

The young inmate shrugs his shoulders and walks on. What an idiot I am! Why didn't I take the bread?

We get up and start walking in the direction from which the young prisoner came. Perhaps we, too, can get some food from the German food wagon. As we approach we see the wagon going up in flames. Someone put a torch to the wagon while dozens of prisoners were inside. Half-burned bodies are rolling in the grass. Others burn inside the wagon. And all the food is going up in flames.

I am very tired. "Let's sit down."

There is a German rifle in the grass. Down below an SS soldier is racing down the embankment. He must have just dropped the rifle.

Bubi bends down to pick it up. He falls.

"Elli, quick! Get that rifle and shoot him! He is not too far yet."

"Shoot? I can't. I can't kill anyone."

"Shoot him or I will!" He gets up and reaches for the rifle. I shriek: "Bubi, don't!"

He is not able to lift it, and the rifle remains lying in the grass.

We sit on the embankment while all about us the inmates

are disappearing. We are almost all alone near the tracks. Suddenly, from somewhere, a round of fire is heard. More shooting. Louder. In the valley inmates are falling like flies. Shouts. More shooting. Cries of pain and large numbers lying in pools of blood among the corn. Shouts in German. *"Zurück in die Waggonen! Los! Los!"* Back into the wagons!

Many are running through the field toward the embankment. Up the embankment toward the wagons.

SS troops close in on them from every direction, shooting. SS from all sides, firing incessantly. Inmates are falling in droves. "Back into the wagons!"

What happened? Where are the Americans?

Within minutes the embankment is full with inmates once again. But so is the green valley. Inmates bleeding, lying prone, lifeless. Striped uniforms stud the green valley with pools of red.

We get up also and hurry toward the wagons. Mommy decides that Bubi will stay with us. We will not be separated.

"How? They will send me into the men's wagons, and you will go back to the other end, with women."

Mommy tears a piece from her skirt. "Here." She ties it about Bubi's head as if it were a kerchief. "No one will notice. You will stay with us in the car. I will take care of you."

In the great commotion no one pays attention to us. Within a short time the boxcar fills to half capacity and the doors are closed shut. The train begins to roll. The sun is setting. It is getting dark and very cold.

The train rolls past the valley of the dead and the dying. Onward. Where to? What has happened?

There are some wounded among us. But they have only superficial flesh wounds. Arm or leg grazed by bullet as they were running for the wagons. Does anyone know what has happened?

Yes, some know. Some girls reached the village and there they heard that the Americans are in the nearby village. Then the German troops arrived. Someone in the village radioed for help. It was believed a train full of prisoners mutinied. The villagers were alarmed when they saw the inmates streaming into the village, stripping the cornfield. They notified the field commander, and he must have called for the troops. It all has been a mistake. We were prematurely told we were liberated. But what about our guards? Where were they? What became of them? They must have deserted during the night. That is why we stayed all those hours in one place. Some of our men must have realized we were unguarded and believed we were liberated. That is when they opened the doors. The Americans are still far away. And we are back in the wagons once again.

Except those who are lying dead in the cornfield. Hundreds. Their expression of freedom was silenced suddenly, arbitrarily. We move on, hungry, cold, and very tired. It is Sabbath eve.

THIRTY-FIVE

Bubi is lying motionless with closed eyes. The train keeps moving all night among high mountains, dark forests. It is very cold in the boxcar. Three sisters from a small village in Hungary huddle in the corner near Bubi. I know them from Augsburg.

"Move," the oldest says to the two younger ones. "Move closer to him. He looks feverish. We will get a little warmer."

They all move closer to my brother who seems delirious. It must be his leg, I think. The wound must have gotten infected again. I should warn them about his lice. They will all be infested with lice within minutes. But I am too weak. And too tired.

Mommy and I huddle together trying to warm each other. Neither of us says anything. What will happen next? Where

are we being taken? The brief freedom, the hunger, the shooting, Bubi with us in the wagon, the cold night, the uncertainty.
. . . Slowly I fall asleep.

The early dawn filters bright sunrays through the small
window. We are moving along slowly. In a slow but steady
rhythm. The train rattles and shakes, bobbing the heads of
pale, prone bodies.

Bubi is still lying in the same position on his back, with eyes
closed. His breath comes in a labored stream through half-
open lips. His face is white except for the large bruise on his
left cheek and the red patches on his cheekbones. The two
younger sisters are lying against his body, asleep. Mommy is
also lying with eyes closed. Many girls are awake but do not
stir. One of them is unwrapping the bandage on her arm. She
bandaged her arm yesterday with a rag torn from her skirt.
Silently she is examining her wound now.

There are a few girls I know from Augsburg, but most of
the inmates now with us in the car are strangers. No one
complains about having a boy in the wagon. Most probably
they do not even notice. The mood is that of deep apathy.
Post-liberation trauma. And hunger manifests itself in loss of
mental effort.

By noon we reach a station and the train stops. The cessa-
tion of movement, of constant rattle and rhythmic shaking,
awakens the inhabitants of the boxcar. One by one they stir,
open their eyes, and pull themselves into sitting position. But
Bubi still lies motionless.

Mommy crawls over to him, stepping over the bodies of
those around him.

"Bubi! Bubi, what is the matter?" She is stroking his face.
He opens his eyes.

"I am dizzy," he says, and shuts his eyes again.

There are loud voices outside. One of the girls crawls over
to the window and peers out.

"There are white trucks with large red crosses on them, and
German soldiers milling about." Her voice is a croak.

The Red Cross. What does the Red Cross want with us? Perhaps they will take the wounded.

There are more shouts, and then someone quite near our wagon shouts in German: "All line up with your dish in hand near the window. The Red Cross is handing out warm soup to you. One by one step to the window and reach out with your dish."

Food! Warm food! In minutes there is a crowd at the window. I untie my dish from about my waist and stand up with great effort. The wagon is spinning about me. Holding on to the wall of the car I walk with difficulty toward the crowd at the window. Mommy helps Bubi to his feet, but then it seems he will fall right down again. She tries to prop him up but both tumble to the floor. I manage to reach them, and the two of us pull Bubi to his feet.

By the time we reach the window, the crowd dwindles. Many are sitting and drinking the steaming yellow soup. Its aroma fills the car. It is our turn. Mommy is supporting Bubi with both hands as he steps over to the window and reaches out with his right hand holding the dish. I stand behind Mommy.

At that moment machine-gun fire is heard. A sudden impact hurls Bubi backwards against Mommy and both of them fall to the floor. Blood is spurting from Bubi's forehead. His hand, still holding the dish, is covered with blood. Machine-gun fire comes in bursts. Everyone about me falls to the floor. Blood is bubbling from the shoulder of the girl next to me. Another one tumbles to the floor, face down, her soup spilled. There is a round hole in the middle of her back spurting blood like a fountain. As I lie on the floor I can see bursts of fire shooting through the walls and zigzagging in the car. One such flash hits the youngest village sister in the left cheek. Her eye splatters on her cheek. She tumbles sideways against her sister.

I grab my metal dish and put it on my head for protection. Whatever happens I must survive. Arms, legs do not matter. I must protect my head.

"Mommy, put your dish on your head. And lie flat on the floor." But Mommy does not hear. She is holding Bubi's head in her lap. She tears a piece from her skirt and is bandaging the bleeding wound.

"Mommy! Lie flat. You will get hit. Put your dish on your head to protect it. Mommy, leave him alone. There is nothing you can do for him. He was hit in the head. You can't help him anymore. Lie down so you are not killed, too. Mommy, please."

I am hysterical. I know this is the end. Yet somehow I want to survive. Somehow, by some miracle. Even though around me everyone is dying, I want to survive. Panic paralyzes me into this one obsessive thought. I want to live. To live. The Germans set up the trap of the Red Cross food trucks in order to line us up at the windows and machine-gun us easily. This is the end. They will keep on shooting until everyone in the boxcars is dead. Yet, somehow I must stay alive. I must. I must live.

Mommy is not concerned about herself. She cradles Bubi's head in her lap unaware of the machine-gun fire which keeps up a relentless barrage. A young girl's leg is torn off at the knee. She sits holding her leg. Now she begins screaming. As she lets go, the lower leg falls to the floor, and the kneebone, a bloody stump, protrudes from her tattered thigh. She is Lilli, the sixteen-year-old pretty brunette with the lovely voice I idolized in Augsburg. I had always wanted to be like her, a petite brunette with a lovely voice. I grab her leg and press it against the bloody knee stump, holding it there. It is still attached by a shred of skin. Lilli obeys my insane impulse, and holds onto the leg, believing that thereby it will grow together again.

"Hold it!" I scream before I take my hands away. "Hold it!" Lilli holds the leg, her hands overflowing with blood.

The shooting has finally stopped. A sudden deadly silence. We look at each other. Did the shooting really stop? Is it all over? We are not all dead. Eight dead, many wounded. And some not hit at all. I am bloody but I know I have not been hit. Neither has Mommy. Bubi lies unconscious but he, too, is alive. He is breathing, and blood is seeping through the rag Mommy had tied about his head. He is bleeding also at the right elbow. He has been shot in two places.

Lilli is sitting in a pool of blood. She is trembling. I clutch her shoulder and ask her if she is in pain. She says no, but she is cold and dizzy. The sister whose eye was shot is alive, too. She is conscious and complains of a headache. She does not seem to realize she has lost her eye. She keeps on asking her sisters if her wound is large, and they keep reassuring her that it is not. One of the three Stadler sisters from Dunaszerdahely is dead and another one, the youngest, wounded in one arm, is bleeding profusely. The middle one, a tall girl with a lame leg, keeps comforting her. The girl shot in the back was their oldest sister, a teacher. Once she substituted for our teacher in Somorja. I liked her better than our teacher and had told her so in Augsburg. It made her happy, and from then on she gave me a smile every time we passed each other. Now she is lying face down on the wagon floor, the hole in the middle of her back oozing dark blood. She is dead.

All at once the doors of the wagon slide open. German soldiers stand in the doorway and tell us to get out if we can. The enemy planes are expected to return and stage another attack. We are permitted to leave the wagons and hide among the trees of the forest. *Los!*

Some start to drag themselves toward the doors. But most are unable to move. The Germans are shouting. *Los!* The planes are coming! I see several German soldiers running up on an incline toward the forest.

"Elli, go to the forest. I cannot move. I have no strength. I am staying here with Bubi in the wagon."

"You must come. Pull yourself together. You can make it."

"But what about Bubi? We cannot leave him here."

I know Bubi is beyond help. I have not heard his breathing

for some time now, but I do not want to leave Mother behind. So I suggest that we carry Bubi with us. I crawl over and lift Bubi by the shoulders. Without protest, Mommy lifts his legs and we start dragging him toward the door. He opens his eyes.

"Bubi! Mommy, he opened his eyes! He is alive!"

"Of course he is alive. You did not know?"

I do not answer. I was wrong. He *is* alive. My God! I begin to cry and tears are dripping on his head as I drag him by the shoulders. At the door Mommy says she cannot get down, she is too dizzy. I let go of Bubi's shoulders but first prop him up in a sitting position. Then I climb out of the wagon and help Mommy down. In the meantime Bubi has recovered somewhat. He says he can get off the wagon with some help. He does not have to be carried. Thank God.

Once outside, Mommy sits on the ground. She is too weak to stand up. I help Bubi down and as he is leaning on my shoulder I start to pull at Mommy's arm to get her upright. People are crawling up on the green hill to the shade of the trees. It is a climb of about ten feet.

Mommy lets herself be pulled to her feet and the three of us begin to cross the tracks, holding on to each other. But there is a wire running horizontally alongside the tracks about a foot high in the air and neither Bubi nor Mommy can step over that. They try but cannot lift their legs high enough. I bend down to lift Bubi's leg but he loses his balance.

Mommy begins to shout: "No use. No use. I cannot go on. Elli, you go ahead. Leave us here."

A low, steady hum of approaching planes. They are back. There is no time.

"Let's crawl under the wagons."

On all fours we crawl under the boxcar. A few other inmates are there. Miriam Stadler and her younger sister are lying on their bellies, the sister's arm still bleeding heavily. The planes are flying low. There is a clearing at the edge of the forest some hundred yards ahead and a plane dives down to spray bullets into the forest where inmates and German soldiers are clustering. It is an American plane! Incredible. So it is true. It was an "enemy" attack. Why would American planes shoot at a concentration camp transport? Can't they see the striped uniforms?

The planes fly overhead, spray bullets in every direction, and fly off. In minutes they return and attack again.

A woman next to me is hit and killed instantly. Miriam Stadler lies on top of her wounded little sister. The planes returned a third time, and I can see the bluish flashes zigzag in every direction. The noise of the low-flying planes is ear-shattering.

Miriam Stadler whispers: "Don't worry, I will not let them hurt you this time. I am covering you. If they shoot here, it is I who will be hit, not you."

Her sister does not answer. She is dead. A bullet in the neck has killed her.

Miriam Stadler goes wild. She crawls out from under the boxcar. She stands there waving her arms at the sky and screams: "God! Do you see me? I am here. Kill me! Kill me! You killed my two sisters. My beautiful talented sisters. And you left me, a cripple. Why didn't you leave them? Why didn't you kill me instead? Kill me now! I don't want to live. What will I tell my parents? What will I tell my mother? Oh, God!"

Mommy calls to her: "Miriam, come here. Come here, fast."

Miriam, in a daze, turns around and crawls back under the wagon. She embraces her dead sister and begins to sob.

The planes are gone. We wait but they do not return.

Miriam sobs: "What will I tell my parents? The cripple survived! And my two beautiful sisters are dead."

We wait a long time. The planes do not return. The attack is over. The Germans and the inmates start to come out of the forest. We, too, crawl from under the wagons. Miriam pulls her dead sister out.

"Back into the wagons!"

Miriam carries her sister on her shoulder. Mommy and

Bubi and I hold on to each other and struggle back into the wagon. Miriam carries her dead sister into the car and lays her next to the older one who is face down near the wall. The wounded lie silently. The girl shot in the eye is dead. Her sister sits next to her, staring vacantly into the air. Two other wounded died while we were out.

The wagon floor is covered with pools of blood. We sit in a dry corner. Lilli lies in a stupor, trembling violently, her leg hanging on a shred of skin.

Two Germans come to the door: "Are there any corpses in this car?"

"Yes, there are."

"How many?"

We count. "Twelve."

Two male inmates climb into the wagon and begin carrying out the dead. They place them on the pebbles next to the tracks. Miriam Stadler pleads with them not to take her sisters away. But no one heeds her pleas, and both of them are put on the heap of bodies facing the entrance of the wagon.

The sun is setting by the time the train begins to pull out. The doors are left open. Miriam stands, staring at the bodies of her sisters as the wheels roll by with increasing clatter and speed.

"Remember, Miriam," Mother tells her, "the anniversary of your sisters' deaths is three days before Lag B'Omer. Today is the thirtieth day of Omer. That is the *Yahrzeit* of your sisters."

I look at Mommy with amazement. How can she have her wits about her at such moments? How can she remember the Hebrew date after what we have just been through?

The train picks up speed. It is getting dark. Sabbath is coming to a close. April 28, 1945.

THIRTY-SIX

THE TRAIN rolls on and on throughout the night. It is bitter cold in the wagon. The door stands wide open. The Germans know that no one will escape. Most of the transport is wounded, some critically and the others are weak from hunger. We have not eaten since Monday evening, five days ago. Or perhaps they do not care whether we escape or not. Everything is drawing to an end. Most of the guards are gone. Some deserted on Thursday before the sham liberation, others during the air attack today. Only a few came out of the forest after the attack. Perhaps some inmates escaped also during the attack. The train is largely empty now. There are only twelve persons in our wagon. I saw several cars completely empty as we reentered the train.

We roll with a steady, loud clatter amid high mountains and deep forests. Lakes glisten with eerie gray light. There is silence in the boxcar. Bubi is lying with closed eyes, his head in Mommy's lap. She sits, leaning against the wall in the corner, her head hanging to one side. Her mouth is wide open. I know she is asleep. Lilli is silent now. She stopped whimpering some time after the train began to move. I touch her. She is very hot. Miriam is silent, too. She is not asleep, though. She is sitting in a far corner, staring ahead. Her eyes seem enormous in the shadowy darkness of the car. The two remaining sisters from the little Hungarian village huddle together, asleep. The girl with the shoulder injury, Judy from Budapest, sits upright in the corner opposite Mommy and Bubi. She is awake. She makes the only human sound in the wagon. She is wheezing. Sometimes she gasps for air, and then Mommy trembles in fright, opening her eyes and promptly closing them again, letting her head fall to one side again. I think Judy must have been shot in the lungs. The bullet must have entered her lungs through her shoulder. That is why she has trouble breathing. I hope we will be liberated soon. She needs medical attention urgently.

Two cousins joined our car after the attack. One of them is injured in the face. Just as they were running to the forest, a blinding flash hit her in the face. Her cousin, Martha, bandaged her face with the kerchief she had received from her father in Dachau. Martha believed her father was in the transport also and she looked for him during the fake liberation on Friday, and then again during the attack on Saturday, but did not find him. As Irene's face was bandaged and she could not see, Martha helped her climb into the nearest wagon, our wagon.

Now they are lying next to me. Both seem asleep. Suddenly, Irene grows restless. She lifts her head and rips the kerchief off her face. Then sits up abruptly.

"Martha!" She begins to shriek. "Martha! I can't see! I can't see anything!" Martha awakens.

"Don't take off your bandage. Your face is still bleeding."

"But I can't see! The bandage is off and I can't see anything! I am blind! Martha, I am blind! My God, I am blind! I am blind! I am blind!"

Her screams awaken everyone. Words of comfort pour from all sides. She is told that it is dark in the car, no one sees anything; and that her blindness may be only temporary, caused by the sudden flash she saw; and that she has lost much blood, she is simply too weak and therefore cannot see; and that her face is swollen because of her wound and so are her eyelids, and that blocks her vision. . . . Finally, she quiets down, and all settle back into lethargic silence.

But Irene does not relax completely. She lies down and begins to talk in a low voice. She talks at first about the attack, describing every detail of the first machine-gun barrage on their wagon. Then about their flight to the forest and the flash which first blinded her and threw her to the ground and then made her bleed profusely. She keeps repeating the description of her experience again and again. With each repetition her voice grows more hoarse. Her phrases begin to slur . . . her sentences become disjointed, confused. But she talks on.

Martha attempts to quiet her. To no avail. Irene does not seem to hear. I touch her gesticulating arm. It is very hot. Then she begins to speak about her family. Her hometown in Czechoslovakia, her mother and father, her grandmother, her sisters . . .

Pale light of dawn floods the wagon. I look at Irene's face. Two empty eye sockets stare back at me. I cover my face with my hands. God! Oh, God! God!

All at once Irene grabs my arm. "Look there! Do you see it? What a beautiful meadow! Beautiful! Do you see it? There!"

She gesticulates wildly. With both hands she points in the direction of the dark wagon wall. "There! Beautiful! Beautiful, beautiful meadow . . . trees . . . birds . . . beautiful . . ."

Then she is silent.

Lilli begins to whimper again. When I ask her if she is in pain, she does not answer. Her mouth is dry. Her leg is not bleeding anymore. Then, in a barely audible tone she whispers: "Water . . ."

With the brightening of the morning light I see that she is very pale. I touch her forehead. It is not hot anymore. I stroke her face gently. I have no strength to cry, I have no tears, no tears at all. Yet I hold a sob deep within. Somewhere deep within I am sobbing. Not in my mind. My mind is blank. My God! I am losing my mind. I am not functioning. In my stomach . . . I am sobbing in my stomach as I am stroking the cooling forehead of pretty little Lilli lying next to the ravaged face of Irene. The seventeen-year-old gentle-voiced Irene. Irene with both eyes shot out. Irene, lying now in silent stupor. My mind is blank. But I have a trembling in my belly.

"Mommy," Lilli whispers. "Mommy. I am going to do it, Mommy . . . yes . . . oh, yes . . ."

Her head falls back onto the floor of the wagon. She is dead.

During the morning hours Irene dies, too. The train rolls on.

All day we keep moving. The hills grow taller as we move through curving valleys, deep valleys with steep rocky walls. The hills are tall and covered with snow. It is bitter cold in the wagon. The rattle of the train pounds on every nerve.

We wait silently for the hours to pass. Silently and motionlessly, we lie on the floor of the wagon. And wait.

The blood has long dried on the floor. The cloth soaked with blood on Bubi's head has also dried, and his torn jacket sleeve hangs stiffly on his right elbow caked with blood.

Irene and Lilli are silent now and their presence hushes the mood of the rest. No one sleeps as the bitter cold wind numbs our senses into a strange state of alertness. No one speaks.

Only Judy's constant wheezing breaks the silence of the wagon. Her painful gasps for air are the only signs and sounds of life among the ten survivors in the boxcar. Our motionlessness and our silence betray reality. We are dead. Dead survivors of a long-lost struggle.

But the train moves on. All day. All night.

When the first flickers of dawn pierce the wagon, I realize that we have been standing for some time. I must have dozed off after all. Everyone is asleep, the dead and the living dead.

I want to look to see where we are standing, but I cannot move. My limbs seem frozen. So I just lie there, waiting. Waiting for the train to move again. For the rattle which has become the only rhythm of life.

Slowly eyes open. But no one moves. No one breaks the frozen compulsion of motionlessness. No one speaks. We wait.

In midmorning sounds reach us. Human voices. A shadow is cast into the wagon and voices seem quite near. With effort I lift my head.

Two tall men in a strange uniform stand in the doorway of the wagon. They look at us with a curious expression. One of them shakes his head and says something to the other. I do not understand what he says. I am very tired, it is difficult to concentrate. Then the two tall men leave.

In a few minutes another man, a heavyset man with reddish cheeks, also in a strange uniform, comes up into the car. He speaks loudly in strangely accented Yiddish: "Are you Jews? Do you understand me? Can you speak Yiddish? Can you hear me? Who can understand me?"

We all stare at him without answering. Finally, Martha, who sits nearest to the entrance, replies: "We understand you. Who are you?"

"We are Americans. But who are you? Are you Jews? Where are you from?"

"Americans!"

We struggle into a sitting position.

"Americans!"

So it has come. We are liberated. It is all over now. We are free. The Americans have finally come. The Americans are here, they have come at last. At last.

"Are you really an American? Where are the Germans?"

"The Germans surrendered. We have arrested your German guards. But who are you? What prison camp do you come from? Are you Jews? Are you men or women?"

"We are women. Jewish women from the concentration camp Dachau. There is only one man among us. There. A young boy. But he is wounded. He can't walk. Most of us can't walk. We are wounded and we are starved. We are unable to walk."

So this is it. Liberation. It has come. My mind is blank. I do not understand. I do not feel. These are Americans. Our liberators. But I cannot feel. I am numb with cold. With hunger. With death and blood and the noisy rattle of the train rolling on and on and on . . .

Mommy is silent, and Bubi does not comprehend. And I am unable to get up. I am too weak. Perhaps in a little while. Not now.

"Can you get off the wagon?"

The tall, red-cheeked American officer is addressing me. He speaks very loud, in very strange-sounding Yiddish.

"I will try."

He gives me a hand and I stand up. He helps me off the wagon. Then he helps Mother.

"My son cannot get on his feet. Someone has to carry him."

Two civilians carry Bubi out of the wagon. They put him on the ground next to the wall of the station house. One by one they carry out all the others who cannot walk. The bodies of Lilli and Irene are also carried out and placed on the ground. The entire station is filled with dead and wounded. And the living, also covered with dried blood, sprawl among them on the ground.

The heavyset American officer now stands at the head of a large group of civilians. He is making a speech in his strange Yiddish.

"Leading citizens of Seeshaupt. We brought you here so that you can see with your very eyes what your government has wrought. Look at these people! Have you ever seen human beings in such misery? Have you ever seen such living skeletons? These are innocent people who were subjected to this horror by your government. Starved beyond recognition, maimed, and killed. Look at the many dead and wounded! Look at the survivors of your concentration camps!"

A distinguished-looking elderly German steps forward and gives a reply. He says they are all appalled and shocked at what they see and claims they knew nothing about concentration camps. They had no idea. They had never heard of such horror. They are innocent. But they will see to it that we are restored to strength as soon as possible. Public kitchens will be set up to feed us, and the citizenry of Seeshaupt will open their homes to provide shelter. They are sorry.

People in the crowd shake their heads and keep muttering, *"Wir haben es nicht gewusst. Wir wissten gar nichts . . ."*

A middle-aged woman comes to me: "We did not know

anything. We had no idea. You must believe me. Did you have
to work hard also?"

"Yes. We worked also."

"At your age, it must have been difficult."

At my age. What does she mean? "Why at my age? It was
difficult because we did not get enough to eat. Not because of
my age."

"I meant it must have been harder for the older people.
What kind of work did you do?"

For older people? What is she talking about? "How old do
you think I am?"

She looks at me uncertainly. "Sixty? Sixty-two?"

"Sixty! I? I am fourteen. Fourteen years old."

She gives a little shriek and makes the sign of the cross on
herself.

"Forgive me . . . please. How was I to know? You are so
skinny. Your face. The bones in your face. I did not know.
Fourteen! Forgive me."

In horror and disbelief she walks away. She casts one more
glance at me as she joins the crowd of German civilians.

In the meantime, the dead and the heavily wounded are
placed on open carts by the German civilians and drawn out
of the station. Bubi is also put on one of these carts. Mother
and I walk right behind the cart. We do not want to be separated from Bubi.

The cart is drawn by two Germans. As we follow the cart, I
feel the world rush by me at an incredible pace. The cart rolls
out of the train station onto an open road flanked by wooden
fences. It churns up dust. As the wheels of the cart roll faster,
Mommy and I keep falling behind despite our desperate effort
to keep up. The wounded lie motionless on the wooden platform of the cart, Bubi among them. We keep losing sight of
them in the dust cloud that follows.

Mother is out of breath. I feel I am going to faint. We must
stop for a moment. The cart disappears. What now?

"Let's rest for a few minutes. We will catch up with the cart. We will find out where it went. First rest."

We sit down at the roadside. In a few minutes a huge, gray army truck full of American soldiers passes by. I wave to them. A tall young soldier with a dark, shiny face throws something to me. After the truck passes, I find it in the dust. It is a bar of chocolate. I pick it up. My hands tremble. Slowly I tear off the wrapping paper and take a bite, then offer it to Mother. It is the first bite of food after seven days. The first bite of food in freedom. A bite of American chocolate.

My mouth is very dry. It is difficult to swallow. Another truck passes. I wave to them and Mother points to her mouth. The American soldiers on the top of the truck understand. Several small objects fly at us. More chocolate bars. Biscuits. We pick them up eagerly but cannot eat them. Our lips are cracked, and our tongues will not move. They feel swollen and covered with some thick paste. I am getting dizzier.

Mother manages to eat a biscuit bar and insists that I try also. I cannot. We stuff chocolate bars into our pockets and struggle to our feet. We must find the cart which took Bubi.

Following the bend in the road where the cart disappeared, we find ourselves in town. A clean, neat little town with white houses and green lawns. Snow lies in patches on the lawns. A long row of army trucks keeps passing us. Packets of sweets scatter at our feet as the trucks roll by on the cobblestones of this strange German town.

At a street corner a cauldron is boiling on an open fire, and a stout German woman is handing out potatoes to a group of inmates. Mother and I join the group. We untie our metal pans from about our waists, and the German woman dishes several hot boiled potatoes into it.

An American jeep roars by. It comes to a sudden stop near our group huddled about the cauldron. One of the officers steps over to me. He reaches into his pocket and hands me a bar of chocolate. I shake my head.

"I can't swallow it," I say in German. "I am very thirsty."

He does not understand. I point to my tongue. Then make a drinking motion. His face brightens. He steps over to the jeep and brings out a metal container. As he unscrews it, the top becomes an aluminum cup. He pours a light pink liquid into it and hands it to me. It is cold and sweet. Pink lemonade.

I drink in large, eager gulps. He pours again. I turn to Mother. She is eating potatoes. She takes a sip but cannot drink. It is too cold, she says. I finish the lemonade and a rush of gratitude overwhelms me. I want to say thank you but suddenly my throat is too tight and my hands begin to tremble uncontrollably. The American officer notices my trembling as I hand him the cup. He places his hand on my head and says something in English. I do not understand. He returns to the jeep and drives off. I sit down on the ground next to Mommy and begin to eat the potatoes. My mouth is not too dry anymore. I can swallow.

As we walk on we pass another steaming cauldron on the street. It is black coffee served by another German woman. Mommy is able to drink the coffee. But I manage only a few sips. I have never drunk real coffee before. It is warm and it feels good. It is a very cold day. But my stomach starts to ache.

Now we are inquiring from everyone we meet about the carts with the wounded. Finally someone says the wounded were taken to the lazarette. Mommy says lazarette means hospital. We inquire after the lazarette until we come to a charming, white, two-storey building marked LAZARETTE in large black letters. But when we get there we find that the wounded are not there. They are instead in a storage house adjacent to the lazarette converted into an emergency hospital. The wounded lie on blankets on the floor, and some of them have fresh bandages on their wounds. Bubi is also lying on a blanket. He has not been treated yet, but he has had something to drink. He is very pale and is still in a daze.

Mommy and I volunteer to help nurse the wounded and ask to be allowed to stay there. A busy German doctor quickly agrees, and I am given a white porcelain wash basin and a white towel and told to wash the patients' face, hands, and feet.

My first patient is asleep. I do not want to disturb him, so I move to the one who lies on the next blanket. He is a very young boy with a bandaged leg. I wash his grimy and bloody face and hands, and when I am about to move on, he asks me for a drink. There is tea in the large kettle in the middle of the room. I bring him a cupful and find he cannot drink it alone. He cannot sit up even with my help, neither can he lift his head. I am surprised. I have not realized he is so very ill. I help him sip the tea slowly by lifting his head slightly. His neck feels very warm. He has a fever.

He asks for more tea and I feed him two more cups, then bring a small wet towel and wrap it about his head. He smiles at me. He says the cold towel feels good.

As I go about my work, sponging arms, legs, faces, carrying the wash basin back and forth for clean water, I keep returning to the young boy to freshen the cold compress about his head. He keeps smiling at my every approach. He becomes my special patient. As soon as I find a little time I sit down next to him and soon discover that he is fifteen and came from Salonika. He was with his father in Dachau, but his father was killed in the train and he was wounded in the leg. I call him Greco, his nickname in the camps. He likes the way I pronounce it and asks me to say it again and again.

In the evening Mother and I are given a room in the lazarette. By the time we get there it is quite late, and I am fatigued beyond anything I ever experienced before. We are allowed to use the showers. After we shower we receive clean hospital gowns and white beds. My first night in freedom. In a clean nightgown, a clean, white bed. But I could not fall asleep. There is a thought tearing at my insides.

What about all the wounded? The wounded in the nearby emergency hospital lie on rough army blankets on the floor. They were fed only tea and soup. Some of them needed serious medical attention but received only superficial care. When

I reported that Greco had fever, nothing was done for him. The only help he got was the wet towel I applied to his head. Not even an aspirin. Others were badly wounded and perhaps needed surgery. They were given first aid only. Nothing beyond that. What will their future be? Will freedom mean life to them?

THIRTY-SEVEN

IN THE morning I saw that there were many empty beds in the lazarette. But the wounded were not brought here. They were dirty and bloody and full of lice. The clean antiseptic German hospital was not to be infected by them. I decided to do something about it.

When I returned to the emergency room I found Greco propped up on a pillow; he was smiling when he saw me. He said I looked very nice. I had washed and found a hairbrush so my hair was parted and brushed to the side. One of the nurses gave me a small jar of hair cream, and with it I managed to accomplish the seemingly impossible: I forced my stubborn yellow bristles into shape. There was a mirror in the room where Mother and I slept. And I saw that my hair had grown in the last few weeks since Augsburg. It had grown long enough to be manageable. I felt grateful for Greco's compliment.

Bubi also looked better. Mother got some cereal and fed him. I wanted to begin feeding Greco's row but the first man on the row was sleeping again. Greco said he slept all afternoon and evening. I thought perhaps it was a good idea to wake him now and feed him some warm cereal. Gently I drew his blanket off his face and touched it. It was ice cold. He was dead.

I ran and called the nurse and she ordered two male nurses to carry him away. No questions were asked. Who was he? Why did he die? What was his injury? Did he have to die? Could he have been saved?

The German doctor came in much later. I told him of the incident and he said I should not worry. He will report it to the Americans.

The Americans? Where were they? I did not see an American ever since yesterday morning at the station. Where were they? Why did no one see to it that the injured were cared for? That all the others were fed? It was all left to the Germans. And the Germans did only what was unavoidable under the circumstances. But the Americans did not see whether all was done that had to be done in order to save the lives of survivors, alleviate hunger and pain. They delivered us to the compassion of the Germans and there their interest ended. A man died after the liberation. Perhaps he could have been saved by emergency surgery. Or by a bowl of soup. On time. Perhaps yesterday. Perhaps I should have awakened him yesterday. Perhaps I could have saved him. And did not. I was too busy with the others. I was sponging hands and faces while this man died.

Someone said there was an American army headquarters in town. I decided to speak to the officer in charge. But it was evening before I could get away from the emergency hospital. The patients had to be fed and cared for in other ways. Most of them had to be given bedpans. Bandages had to be changed. There was only one German doctor and two nurses, and there were hundreds of wounded. Most of them were feverish, and many of them had constant diarrhea. It was impossible to leave. Or to find time to rest. Or even go to the bathroom.

There were no toilet facilities in the emergency hospital. The doctor, nurses, Mother, and I used the toilet in the lazarette across the street. I found no time to go there. I ran behind the bushes in the garden of the hospital. As I was crouching in the shade of the thicket, my leg brushed against a cold object. It was a human head. I looked closer. It was the man who died this morning. Farther in the underbrush I saw three more bodies, two men and a girl. The girl was injured in the arm, but the two men did not appear wounded at all. Why did they die? My God, how many more dead are scattered in the gardens of this lovely resort? How can this be happening? Help me, God, please. What shall I do?

Suddenly I remembered Judy. Where could she be? She was not in our emergency hospital. Where did they take her? I did not remember what had happened at the station to the others. The whole thing seemed foggy and confused. It was only yesterday. Yesterday?

Since yesterday I have had a constant stomachache. It is cold. Today, May 2, it was snowing lightly. I am cold and have a stomachache, but have no time to think about it. The wounded need care, and Mother and I are the only people to work here besides the three Germans. Where are the other liberated ones? What became of them? What are they doing? Since yesterday I have not seen anyone but the wounded and the dead.

In the evening Mother and I went into town. It was not quite dark, and we could see it was a beautiful little resort with villas along tree-lined streets. The houses hugged the northern end of a beautiful lake. Later I found out that the name of the town derived from this fact. Seeshaupt, the head of the sea. The lake, a small sea, is called Starnberger See, a scenic lake about forty kilometers in length and eight in width. All around the Starnberger See there are resorts like See-shaupt—clean, graceful, and tranquil. Untouched by the war.

In the middle of the town several army trucks converged about an antiaircraft gun. A series of shots was heard and the soldiers gazed up at a plane directly above. The plane shook with every charge. Then it started careening down in a wide arc, in flames and smoke. The Americans applauded.

We moved on. Tanks and armored trucks passed with an awful noise. A soldier with a shiny black face threw a package of biscuits toward me. As I picked it up he flashed a happy smile. I had never seen a Negro before today. What an unusual face! Black and glowing. And the wide smile full of brilliant white teeth! How very white. It makes you feel good. Warm. Almost happy. A good, kind smile, a good, kind face.

We shouted to him: "Commandant!" We wanted to see the red-cheeked officer who was in charge yesterday. At the time of the liberation. He must be the commandant of this army.

But the splendid black-faced American just smiled and waved to us as the tank passed by. Others came, but on the other tanks the soldiers were preoccupied and paid no heed to Mommy and me. It was cold and damp. We reached the main square. There were many people congregating about several green tents. Outside the tents stood a cauldron and a tall, heavy American soldier was ladling steaming food into bowls, and another soldier was handing them out to a motley crowd. As we drew nearer we saw that there were several concentration camp inmates in the crowd. They told us that this was the American army headquarters and you could get food here once a day. We asked them about the officer in charge and they pointed to a tall, thin officer with very short red hair and said that he was a Jew and spoke a little Yiddish, American Yiddish, but that it was possible to understand him and he also understood us. His name was Captain Kline. We could speak to him. He was a good man and would listen to us.

I approached the tall red-headed Jewish–American and told him about the wounded in the lazarette and that there was no one to take care of them or feed them. Here they are serving German civilians and the inmates are dying of their wounds and of hunger. I started to cry as I spoke and I am afraid I did not make a very good impression. My Yiddish was halting and mingled with German. He did not seem to understand me. I was crying like a fool when I finished.

He looked at me and said nothing. Mommy was talking now.

When she told him the same things with more emphasis, he

said: "I understand. But listen. The war is still going on. You understand? We are fighting here. Right here, outside of this town a battle is going on. There is no one who can do anything now. Not until the war is over. The war, you understand. It is not over yet. Maybe tomorrow it will be over. Maybe in two or three days. Not today. Today there is still fighting, understand? Are you hungry?"

I was hungry and cold. My shoes were soaked through with snow. I had no stockings and my toes felt frozen. He took out a handkerchief from his pocket and handed it to me. I blew my nose. Strange. The handkerchief was paper. Soft thin paper. A paper handkerchief. I carefully folded it and put it in my pocket. I must show this to Bubi. A paper handkerchief. He will never believe it.

The red-headed Jewish–American called to the stout soldier who was ladling the food, and he handed him two bowls full of food. They were for Mommy and me. It was hot stew. With small pieces of meat. Hot and spicy. It warmed my whole body. But the choking sense of misery remained.

He said there was nothing that could be done until the war was over. But inmates were dying every day. When will the war end, who knows? How many more will die until then? I cannot believe nothing could be done. There was time to feed the Germans of this town. There must be time for the inmates whose lives were at stake. There must be some way. The Germans could be organized to help.

I stepped over to Captain Kline.

"Something must be done now. If someone just came to the lazarette and saw. To show the Germans that the Americans care. Then they would do more to help. Something must be done."

I was not crying anymore. The American listened.

"Okay," he said. "Okay, someone will go there tomorrow. Maybe I will go there. But don't cry."

It was late by the time we got back to the emergency hospital. Most of the patients were asleep. Bubi was asleep, too.

But Greco was awake. He asked me for a drink. He was hot.

After I gave him the drink I was going to tiptoe out of the room and go across the street to our room and sleep. I was very tired. But Greco asked for another cup of cold tea, and after I gave it to him, he said he felt a lot of pain in his leg. I decided to send for the doctor but he was nowhere to be found. A nurse gave me some aspirins for Greco. Finally, at about midnight, he fell asleep and I went to my room.

The next morning was sunny and much warmer. I slept late. It was almost eight o'clock when I got back to the emergency ward. Mommy was feeding some patients. Bubi was up and about. He was sitting in a chair and eating. I went to see Greco. He must have slept through the night. When I left him last night, he was sleeping peacefully.

But Greco's mat was empty. The blankets were disheveled and he was nowhere. I asked the nurse in the next room.

"Which one? Greco? *Ja*, the Greek boy. He died during the night."

"That can't be! I was with him until midnight. He was better. He fell asleep."

"I don't know. I think he is dead. A young boy. Greek. He was taken away early this morning."

"Taken away? Where? Where was he taken?"

"I don't know. The dead are taken somewhere. I don't know where."

That cannot be. Greco cannot be dead. I took care of him. I took special care of him. He was not so sick. He was better. Last night he said he felt much better. How can he be dead now?

The other patients confirmed what the nurse had said. He died during the night and was taken away in the morning.

Oh, no. No. He can't. Greco can't be dead. He survived. He could not die.

I ran into the garden. But there were no corpses in the bushes. Greco was taken somewhere else. It was a warm, sunny morning. I walked among the trees. And then convulsive sobbing took hold of me. Greco! Greco! I cannot bear your death! I can't bear it! A violent spasm of nausea took hold of my intestines. I began to vomit. But the nausea kept rising in waves, and I had to vomit again and again. My tears were tears of disgust. I was disgusted with myself, with the mess I made in the garden, with the taste and smell of vomit. I hated my guts.

I was shaking. The vomiting left me too weak to cry, too sick to grieve. Yet the pain of Greco's death was sharp and unbearable in my belly. It oozed through my bowels like burning acid. I had to vomit again.

For days I walked about fighting waves of nausea. Mommy thought I was getting sick. Just now when Bubi was getting better.

But I was not sick at all. I was almost too tired to nurse the patients as I had before. I did things automatically, and then in the evening I fell into my bed exhausted. Daily I went into the garden, and there, among the trees, I threw up. I did not feel better after my daily vomiting, but I felt it had to be performed. It was a ritual.

It was there, among the trees, that I heard the bells. A hundred church bells ringing, ringing, long and loud. Church bells of this town and of other towns far away. What was it? What was going on?

It is the end of the war, I was told. Germany has surrendered to the Allies. It was Shabbat noon. The seventh of May 1945.

THIRTY-EIGHT

WE STAYED in Seeshaupt one more week. Bubi recovered sufficiently to leave the lazarette during the day. So he started to walk about the town. He brought us news of large groups of prisoners who were looting the town; they were mostly Russians from a nearby POW camp. He saw beautiful art treasures destroyed, furniture axed to pieces, a piano smashed, chandeliers shattered. Lovely Seeshaupt was beginning to experience the war.

One day he brought me a lovely white-and-red print dress and a white blouse. He found them in an abandoned villa that was being ransacked by the Russians. If felt strange to touch the lovely fabric of the dress, to try it on. It was too large for either Mommy or me. The owner must have been a huge woman. Not fat, only tall and strong. We folded the blouse and dress and put them in a paper bag. Perhaps one day they would fit.

Mommy and I went to town only in the evening. There was much work at the lazarette. But at the end of the second week several patients left the emergency ward and others were transferred to a general hospital in Gauting. And we—Mommy, Bubi, and I—were going to Munich. There, in the Flack Kaserne, a transit camp was set up. From there transports were leaving for home. We decided to get home as soon as possible.

During the second week of May the weather warmed up and Seeshaupt was glowing in the reflection of the shimmering See. The night before we left the resort town, I walked along the lake shore until I reached a small pier where sailboats were anchored. I sat in the grass and watched the stars light up in the reflection of the calm water. Suddenly, gay laughter rippled the darkening breeze. In a larger boat two Americans sat and in their embrace two German girls lolled, shrieking with delight.

Blood rushed to my head. Americans with Germans, frolicking! One week after the end of the war!

How could they? Our liberators cavorting with our murderers. How could they do it?

As I watched them, my alienation became a heavy burden. It sat like a leaden weight. The war was over but I remained prisoner. The enemy became friend but I remained a stranger. An outsider. Even with the Americans, our liberators. Oh, God, what is liberty? What is a liberator?

THIRTY-NINE

WE WERE taken to the Flack Kaserne in large American military trucks. The Flack Kaserne was an enormous German army camp a few kilometers outside Munich. We drove through Munich in order to reach it.

Munich lay in ruins. Entire streets in huge heaps of rubbish, rows upon rows of houses like halved skeletons. Sections could boast not a single house intact. Broken pipes and smokestacks rose to the sky like paralyzed shrieks. A bathtub hung in the air dangling alonside a wall which stood dangerously erect amid a sea of ruin. A church tower protruded sideways in a particularly colorful heap of masonry and bricks. Glorious Munich, birthplace of Nazism!

Vast stretches of Flack Kaserne were studded by neat rows of army barracks abandoned by the German army but now occupied by refugees of different nationalities. Each barrack flew a different-colored flag. We were ushered into a block through an entrance marked by a huge picture of Tito draped in red and green. I had never seen that congenial fat face with the full toothy smile before. It was Bubi who recognized it. He remembered it from the newspapers back home.

"That's Tito up there. This must be the Yugoslav Block."

"So that is Tito. Handsome. What a handsome smile."

Tito had been a hero to us in the first years of the war. His escapades against the Germans had made daily headlines. I was glad to be placed in a Block graced by Tito's picture. I knew I would like the Yugoslavs.

We were given a room with three beds. There was nothing else in it except a single chair in one corner.

We put our bundles down; we had some belongings now. We had been issued blankets and sheets and towels, and I had received a comb, a hairbrush, and a toothbrush in the laza-rette. And, of course, there was the dress Bubi brought me in Seeshaupt.

We needed a table, chairs, and hooks to hang our clothes. A short, fat man with a heavy Slav accent and an armband was running busily about, so we asked him for a table and some chairs, but he said there weren't any and hurried on. But later Bubi discovered that some of the other rooms were fully and quite luxuriously furnished. One of these rooms was open and looked unoccupied, so we decided to "organize" the table and the chairs. ("Organize" was the term used in the concentra-tion camp for the acquisition of any necessity—food, articles of clothing, etc.) The next morning we grew bolder and or-ganized the rest of the furniture—a chest, night tables, even a carpet. Our organization now resulted in a well-furnished, pretty room for the three of us. There was excitement in set-ting up this room—a strange, unexpected joy. We had a home. And we delighted in it.

Bubi discovered an empty barrack whose attic was stocked with many useful objects, among them a typewriter. He called me, and the two of us carried it to our room. It was very heavy, and Bubi almost dropped it as we were dragging it down the stairs. Our joy was unbounded. A typewriter of our very own. Mine, said Bubi, but you can use it, too. Thank you. We had no paper. So our next project was to "organize" paper. From somewhere.

In the attic Bubi discovered a large can of some kind of brown ointment. It was smooth and greasy, and he decided to apply it to his body. His body was still covered with sores that refused to heal. Some were oozing pus. He thought that the smooth, brown cream might prove to be therapeutic.

The ointment smelled just like peanuts. When Bubi asked

me to apply it to his back, I could not overcome the urge to taste it. It was delicious. A flavor just like peanuts. Amazing. A skin ointment made of peanuts. Bubi did not allow me to taste more. It might be harmful. We were having trouble with our bowels. All of us were having violent diarrhea since liberation. Especially Bubi. His diarrhea was so bad that for weeks he was unable to control his bowels. So he forbade me to eat from the brown ointment, no matter how delicious I thought it was.

But the peanut butter did not help Bubi's sores. The burning itch continued. It even made the pain worse, so Bubi had to wash it all off again. He found a green liquid smelling of alcohol in the attic, and now he tried that. But the green liquid turned into a solid glaze on his body and caused excruciating burning. It would not come off. The only way he could tolerate the pain now was by lying in a bathtub filled with cold water. By now, we had also organized an aluminum bathtub, and Bubi lay hours in a cold bath.

There was a knock on the door and two husky men came in smiling.

"Hello," said one of them with a thick Russian accent. "Is this your room?"

"Yes," I answered, "our room."

"Nice room. Very nice room. *Vochem Charasho*, very very nice." He looked around and nodded to his companion.

"Okay. Out! Fast. Get out. We are moving in." He stepped to the door and opened it wide. Two young women with bundles came in and the man put one of the bundles on the table.

"This is our room now." He stood menacingly over Bubi. He was husky and he meant business.

Bubi and I looked at each other. Just then Mommy entered. Her face reflected the surprise and confusion we felt. "What's going on?"

We did not know.

"Davai! Davai!"

Our visitors were impatient.

"Out! All of you! Out! Quickly!"

Bubi got out of the tub and began to dress. Mommy and I collected our things. We tied them in a bundle and dragged the bundles out of the room. The Russians began to spread their things matter-of-factly. The room was theirs now. As simple as that. And we were out in the hallway. Homeless, once again. Where to now?

The busy fellow with the armband suggested that we try the the next building. We carried our bundles into the next Block and found an empty room.

The job of organization began once again. We were experts by now. Soon our empty room was transformed into a new home—a table, some chairs, a lamp, even a colorful rug.

"Those Ruskis did us a favor. This is a much nicer room."

"Shh . . . not so loud. There are Ruskis in this Block, too."

FORTY

EGON HAD a large circle of followers. Girls. Like butterflies about a very tall flower, budding girls with wavy brown hair and round breasts flocked about him constantly. Girls of eighteen to twenty blossomed into womanhood within weeks after the liberation. Lusty, yearning, urgent womanhood. And they clustered about the few men in the camp, reawakening males within tired skeletons.

Egon was more popular than most. He was masculine in his shabby trousers and threadbare T-shirt. He exuded a serenity and worldliness the girls found irresistible. They loved him. He walked about with a lanky, careless posture followed by bright girls wherever he went. Into town, within the camp, or on his famous picnic ground at the edge of the camp—he had an entourage of five or six of the prettiest girls.

One of them was from Dunaszerdahely—Lici—perhaps the sexiest of the lot. One day she invited me to join them on a picnic with Egon. I was hesitant about it at first, but then I agreed. I had no friends here in the Flack Kaserne.

In the afternoon, Lici and I walked to the spot where Egon's daily picnics were held—girls and a basketful of apples. Where did he get the apples? It was his organizational secret.

As we approached the group sitting in the tall grass, Egon turned his short-cropped head toward me. He had gray eyes. As he looked at me, I felt I was turning red from head to foot. Lici introduced me. Egon kept on looking into my face. I felt uncomfortable.

"Sit down, Elli, and have an apple." His voice was kind.

I did not join in the conversation. I did not know any of the people they talked about. I had nothing to say. From time to time Egon looked at me as if he was trying to remember something. It made me self-conscious and quiet. The mocking tone Egon and the girls used was unfamiliar and intimidating. Egon noticed my discomfort and started to talk to me in that friendly, fatherly tone he used at first. Soon we were engaged in serious conversation. The girls chatted on.

Egon gazed steadily into my face with those puzzling gray eyes. Suddenly, he said: "You are a beautiful girl, Elli."

Blood rushed into my face. His face was very serious as he said it. I did not understand. I stammered: "I am not pretty at all."

"I said you were beautiful. Not pretty." After a pause he continued: "One day you will believe me. Now you are still too young. How old are you?"

"Fourteen."

"My God! Fourteen? You are like a young woman. A mature young woman."

This, too, he said like an affectionate father, and his eyes searched my face with a puzzling curiosity. Then, abruptly, he rejoined the group. He was lighthearted and bantering once again. He began to flirt with Lici. When he pinched her the others howled with wild laughter. But I hurt deeply.

Why can't I be just a little older? Why can't I gain weight faster? I am a long, shapeless stick. And my hair. It's straight like a boy's. My chest is flat and straight like my hair. No wonder he speaks to me in that fatherly tone. And with the other girls he speaks like an equal. A man to women. Me, he treats as a child. He is sorry for me. That's why he called me beautiful. With Lici, he flirts because he can see she is an attractive woman. She is nineteen. When he looks at her and all the others, he is gay and playful. But when he spoke to me, he turned solemn. I don't need his pity.

I was silent for the rest of the afternoon. By the time I got back to our room, I was miserable. Mommy asked what was the matter and when I did not answer she assumed I had a stomachache. I always had a stomachache. Other girls dressed up in pretty dresses which they got from boyfriends who had organized them from Germans, and fussed with their hair, and ran around Munich with handsome Americans—and I had a stomachache. I gained weight very slowly because I had stomachaches and could eat very little. I remained skinny and unattractive while other girls blossomed into shapely young women. I was a sticklike boy. Instead of putting on a golden tan as the others did, I got freckles on my nose. And my hair was getting lighter and more like straw. Why did I ever meet Egon?

Lici and two of her friends came to our room on their way back from the picnic.

"Elli, why did you leave so early? The picnic was lots of fun. Egon said you were nice. It's a pity you left so soon."

"She has a stomachache," Mother said.

The next day Lici called for me again, but I did not go to the picnic. I did not want to see Egon ever again. Instead I lay in bed all afternoon and listened to the mournful tunes a young Yugoslav was playing on his harmonica. I thought my heart would break.

Bubi went on an expedition looking for a bathtub. Mommy was cooking. We had received large blocks of frozen meat from the Americans, and Bubi had organized some onions and potatoes. Mommy was making goulash.

After supper I went for a walk in the camp. The Russians sat in groups, one of them played the harmonica and the others sang along. Some Yugoslavs were telling stories or jokes at the entrance to their Block. Loud, raucous laughter. The road was dark, a hazy moon lit up huddled silhouettes. A group of Jewish girls approached. They spoke Hungarian, and I recognized them as Egon's friends. Egon was not among them.

I walked beyond the row of Blocks, out into the open. The sounds of the camp died away. A soft breeze ruffled the tall grass. In the pale light of the moon every clump of earth looked exaggerated, eerie.

The sound of a motorcycle cut into the hush of the summer evening. I stepped off the path as the motorcycle roared past me. It stopped. The tall man in a helmet and an American army jacket turned around. It was Egon.

"I thought it was you, Elli. Good evening."

"Good evening."

"Are you alone?"

I did not answer.

"You are always alone. Why?"

"Are you sorry for me? Don't be. I am happy."

"I did not ask whether you were happy. I asked why you were alone. I am sorry if I offended you."

"I am not a child. You don't have to talk to me like that. Just because I am younger than the other girls. I am not a child."

"I did not mean to hurt you. Forgive me. No, Elli, you're not a child. In many ways you are older than the other girls. Believe me. In many ways you are a mature woman. They, the other girls, are growing children. You are different."

"In what way am I different?"

Was he joking? Or patronizing again? I could not make out his face.

"You are . . . at fourteen, you are a grown woman. There is a maturity about you, a wisdom, no other girl here has. And you are in a strange way . . . very . . . attractive. You see, I should not say this to you . . . forget it. Anyway, forgive me if I offended you in any way."

"No. It is I who should apologize. I misunderstood you, I am sorry."

"You know what? Let me take my motorcycle to my room and let's take a walk."

It was the most memorable walk of my life. Egon told me of himself. He told me of things he never spoke of before to anyone. About his wife from whom he had been separated four years earlier in Berlin and never heard of again. About his brother who died at Dachau. About his fears. He was afraid to go home. He was stalling needlessly for time in this camp. German Jews were repatriated weeks before, but he stayed behind, afraid to face the reality of a new life without family or friends. He did not believe any member of his family survived. Not his wife, not any of his friends. He did not want to see his house or his parents' house again, yet had no courage to turn his back on his past and go to Palestine. He was afraid of a new start in a new country in strange surroundings. He thought he was a coward.

I tried to comfort him, but instead I began to talk about other things. About my hopes and plans. About the friends I hoped to meet again. About our little town.

It was past midnight when we walked back to camp. Luckily Mommy did not mind the late hour, after Egon apologized to her. He asked to see me the next evening again, promising Mommy that we would be back much much earlier.

But the next walk was almost as long. We had so much to talk about. Egon was cheerful. He said his talk the evening before helped him. He did not elaborate. He asked me to talk about my home and of my expectations. So I told him I wanted to go on with my studies. I had so much to catch up with. And that I wanted to become a teacher. And a writer.

"How about marriage? In your plans for the future, where does marriage come in? Do you have an ideal mate?"

I wanted to tell him my ideal mate was tall and lanky with short-cropped graying hair, gray eyes, was forty years old and plagued by fears and uncertainties. But I did not. Instead, I told him I could not see that far into the future. I knew I would not be married young because of my studies. And I was not going to stay in Czechoslovakia. I was going to go to Palestine. Marriage was too difficult to contemplate that far in the future.

Egon said he hoped I would meet my ideal mate eventually and that I would be happy. When he said that he sounded very sad. I laughed and asked why he wished me happiness in such a sad tone. He did not answer.

We saw each other daily for over a week. Our walks became the most important thing in my life. I counted the hours and the minutes until the moment he would knock on our door. I learned to relate to him in a manner I had never related to anyone. Except to my mother, perhaps, when I was younger. We got to know each other in subtle, sensitive ways. We were in tune.

One evening he held a small package wrapped in newspaper. As soon as we reached the path beyond the last barrack, he handed me the package.

"It's for you. Open it, Elli."

A dainty silver bracelet. He took it from my hand and put it on my wrist.

"Do you like it? I found it in Dachau over two years ago. Kept it concealed in the lining of my camp uniform. For two years I managed to keep it safe. Now it's yours."

"It's beautiful. But why are you giving it to me? Why don't you take it home. For your wife. You kept it safe all these years for her."

"Yes. I kept it for Else. And if I will ever meet Else, I will buy her another bracelet. This one I want you to have."

"Thank you."

We walked on in silence. A strange, bittersweet happiness tightened my throat. On the way back to the barracks Egon said: "Elli, promise me you will wear the bracelet. And whenever you'll wear it, you'll remember me."

"I will. But we are not leaving yet. Our transport may not leave for another two weeks. Or longer. We will see each other many times before that."

"Listen. I don't know if I'll see you tomorrow. Or the day after. I do not know yet. I may not be able to see you for some time."

"But why?"

"Listen. I can't explain. Perhaps in a few days I'll be able to explain it to you. Understand?"

I did not understand. I was frightened.

Near the barrack Egon took my hand and kissed it. "Good night, Elli."

"Good night."

In the room I took off the bracelet and wrapped it in a handkerchief, and put it on the bottom of the dresser drawer. Right under my poems.

The next day I wandered about the camp aimlessly in hopes of meeting him. I saw Lici and the others, but he was not with them. The next day I almost broke down and asked Lici about him. But I held back.

Two days later Lici came to our room.

"Remember Egon? He left. This morning he left abruptly. He came to our room to say good-bye and left without any explanation. He said he was going to Berlin. Last night we saw him but he said nothing about leaving. And this morning he left for good. Just like that. It's not like Egon to act like this. All the girls are terribly shocked. Judith can't get over it. She had a bad case of it, you know. We all liked him a lot. But Judith . . . Poor kid."

When she saw I did not answer, she said: "You knew him only briefly, but the other girls miss him very much. He was a great guy. I wonder what made him leave so suddenly. He had said he was going to stay here long after we will be gone. And now he left so suddenly. I am sorry you did not know him better. He was really a wonderful guy."

Lici was right. I knew him only briefly. But I knew him for a lifetime.

FORTY-ONE

In the middle of June the transports began. First to parts in Germany and Austria. Then to Czechoslovakia. Hungarians, Poles, Ukrainians, Rumanians and Russians were to be last.

One of the Blocks served as delousing headquarters. Ever since the liberation we had been deloused serveral times. A white powder was sprayed under our armpits, on our hair, and between our legs. Bubi's lice were a hardy lot. They were flourishing even now, six weeks after liberation. We hoped this delousing, somewhat more thorough, would deal them a final blow. We had no wish to transport Bubi's lice to Czechoslovakia.

We were injected with all kinds of stuff. Then from the top of an American army truck we were handed small packages, our food ration for the road. The kit contained canned meat and fish, biscuits, a piece of soap, a toothbrush, and toothpowder.

The trucks arrived. Large American army trucks. High, open trucks. They were driven by handsome, young Americans with shiny black faces. Their quick, bright smiles, their brilliant white teeth—they are simply amazing. They must be good men, these black young Americans. Their smiles give them away.

One by one we climbed onto the trucks. There were seats, metal planks, flanking the three sides of the open back, and we sat in a tight row, our luggage in the middle, a large, bulky heap.

Mommy, Bubi, and I climbed on. Our luggage—a long, gray duffel bag and two smaller bundles made of sheets and three green army blankets—was tossed on top of the heap. As the trucks took off, some ten to twelve trucks in all, we waved good-bye to those we were leaving behind—friends who were to be repatriated later, to Hungary, Rumania, and Poland.

The roar of the engine. A sudden rush of open air. Wildly waving arms. We are off. The camp recedes into a bluish haze and the hills come rushing to meet the trucks zigzagging through roads curving upward toward the sky. Suspended between sky and the Bavarian Alps. Tunnels dare the tentative sensation of freedom. Deep precipices. Wide-open sky. Whistling rush of unbridled wind. Freedom, exhilarating, intoxicating, threatening. I grip Bubi's arms. His eyes are closed, his chin raised. He is drinking it in through wide-open nostrils.

"Fast, isn't it?"

"Wonderful. Just wonderful. These black Americans, they call them Negroes, they are the best drivers in the world!"

"How do you know that?"

"I read it somewhere."

He knows everything. The curves, sharp, dizzying curves upward on the snake path. I am glad Bubi knows the Negroes are the best drivers in the world. I am not going to be afraid.

The trucks rush nonstop all night. The sky is deep and the stars are breathtakingly brilliant. It is paralyzingly cold even under the blankets. My jaw is stiff from a thousand shivers. Aren't they ever going to stop? Don't they have to rest? They have been driving since yesterday morning.

"There are two of them. They are taking turns."

We are still rising closer to the sky, to the myriad stars.

"These are the Austrian Alps. They are much higher. Soon we will reach the slopes of Bohemia. I hope it will be daylight by then. It's a shame to miss all this scenery. Do you hear?"

"What?"

"There is a river down below. I can hear. There must be a waterfall nearby. I wish we could see all this."

I had heard the murmur. But to me it was a concert of sky and wind and the incredibility of freedom.

By noon the next day we arrived at Pilsen in the heart of Moravia. A charming town of Gothic severity softened by flower pots in almost every window. In the town square the trucks came to an abrupt halt. Finally. We will rest here.

The drivers came to the back and smiled wearily. One of them said something in English, and then both of them began to unload the luggage. With a wave of their arms they indicated to us to get off. We obliged, somewhat uncomprehending. As soon as we got off, the trucks drove away. Away they roared in a show of indifferent efficiency. The motley gang of dusty, weary cargo of the mighty American machines began to scatter in every direction. We were free to go anywhere now. This was Czechoslovakia. We were home.

Soon there was only a small group in the shade of the town hall who, like the three of us, just stood there trying to decide what to do. Those who left were from Bohemia or Moravia, and they headed for the local station to catch rides to nearby towns. We had to get to Slovakia, farther east. And we did not know how.

A policeman approached us. One of the men spoke Czech, and he became the interpreter for the group. There were freight trains going almost daily to the east. The best thing for us to do was to go to the station and inquire about the next freight transport to the east. The policeman saluted politely and left us. We started to gather our belongings. Then the little crowd began to move hesitantly in the direction the policeman had indicated. It was getting warm. Our gray duffel bag was too heavy. The enormous typewriter weighed it down. Bubi and I dragged it until the end of the street but could not carry it farther. We decided to leave the duffel bag in town with one of us in charge while the other two carried the smaller bundles to the station, then return for the duffel bag. Mommy volunteered to stay.

Bubi and I found the station without difficulty, and to our joy there was a freight train right there ready to leave for Pressburg in the morning. A stationmaster permitted us to leave our bundles in one of the cars and return to spend the night in it. A train leaving for home in the morning! Mommy was delighted with the news. She found a wicker broom and swept the freight car clean. We spread our blankets, opened our ration kit, and dined in the spacious luxury of an empty, cool wagon. The wide-open sliding door allowed the light and air to flow into our haven but the roof and walls provided shade. What a stroke of good fortune!

By nightfall several other passengers filtered into our quarters. Some we recognized from our transport. Others were total strangers, looking for a ride east. All refugees, displaced by the war, heading home. Soon the wagon was full. Filled with a mood of expectation. A pervading sense of waiting. For tomorrow.

It was noon before the wagons began to roll. Slowly, with clumsy, hesitant clatter, the couplings jerked. Wheels stirred into motion. We were moving. The tenants of the wagon sat up, alert. We were moving at last.

Mountains softened into rolling hills, then smoothed into wide stretches of open fields. We were heading east toward the lower lands of the Danube Valley. Home. The foliage was becoming familiar. The dramatic beauty of dark-green pine forests was now exchanged for the reassuring mildness of grassy slopes, cultivated plains, studded by an occasional oak or clusters of acacia. Goats were grazing near a narrow creek, and quite near the tracks several cows sprawled under a leafy birch. We were getting closer to home.

But soon the train halted near an obscure station in lower Moravia, and we spent the night there, standing, motionless, numbed by the urgency of our yearning to go on. Days and nights were spent in containing that urgency while the train moved in sparse installments, stopping for long stretches of senseless waiting.

On the Sabbath, on the morning of the fourth day, the train pulled into the outskirts of Pressburg. It stopped several kilometers from the station, long enough for us to get off. And then moved on. As the wagon with our companions passed us, we waved to them, and they waved back, rapidly disappearing into blinding sunshine. And we—Mommy, Bubi, and I— stood there in the sun-drenched open field with the grimy luggage at our feet and the towers of Pressburg in the immediate yet hazy distance of the midsummer heat. We were almost home.

FORTY-TWO

WE LEFT Mommy under a solitary tree and walked into town. Large, jagged cobblestones. Hilly, narrow winding streets under the shade of gnarled ancient trees. Medieval buildings, gray, shuttered, with arched doorways. It was Pressburg. Familiar, fondly remembered, tired old city, now empty and drab. Under the cling-clang of our uneven footsteps on the pavement, Pressburg slowly slid out of the realm of a dream into a vague, undefinable reality.

This was Pressburg. Not as I remembered it, the glamorous city of a seven year old's fantasy. It was the city that survived the war and the occupation. It was deserted and melancholy and much smaller than the city that dwelt so vividly in my memory.

Bubi knew Pressburg. He had been at school here before the Hungarian occupation of the Upper Country drew an unpassable border between Pressburg and Somorja, and he was brought home by Daddy. He remembered the streets and knew which turns to take to get to the Jewish quarter. We were heading for the Jewish quarter. Perhaps we would find Jews there. Someone who would direct us to a place to stay over the Sabbath. On Sunday we will go on to Somorja. Somorja is less than twenty kilometers east of Pressburg.

A solitary streetcar, a faded yellow contraption, wound its way up on Michalovska Street. We followed its course and reached Zidovska Street, the center of the Jewish section. A woman shook a dust rag through an open window. The first human encounter in Pressburg. Bubi asked her whether there were any Jews in the neighborhood. She pointed toward Svoradová Street. There were some Jews in a building there, she thought it was Svoradová seven. Or nine. At any rate, in one of those buildings.

Svoradová seven turned out to be a public kitchen for repatriates. There were at least twenty people there, young men and women, busily eating at tables covered with white tablecloths.

It is not a mirage. It is indeed a dining room with young Jews eating at tables set with food. White tablecloths. Steaming food served in white porcelain plates. Young Jews, dressed in clean clothes, neat and pressed. The smell of warm food. The buzz of conversation. A scene vaguely remembered from a distant dream. Or from a picture in a book somewhere.

We stand on top of the stair near the entrance, Bubi and I, and do not move. A big clock on the opposite wall shows five minutes after one. This is not a mirage. The hand of the clock shows the time. It is five minutes after one. We must have walked for hours. It was early morning when the freight train let us off near the station: The sun was far to the east. I look at Bubi. He also stands, motionless. As if in a dream.

A young man approaches us. He tells us to come in. To sit

down at a table. Two girls bring us food, some kind of a soup
or a stew, I don't know which. It is warm and it tastes heav-
enly. There is bread on the table. Bubi eats a lot of bread. My
stomach begins to hurt. I cannot eat more. "Eat," says Bubi.
"We haven't eaten since Thursday morning." I know. I'm terribly hungry but I have a stomachache. "Eat," says Bubi. And
he eats some more bread.

There is a school where repatriates can sleep, we find out.
We head back to the station. To bring Mommy. Bubi puts
some bread in his pocket. For Mommy.

As we pass a street near the outskirts of the city, Bubi
recognizes a girl at a window. He stops to talk to her. She
turns out to be the sister of Bubi's friend from school here in
Pressburg six years ago. She invites us in. Two sisters live here
alone. Their family has not returned. It is a big house full of
furniture, even bric-a-brac and curtains. They ask us to stay
with them instead of going to the public haven for repatriates
in the school. Bubi says good, this house is much nearer to the
station.

By the time we reach Mommy under the tree she and the
luggage have turned into a dark patch on the field. In the thin
grayness of twilight we drag our belongings on the cobblestones.

We stayed in the Donath house for over a week. There is no
transportation to Somorja. It is Samorin, now, once again.
The Hungarians are gone from Samorin. Bubi's wounds are
still wet, festering. His leg is swollen and hurts every time he
steps on it. But a week later he ventures onto the street. With a
beaming face he bursts into the house. He met a farmer from
Úszor, a village near Samorin. The farmer offered to take us
on his cart until Úszor, about four kilometers from Samorin.
But he was leaving immediately.

We packed in a frenzy. In a matter of minutes we were
dragging the duffel bag on the cobblestones once again toward
the station. The cart was half full with packages, but we managed to get our luggage and Bubi on, too. There was no room

for Mommy and me. Bubi sat on the duffel bag, his bad leg carefully draped over the typewriter. The horses started at a slow trot. Mommy and I walked behind the cart with all the vigor and speed we could muster.

Near Úszor another horse-drawn peasant cart picked us up all the way to Samorin. Mommy and I sat on the wagon now, luxuriating in its comfort.

Samorin lies enveloped in a hot summer haze as we approach the end of the town. Dust obliterates some of my vision. My stomachache creeps lower into my abdomen. The dull pain turns into sharp stabs. The peasant cart turns the corner. There on the small hill in a deserted square stands our house. Large patches of gray on its faded yellow walls. A battered sign above the shuttered store window—FRIEDMANN MÁRKUSZ, VEGYESKERESKEDÉS. Mark Friedmann, Grocery. The house is small and so desolate. The windows empty and dark. The gate stands ajar.

"Here," says Mother. "Stop right here, please. And thank you kindly."

The farmer loosens the reins. The horses stop abruptly, jerking the cart to a sudden halt. He gets off the seat and helps us put the luggage on the sidewalk. Then, with a clatter and a cloud of dust, the wagon is off. We have arrived.

Open gate. Dark, empty courtyard. Bare rooms covered with dust. And something else. In the middle of every room there is a heap of human excrement.

Where is everything? The furniture, the bedding, the carpet, even the well pump is gone. There is nothing left of our home. The bare walls. And where is Daddy?

"At least they did not strip the doors and the windows. We should be thankful for that."

Mother, the optimist. What about Daddy? Why hasn't he arrived yet?

"Perhaps Daddy is staying with someone else. He did not want to be here alone in this empty house. Soon we'll find out."

Bubi limped into town to find out. Mommy sent me over to the Plutzers to ask for some straw and to borrow a broom.

The Plutzers' farmyard is long. But I notice the kitchen door is open. I approach it timidly. Mrs. Plutzer is in the kitchen. She turns to me and I greet her, my heart beating in my throat. She stares at me. Then gives a shriek and makes the sign of the cross on her chest: "Jesus Maria! Jesus!"

She grips my shoulders. "Ellike! You're here! You're alive! Where is your mother? Your father? Alive! Oh, Jesus!"

I told her about Mommy and Bubi, and that we have just arrived. And that we need some straw to sit on and a broom. Mrs. Plutzer yelled to her husband, and he came to shake my hand. He is a tall, proud farmer with a shy hand shake. She grabbed a broom and he went to the shed to bring some straw. Incredulous, Mrs. Plutzer flew across the street and held Mother in a long embrace.

"Jesus is kind. You're alive! I never thought, sweet Maria, I never thought!"

We swept the rooms clean and spread the straw in the bedroom. The metal stove still stood in the kitchen. Mrs. Plutzer ran to bring some milk and eggs. Mommy pulled out of our duffel bag the two pans we brought.

"From now on, children, we will eat only kosher, once again."

One of the pans was designated for milk dishes and the other for meat—if we will ever get some. In the dish for milk she boiled the potful of fresh milk Mrs. Plutzer brought. Bubi had returned in the meantime, and we sat on the kitchen floor taking turns in drinking the hot, foamy milk. We were home.

FORTY-THREE

DADDY HAS not arrived yet. There were thirty-two people, thirty-two young Jewish boys and girls who returned. Our arrival made the number thirty-five. They all congregated in a public kitchen in the middle of town. The public kitchen survived as a meeting place, a nerve center of news of arrivals, a social hall. There we found out that Daddy is on his way home together with Misi Lunger and Mr. Weiss of Nagymagyar.

Our group of thirty-five survivors became a close-knit family. Most of our time we spent in the kitchen someone named "Tattersaal" in the company of each other. Girls volunteered to do the cooking and serving, the dishwashing and cleaning, and the boys carried the supplies from the government office which allocated the food for us. There was a weekly money allowance for each repatriate. This too was distributed at the Tattersaal.

Groups of survivors heading east passed our town, and they too found a home at the Tattersaal. They brought us news of the outside world. News of recent arrivals in neighboring towns. Names of survivors trapped in other parts.

Then, one day, two weeks after our arrival, Misi Lunger came home. Daddy was not with him. He told us he had parted ways with Daddy some time ago, but Mr. Weiss of Nagymagyar can tell us more about him. Several days later news reached us that Mr. Weiss had arrived in Nagymagyar. Bubi decided to go there at once.

There was no transportation. Some trains passed Samorin station loaded with Russian soldiers, but they did not stop. The freight trains slowed down a bit, so it was possible to get on them, but they would not slow down at a small village like Nagymagyar. It would be impossible to get off there. In the

meantime all three of us went to the train station every afternoon at five. We felt Daddy's arrival imminent. Misi Lunger
and Mr. Weiss from Nagymagyar, the two men who were with
him, have arrived. Daddy also will be home any day now.
Who knows what caused his delay.

The freight train slowed and several refugees jumped off.
Daddy was not among them. They were from nearby villages.
They did not know Daddy. After several days of our futile
waiting at the train, a Samorin cattle dealer told Bubi he
would be going to Nagymagyar with his wagon and would be
glad to take him along. The wagon was to leave early next
dawn.

It was still dark when Bubi left the house. Mommy and I
walked him to the gate. I felt a tinge of regret that he would be
the one to get the first news about Daddy and not I. But
Mommy would not let me go: It was a long and hazardous
trip for a girl. The countryside was full of roaming Russian
soldiers.

About 10 A.M. Bubi walked into the kitchen. His face
ashen. "Bubi! You're back so soon?"

"I did not go."

"The man did not go to Nagymagyar after all?"

"The man went. I did not go."

A cold hand stopped the beating of my heart. Mommy
looked into his face and said very quietly: "Bubi, what happened?"

"We hung around for a long time before he was ready to
start. Then I climbed up next to him in the driver's seat. He
said, 'Look, kid. It's a shame you should make this long trip
for nothing. Misi and the others told you to go to Nagymagyar
because nobody wanted to be the one to tell you. But I can't
take you for this ride just for that. I'm going to tell you the
truth about your father. He is not coming home. He died in
Bergen Belsen two days before his liberation. Misi and Weiss
from Nagymagyar buried him with their own hands.' And so I
did not go to Nagymagyar."

Mommy froze. I gave a shriek and ran into the yard. Bubi followed me.

"Come inside, Elli. There is the law. I have to make a tear in your dress. And then we have to sit *shiva*."

In the kitchen he turned to Mommy. She sat on the ground staring into the vacuum.

"We can sit *shiva* only for an hour. According to the law if the news of the death reaches the family after the lapse of the *shloshim*, the thirty-day mourning period, they may sit *shiva* only for an hour instead of the week. Daddy died in April and now it's July."

When Bubi gripped the collar of my dress to rent a tear into it, I began to scream with the savagery of a wounded beast. Slowly Bubi forced me to sit on the ground. It is the law of the Jew.

FORTY-FOUR

THERE IS nothing to keep us here any longer. Daddy is not coming home. Neither is Aunt Szerén. She had gone to the other side. And now we know. The very same day, perhaps less than an hour later, she was dead. The crematorium was near, we had seen the smoke. Aunt Szerén was gassed with the others, the older men and women, the children, the mothers. My darling Szerén *néni* with her frightened eyes. They say they were pressed tight in the gas chambers to save space. To save gas. They were naked and they struggled for air, in the last moments trampling on each other. The stronger ones trampled the weaker ones under foot. How long did they suffer so, my God? Was Szerén *néni* badly trampled my God? And little Tommi? Gallant little Tommi, was he a gentleman in the gas chamber? God?

There was nothing to keep us here. Mommy and Bubi decided to go across the border to Hungary where the rest of our family had lived and see who survived. We decided to leave at once.

The trains ran seldom and at irregular intervals. We went to the station and waited. Some three hours later a trainful of Russian soldiers pulled into the station. There were soldiers hanging on the sides. Some even sat on top of the cars. Before we reached the cars, the train began to move again. Bubi was already on top of the stairs, and I was helping Mommy to reach the first rung while the train began to speed up. She held onto the railing and heaved on the bottom rung. I was still on the ground when a Russian soldier lifted me on his shoulder and handed me to a comrade leaning out of the window. In a moment I was in the car, and my gallant champion was, too, with an incredible leap through the window.

There was a mood of triumph and good cheer in the train. The soldiers applauded my spectacular entry and immediately crowded about me. They offered me their seats and welcomed me in rapid Russian. I did not understand a word even though I had begun to pick up some phrases and had been able to communicate with the Russians in Samorin. But now it was all so foreign. I did not see Mommy and Bubi and wanted to tell the soldiers that they were outside on the steps and I wanted to join them there. The soldiers did not understand me and did not let me leave the car. Finally, with much gesticulation, they got my point and soon Mommy and Bubi were shoved into the car practically above heads and prone bodies.

There were bodies everywhere. Some were lying on the floor of the train, others high up in the package compartment, or on top of each other on the seats. I alone displaced three soldiers, who had occupied a small space on a seat near the window and now stood in the aisle, so that I might sit in comfort. I pulled Mommy down next to me and Bubi found a place high up on the package rack.

The train was heading for the Carpathians eastward. We had to get off in Komarom, cross the town and a small wooden bridge on foot, and board another train heading for the interior of Hungary. The wooden bridge was the border. There was border inspection but no papers were required. The borders were open. Only our luggage was inspected. We were told they were looking for weapons. If you had no weapons on you, you could cross the border unhampered.

The next train was to leave only in the morning. It was late afternoon now, and it began to rain. A leaden, chilly spray of relentless mist. We had packed an army blanket. Wrapped in it, the three of us as one bundle spent the night at the Komarom train station. We were in Hungary now, the Hungarian sector of Komarom, and it was obvious that Hungary was more devastated by the war than Czechoslovakia. There were no stores open, not even vegetable or fruit stands were visible. What happened to the food crop of Hungary? Where did it disappear?

We had part of our loaf of bread and some green peppers. So we were not really hungry yet.

At dawn there was a bustle in the station, and we quickly picked ourselves up and rushed outside. Just on time. The train had come and was in motion already, leaving the platform. With practiced skill we leaped on the metal stairs and held on to the railing for dear life. In stages we filtered into the train. At each stop we managed to wiggle our way higher on the stairs among the many passengers hanging there. This time there were civilians among the crowd of Russian soldiers. By the time we got into the interior of the train, it was high noon and the car was stifling hot.

Late in the evening we reached Budapest. The train did not go any farther. We got off and followed the crowd into the wide-open avenues of the once proud capital, now dark and uninviting. There were several Jews on the train. We joined them, heading for repatriation headquarters in the inner city.

The Jewish school building had been converted into refugee headquarters. As we arrived, we were each given a bowl of food and a blanket to sleep on. Bubi found an army cot and set it up for Mommy. She slept in royal comfort while we slept on the ground. There were bedbugs crawling about. Several times I was awakened by the bite of a bedbug. I had never seen a bedbug before this. They were quite pretty, well-shaped, and a pretty red color. Bubi said I was stupid for thinking they were pretty, and that they were red only after they drank your blood. They must have drunk quite a lot of my blood; I was full of bites. It was a restless night.

In the morning we were registered by the authorities at a table in the schoolyard. Every new arrival received twenty-two pengös. They did not believe I was Jewish even though I showed them the tattooed number on my arm. They brought me a Hebrew prayerbook, and I read. This was my proof. I asked, "What if I could not read Hebrew? Many Jews can't. What is their proof?" You have to bring witnesses, they said. I did not argue the point. But I thought, what if there are no witnesses? How do you prove you are a Jew?

We found out that the Starck family, Mommy's cousins, had survived in hiding, and now lived at their old apartment. They were overjoyed to see us. Tibby, their son, hugged me exuberantly and then surveyed me.

"Where are your braids?"

The question sounded like voices coming from a deep vault. As they reach the open air, they become distorted beyond any relation to reality. My braids. Where are they, indeed? In Auschwitz. Or in a world beyond my grasp. Beyond recall. My braids are gone with the storm that blew my life into irrelevancy.

"And your freckles? You used to have rosy cheeks and freckles on your nose. Now you are pale, and there are no freckles. You are much too thin. And taller than I. You are very tall."

"Sorry. No braids. No freckles. No rosy cheeks. Just me. Much too tall me." Poor Tibby, how will you bear the disappointment?

We spent several days in their apartment. They shared their

rations with us and we brought them some food from repatriation headquarters. On the third day, Sanyi, my cousin from Kisvárda, came to see us. He was in Budapest. On *hachshara*. That meant, he was trained to go to Palestine. Trained as what? Just trained. Don't ask any questions. It was only later that I understood. The *Haganah*. He was trained to fight. The Arabs. And also the British. Sanyi was twenty and a Zionist. He volunteered for *hachshara*. He said his parents have not yet returned, but he had heard that two of his sisters are on the way home. Magda, the younger one, had been ill, but that she is better and the two of them may be arriving soon. He said he was waiting for them and then would leave for Palestine.

I had had a crush on Sanyi when I was visiting in his home in Kisvárda. I was nine and he was fifteen, and he began to pay some attention to me after I confessed to him that I hated to play with dolls. Then he told me a secret. He told me that he had had a cousin visitor just three weeks before who played with a porcelain doll all day long, singing to it and talking to it. He could not stand it, so when she was not looking he snatched the doll and buried it in the garden. The little girl, heartbroken over the disappearance of the doll, cried until they took her home. Sanyi was delighted. His plan worked. He took me into the garden and together we exhumed the doll. He wanted to play catch with the doll. I agreed, even though I felt sorry for the doll. And for the little girl. But my infatuation with this strong older cousin did not allow for personal scruples. We played catch with the muddy doll.

Now five years later, Sanyi is heading for Palestine, to help free it from the British and protect it from the Arabs.

I wanted to remind him of the doll. But the thought became distorted on its way to the surface from a deep vault. The doll, the braids. Disintegrated in a world of make-believe.

The next day we continued our journey, and I did not see Sanyi again for a long time.

We arrived in Miskolc Friday afternoon, Mommy and I. Bubi stayed in Budapest. In Budapest we had heard that my

Mother's younger sister, Aunt Cili, and her husband, Uncle Márton, are in Miskolc. We heard nothing about their son, Imre, and Mommy thought it would be painful for Aunt Cili to see my brother, a boy of Imre's age, if Imre were not home yet. So Bubi remained in Budapest to await our return.

We found Aunt Cili's apartment in Szécsényi utca. A long courtyard. A small entrance. A kitchen. On the table a white tablecloth. White candles in silver candlesticks. Sabbath is awaited. But there was no one in the kitchen. As we enter, slowly closing the front door behind us, Aunt Cili emerges from a side room. She looks puzzled for a moment then gives a shriek. Her tight, almost frantic embrace melts away the backdrop. I stand on the parched earth in Auschwitz and Aunt Cili, in long gray prison garb, head cropped to the scalp, holds me close, rocking me back and forth, weeping. Her tears feel warm against my cheek.

"Lórika! Elli! My God. My God! You are alive. You are here. How did you get here?"

By the time Uncle Márton got home, we had washed and changed. During the entire journey we had worn the same dresses. But now Cili *néni* gave each of us, Mommy and me, a clean dress to change into. I felt clean and festive. Uncle Márton's surprise and joy at seeing us filled me with sorrow. I did not know why.

My sadness increased during the Sabbath meal, the first meal ever since we left Samorin. The vacuum was unbearable. A deep, nagging emptiness. We did not speak of Imre. Nor of the others. But Aunt Cili began to cry silently, and I left the table to cry in the other room.

The next day we told them that we wanted to go to Sátoraljaujhely to look for the others. Aunt Cili knew of no one else who returned, but she did not stop us from going. Maybe since then . . . Uncle Márton would go with us.

The nagging emptiness turned into an agony during our stay in Miskolc. A week later we moved on.

In Sátoraljaujhely, the magnificent house of Mommy's

brother, the chief rabbi of the Jewish community of the entire
county, stood bolted. The handful of survivors congregated in
the community kitchen in the synagogue yard. They knew that
their chief rabbi and his wife had died in the gas chamber.

"When I saw his beard shaved off," said one, "I knew it was
the end of us all. Rabbi Roth was the pride of the entire
county. His tall, elegant figure, his eloquence, his gentle
humor inspired us all until the end. His humiliation by the
Nazis was a death blow to the community. He was seen taken
into the gas chamber."

Mommy trembled visibly.

"Thank you," I said. "Let's go now."

"You knew him?" asked the man.

"Yes," I said, "we knew him."

We went to Árpád utca where Aunt Perl used to live. A
large house inhabited by a family of six children and my
grandmother, Daddy's mother. We had met Suri and Hindi in
Auschwitz and become separated from them and Aunt Cili
when we were taken to Plaszow. They may be home now, just
like Aunt Cili. Then there was Bencu, the eldest, Elyu, the
next boy and all the younger children. My aunt and uncle
were also young. They may have all survived. I did not dare to
hope about my grandmother.

The large, sprawling house on the corner was unchanged.
The storefront, a grain depot, stood ajar. We went in and
found the house bustling with young people. Girls and boys
sat on straw in the depot, apparently listening to a lecture.
They were a Zionist youth group on *hachshara*. The Schreiber
house served as headquarters.

"Where are the Schreibers?"

They did not know. They have been using the house ever
since the beginning of March, almost six months now, and no
one of the family has appeared.

"No one? Not one?"

"No. Nobody heard of them."

There was nothing for us to do but head for the station. We

did not go to Kisvárda, since on the way to Miskolc we had met
people from there who told us the Roth house in Kisvárda was
locked and no one of the family had returned. Nagyvarad and
Temesvár were the last remaining towns where Mommy had
brothers before the war. But we heard that both cities were under Rumanian occupation now, and it was impossible to get into
that country. We decided to return to Budapest for Bubi, and
then back to Czechoslovakia.

At the station we parted from Uncle Márton. Just before he
boarded his train for Miskolc he told us he knew Imre was
dead. He froze to death in a Hungarian labor camp. Aunt Cili
did not know it yet.

His face was distorted with pain as he said these things
rapidly, tonelessly. Cili and Márton's affection for their only
child had been the talk of the family. At seventeen he froze to
death in Hungary, a few kilometers from his birthplace while
his mother was in Auschwitz and his father on the Russian
front, digging ditches for the Hungarians.

"I have not told her yet."

His words were barely audible. I knew his agony was doubled by the anticipation of her pain.

"God bless you." Mommy's voice trailed into a sob. "God
bless you."

As his train pulled away, the Budapest train rolled in. We
ran to meet it but it looked hopeless. It was overflowing with
passengers, Russian soldiers and civilians. We decided against
attempting to board it. There was no room even on the lowest
rung of the stairs.

The next train came only late in the evening. It was also
crowded, but we managed to get on.

Here, too, a Russian soldier made a place for me on a seat
between himself and his comrade. When I pointed to Mommy
and told him she was *moia mat*, he told one of his comrades to
let her have a seat. The fellow sat on his knapsack, and
Mommy sat on his seat.

The trip to Budapest was pleasant. The Russians were

friendly and gay, singing all the way and keeping the beat with rhythmic applause. My Russian soldier, a very young blond boy with high cheekbones, wanted to teach me Russian. He ignored the general merriment. Instead, he pointed to different objects in the car and made me repeat their equivalent in Russian. He was very absorbed with this exercise, taking his teaching task seriously. I enjoyed it, too. For me, learning a new language was great pleasure. Halfway to Budapest I learned over two hundred words, and he made me repeat them in front of his buddies during a lull in the singing and drumming. My performance delighted them so much that they went wild with applause. All at once they began singing a popular song I remembered from my Samorin Russians, a lively number about a girl named Katyusha. It was in my honor.

This strange, new world of almost childlike innocence of the Russian soldiers acted as a magic potion upon my aching, starving soul. Like a warm whirlpool, their spontaneous acceptance of me swirled around me in a dizzying sensation of happiness. I closed my eyes and for a moment allowed the incredible sensation to carry me in a wild circular motion. For a daring moment. Then, the gnawing emptiness returned. I thanked them in Russian and again they began to applaud.

Our journey was suddenly interrupted. The train could not proceed. The lines ahead were bombed out. All disembarked, filling the small way station beyond its capacity.

The next train was a freight transport. Mommy and I got room in one of the closed wagons. My Russian friends had gone to town to spend the rest of the night, as we had all been told that the next passenger train would come only in the morning. But Mommy and I wanted to go on as soon as possible, and now were glad to find room in a freight wagon. There were other passengers in the wagon, and we soon found out that they were Jewish refugees returning from different camps. This train was going to Budapest on a roundabout route, on reconstructed railway lines. We were warned it might take days to get to Budapest. But we were determined to stick with this transport and get there no matter how long it would take.

This was a very different lot from the company of Russians. These were tired and uncommunicative. Some had been home already and had found no relatives. Now they were heading for the capital to start a new life. Others were searching for ways to get to Palestine. There was seventeen-year-old Greta, a small, underdeveloped little girl who was traveling about looking for someone to adopt her. Next to her sat a middle-aged man, a gynecologist from Budapest who was returning from the Russian front. When the girl fell asleep, he confided to me that he would adopt her if his family in Budapest would agree. He was going home first to discuss it with them. He did not want the girl to know of his plans in advance so that she should not be disappointed in case the family decided against it.

I met them both in Budapest later. He had adopted her. She was beaming. But the doctor was a broken man. No one of his family survived. Now Greta was his only relative.

Bubi was relieved to see us. The two weeks he spent in Budapest were eventful but he did worry about us. There had been hangings of Hungarian Nazis, members of the Arrow-cross. Public hangings preceded by public trials. The hangings made a deep impression on him. But he refused to describe them to me. It was extraordinary, he said, to be free and to know it is not one of your campmates hanging on the rope for stealing potatoes. It is not your turn to be the next. You are there merely as a spectator. A voluntary spectator.

I soon had a chance to witness a hanging. As I arrived at the public kitchen to pick up some bread, I noticed a commotion in the yard. Some twenty young boys were dragging a fat man toward a pole. On the pole hung a rope, and one of the boys quickly tied a noose at its end. The fat man struggled and pleaded innocence. A group of men and women screamed obscenities at him. Several of them cited incidents of his atrocities. While the man pleaded and begged for them to deliver him to the authorities, someone threw a stone. It hit him on the brow and he began to bleed. I covered my face and started to push my way out of the crowd. I had to get away from there. But the crowd was closing in. A loud, hoarse shriek propelled me around. The man was dangling in the air, kicking with his fat legs. Fast. I tried again to get away from there.

The crowd goes wild. Inarticulate shouts of the clumsy helpless man. The crowd is very loud now. And then, silence. What is happening? The man, a large loose bundle of clothes, a gray business suit carelessly dangling at the end of a shabby rope. An effigy. A hastily stuffed, haphazardly overstuffed effigy of a man. It dangles, slowly swinging. As the silent crowd watches, it lowers with a muffled thump to the ground. The crowd goes wild again. Some fall upon the body with frantic blows. Some tear the clothes. His hat, a green velour hat with a small feather, is passed from hand to hand. What does it all mean? I feel deep sorrow. Nothing but sorrow. Coward, my brother would say.

FORTY-FIVE

THE SUN filters through a threadbare curtain of clouds, and despite the cool breeze it promises to be a brilliant day. The bittersweet brilliance of autumn. A poem by Petöfi comes to mind. The flowers still bloom, the birch is still wrapped in green but patches of snow brighten the dark green meadows, and the hint of winter subtly saddens the heart. Petöfi, my favorite. "At the end of September . . ."

I am on my way to school. I am back where I left off nineteen months ago. I registered for the fourth grade of the secondary school. The language of instruction is Slovak now, the entire faculty is new, and so is the student body. I see no familiar faces. My former classmates graduated last year when

I was in Auschwitz and now they have gone to parts unknown. Many of our Hungarian neighbors were resettled in
Hungary during the last few weeks, and Slovaks from Hungary were brought in their place. The Czechoslovakian flag
flutters now on a new flagpole, protruding like Pinocchio's nose
from the center of the school's facade.

It is a happy feeling to be back at school. Slovak comes easy
to me. It is familiar from sounds remembered from early
childhood long ago, from little ditties and poems that still survive at ready recall. And Russian is easy because it is beautiful
and melodious and romantic. It is the language of poets. I
learn Russian with the eagerness of an adventurer. It has the
promise of fresh sounds, of brisk, temperamental robustness.
It is good to learn Russian when your soul yearns for solidity.

Bubi is in Pressburg. He went to study at the Yeshiva. But
the Yeshiva did not materialize, and he enrolled instead in a
course which prepares students for graduation from gymnasium—*maturitny kurz*. He has learned Slovak fast, too. He
remembered Slovak from his days in Pressburg before the war.
Bubi learns everything fast. In a year or two, when he com-
pletes this course, he will pass a special examination designed
for survivors of the camps and then he plans to enter the uni-
versity to study architecture. He is brilliant in math and has talent for drawing. We all believe he will make a great architect.

Mommy is busy sewing dresses for the *barishnas*, the
women of the Russian Army, in exchange for eggs, flour, live
chickens, even light bulbs. There are no goods in the stores.
Even if there were, we have no money to buy them. It is a
blessing that Mommy can sew. How else would we live? The
Russians alone have supplies, and we get them in payment for
her work. The Russians alone have fabrics for clothes, so they
are practically Mommy's sole customers.

Our house is always filled with *barishnas* and their friends,
five *tovarishes* to every girl. They spend hours at our house,
waiting in the kitchen to try on a blouse, or for the finishing of
a special gown for a special occasion. They fill the house

bringing along their harmonicas, their balalaikas, their good humor, and voices. I learn Russian from them, and they love it. I interpret for Mommy when taking orders for a new frock, or when bartering for the price. It is fun. The Russians are fun.

But they do not understand us. They like us, Mommy and me and Bubi while he was still at home, because we speak a little Russian. We receive them in our house and deal with them honorably. But to them we are like the rest of the local populace, foreigners under occupation. They do not appreciate our special situation, our special pain. To me they are special. They fought the Germans and won. They saved us. I am suffused with gratitude, in every gesture toward them, in every encounter with them. That is why I love their language, their poetry, their music. I help Mommy sew those blouses and dresses late into the night, so that next day I should experience the glitter in the eye of a young *barishna* at seeing her ordered garment ready even sooner than she expected and prettier than she dreamed. But to them we are not special. While the rest of the populace, Slovaks and Hungarians alike, despise them as crude and primitive enemies, I adore them as heroes. But they do not know the difference. They do not know us. And do not care.

School is fun, too. I have an obsession to study, an unquenchable thirst. A compulsion to imbibe more and more and more, to fill an emptiness almost unbearable. I want to reach out and touch life, and obliterate the gaping void. I reach out. I am studying Slovak, Russian, math, psychology, and biology. I want to become a physician or a nurse or a teacher. I need people. I need people who need, and I want to give. I reach out and there is nothing. Void.

There is Palestine. I start to learn Hebrew. It is more difficult than the other languages because of the different script. I found a Hebrew textbook in the rubble of the synagogue and started to teach myself. I knew the printed characters from the *sidur*, the prayerbook, but not the written letters. And of course, the meaning of the words is new. Next year I will enter a Hebrew teachers' course in Pressburg. I want to go to Palestine.

I want to go to Palestine and live among people who share my void. When I look at a child and see little Frumet and Yingele and Tommi and Suzie and the little boy with the yellow clown from Lodz marching to the gas chamber, my insides turn numb with the pain of emptiness. I want to hear the echo of that void reverberate in the gut of my fellow student or fellow shopper or fellow pedestrian. When I reach for a cake of soap and my fingers cringe from the memory of soap made of pure Jewish fat, I want to glimpse horror in the eyes of the next person sharing that bar of soap. The void. Can it be filled? Perhaps it can be shared. Perhaps in Palestine.

But I have a problem. Mommy says I cannot go to Palestine. Bubi has submitted papers to go to America, and soon he will leave. We must stay together. We cannot be separated again. We all should go to America. We should follow Bubi to America as soon as we can.

So I am learning English, too. Perhaps Bubi will not get to America. We will then all go to Palestine. If he does, and we all go to America, I have to know English. I want to continue my studies in America. And then, one day, I will get to Palestine after all.

Our little group of survivors carved a road for itself, each in his own way. Several boys and girls married. Several left town to seek better futures in larger, more promising circles. But the Tattersaal is still in existence. Even though many prefer to keep a private kitchen, it continues to function as a social center for all of us. We meet there daily. We grow into a family. And those who left keep in touch by coming for frequent visits.

News of others reaches us daily. Of those who are not coming home. Those who went to the gas and those who died later in one or another camp, or on the highways of Germany—on death marches. And of those who died after the liberation on their way home.

Each piece of news is one more blow. Each loss adds to a deepening sense of isolation.

I think of my poems often. What became of them? Is Pista Szivós, the young Hungarian ghetto guard, keeping the notebook for me? Is he awaiting my return as he vowed? Is he there now, back home in his little village beyond the Danube? That little Hungarian village is not far from here, some sixty kilometers from the other side of the river. At first I thought I would go there, as soon as official travel to Hungary became possible, and retrieve it. I would once again cross my beloved Danube on a boat and retrieve the notebook which contains my innermost self. I yearned for my poems. I longed to see them, to read them again. But now I know I will not do it. Now I know I will never go to the little Hungarian village in search of a thing to which I am not entitled. I have no right to such self-indulgence. Our entire world rose up like smoke into nothingness, all those achingly dear to us. They are all gone, robbed of life. How dared I even dream of such passion for self? How dared I violate the agony of Auschwitz?

I must relinquish my poems. There is no other choice. I must not think of my poems. I must move on.

I have new friends. The boys and girls in my class are Slovaks recently settled in town. It is a friendly and cheerful bunch, and we spend our afternoons together taking walks about town, discussing our studies. They are eager, new in the area and glad to learn about it.

There is a new boy, Yuri, who came from Moscow. His father is a Communist. Yuri is older than the others and more mature. He is my special friend. He is tall and has a large mane of light brown hair. He teaches me Russian, and I teach him Slovak, and we find each other's company indispensable. He is very serious about his work in school, more serious than the others, and I know he will get into the engineering school in Bratislava, his dream. His second passion is his motorcycle, and he promised to teach me to ride it. Now I am not old enough to get a license.

"By the time I will be old enough to get a license I won't be here."

"Why do you want to leave here so desperately?" His voice is puzzled.

His puzzlement disturbs me. I had told him about my hopes of getting to Palestine and my simultaneous preparations for America. And I had explained my search for a home. But he does not understand.

"Czechoslovakia is helping the Jews in Palestine. We are the best friends Palestine has. It is your home, your country. Why do you want to leave it?"

"I told you. It is not my home. Not anymore. I am not a Slovak or a Hungarian. I am a Jew. A Jew. A Jew has a home in Palestine. Or he may find a home in America. Not here. Not in any country in Europe. Never. This soil scorches the soles of Jewish feet. We must leave."

"You are wrong. So wrong. The Communists want to fight for the Jews, in Palestine, everywhere. The Communists are brothers to the Jews. This is your home. Your country, your people."

His voice begins to rise with the heat of his rhetoric. His eyes are riveted to the ground where a few new blades of green grass are emerging. It is early spring. We are on our way to the Danube. His first walk to the bank of the river. And my return to it.

With his right foot he stamps on the moist ground. Dramatically he says: "You see this brown earth? This is your land. Yours and mine. Ours. This is your homeland. It belongs to you. And you belong to it. This is your birthplace. Your motherland. Your motherland."

Does he know the pain he is evoking? Does he know the pain of the uprooted? This was my country once. This was my home. Once. Long ago. The path through the pasture is my path, it is my childhood playground. I can hear Daddy's firm, light footsteps next to me in the grass. I can hear his voice, his rhythmic breathing, and his sudden laughter at the shepherd's vulgarities. I can hear Mommy's cheerful chatter, Szerén *néni's* soft singing. I can see Bubi and his friends striding ahead with fishing gear, partially swallowed up by tall grass. I can see the swaying poplars tower in the distance and the delicious deep-dark forest loom far beyond. I can sense summer flies buzz about my head and hear the croaking of the frogs get ever louder as our little expedition approaches the river. I can smell the mist of the rippling water mingle with the odor of wet moss. Each step assaults me with the memory of rising excitement, the childish joy that the Danube, this generous magnetic river generates. I recall the dust that rises among patches of green and the feel of the sticky lemonade jug brushing against the side of my bare leg. I can still hear the peals of church bells filter through glittering dust particles in the sunshine and echo long and booming in the shady forest. It is all part of the fabric of my inner life—the Danube, the meadow, the Carpathian Mountains, and the town. Without it I am not whole. Without it, I will never be whole. Yet, I do not belong to it anymore.

"I do not belong to it anymore."

"Where do you belong?"

"Where do I belong? I don't know. Not yet."

I do know. But I cannot tell him. He would not understand. How can he understand the void, the all-pervading emptiness? How can anyone understand the aching that is Auschwitz? The compulsion to fill the void that is Auschwitz? The search, the reaching out. The futility. The irrevocable statement that is Auschwitz. Who can understand the inconceivable futility that is Auschwitz. The loss of perspective. The loss. The total, irreconcilable loss.

I belong to this void. Nothing can change that. Nothing. My search for a home, for human relationships, for knowledge. This is one unalterable allegiance. This is where I belong. To Auschwitz.

"Do you think you belong to Palestine? Palestine is a strange country for you. You will not be happy there. You will long to come back here. You'll see. America is not for you either. You will want to come back here. You'll see. I know. Our family always talked of going back home. It was our single, constant dream, to return to our birthplace, our home. You, too, will miss your birthplace, your motherland. You will remember my words, Elli. You'll see."

I do not hear his words. We are not walking on the soil of the same planet. We do not speak the same language. It is all so useless. Such waste. Yuri and his convictions. His eager, youthful idealism. His naïve attempts at persuasion. His hollow talk.

We reach the river. A cold breeze snaps at our legs, our faces. Clear ripples foam at the edges of the dark blue stream, sending a mist against our cheeks. The poplars greet us darkly with a mute, secretive hello. It is too early to sway and dance. The sunshine has not arrived yet. It is too early in the spring.

Yuri throws a pebble into the water, and it skips on the shimmering surface again and again.

"Great!" he exclaims. "I did it. Three times. Did you see? What a wonderful water. What a beautiful river. Beautiful. The beautiful blue Danube."

I watch the clear dark water surge rapidly downstream. It flows on with the immutable dignity of life.

"Yes. It is a beautiful river. I love it."

The chilly mist sends a sudden shudder up my body.

"Are you cold?"

"Yes. It is quite cold. It is too early in the season to come to the Danube."

"I guess you are dressed too lightly. Pity I have no jacket to lend you. Let's start back. You will warm up as we walk through the field. It is less windy there. We will come back another time. Soon."

With a gentle touch on my back he directs me away from the shore. We head back to town. I sense the heavy pull of the beloved river. Without turning I follow Yuri's brisk footsteps. I do not whisper good-bye, even though I know I will never see the Danube again. I had said my good-bye long ago.